FAITH, FAMILY, AND FILIPINO AMERICAN COMMUNITY LIFE

FAITH, FAMILY, AND FILIPINO AMERICAN COMMUNITY LIFE

STEPHEN M. CHERRY

RUTGERS UNIVERSITY PRESS
NEW BRUNSWICK, NEW JERSEY, AND LONDON

Library of Congress Cataloging-in-Publication Data

Cherry, Stephen.
  Faith, family, and Filipino American community life / Stephen M. Cherry.
      pages cm
  Includes bibliographical references and index.
  ISBN 978-0-8135-6205-6 (hardcover : alk. paper) — ISBN 978-0-8135-6204-9 (pbk.
: alk. paper) — ISBN 978-0-8135-6206-3 (e-book)
  1. Filipino American Catholics. 2. Immigrants—Religious life. I. Title.
BX1407.F55C44 2014
282.089'9921073—dc23
2013010362

A British Cataloging-in-Publication record for this book is available from the British
Library.

Visit our website: http://rutgerspress.rutgers.edu

Manufactured in the United States of America

For my wife and best friend, Emily
And for our two wonderful children, Amelie and Wesley

CONTENTS

ACKNOWLEDGMENTS

This book would not have been possible without the love, dedication, and support of many people. First and foremost I owe a great debt of gratitude to the Filipino Americans in Houston whom I surveyed and interviewed. I am thankful to all the individuals and families who graciously welcomed me into their churches, prayer groups, and homes, and took the time out of their busy schedules to share their lives with me. They inspired me with their words and stories and fed me well along the way. Although the majority of them remain anonymous and unnamed, this book is about them and would ultimately not have been possible without them. Of those named, I am especially grateful to two people in particular, Elena Salazar and Norma Benzon (1948–2010). I owe a special debt to Elena. She knows why. Sadly, Norma died after a long battle with cancer during the writing of this book. It is my hope that the spirit of this book honors her and her tremendous commitment to serving the Filipino American community.

Research for this book started when I was a graduate student at the University of Texas at Austin. Long before I started my dissertation, however, Steve Warner's guest lecture on the de-Europeanization of American religion at a university brown bag series made me realize just how understudied the Filipino American community was. I am forever grateful to Steve for pushing me to pursue my interest in the role of Catholicism in the community. From the beginning of my research for the dissertation, I knew that the study had the potential to be a book. Towards the end, however, I also came to realize that it was missing something that would require me to take the project into new directions. I would like to thank all the members of my dissertation committee—Chris Ellison, David Leal, Sharmila Rudrappa, Steve Warner, Bob Woodberry, and Michael Young—for their suggestions and sage advice in shaping the project beyond the dissertation. They all, in some way or another, encouraged me to reenter the field to collect more data or rethink some of my underlying theoretical assumptions about the project. Sharmila in particular pushed me to rethink everything from a more Asian American Studies perspective. Both Chris Ellison and Michael Young, my co-chairs, also encouraged me to reexamine my use of culture and ground it in terms that were more accessible. I took all of these suggestions to heart and the results are in this book.

Beyond the dissertation and the shaping of new research for this book, I am indebted to Chris Ellison and Michael Young for their continued support and mentoring. Always a phone call or email away, their advice has continually aided my growth as a scholar. I am also thankful for the support of Helen Rose Ebaugh. Although she was not a member of my original dissertation committee, she took a keen interest in my work while I was in graduate school and has been a true colleague, friend, and mentor ever since. A number of other people helped to shape this book. I benefitted greatly from the anonymous reviewers solicited by Rutgers University Press as well as from the encouraging feedback and suggestions of Peter Mickulas. Peter was a champion of the book from the beginning, and a first-time author could not have asked for a better guide and editor. Graduate students Kody Allred and Angela Miller commented on early drafts of the book and also provided invaluable help with several aspects of data management throughout the project. Angela in particular continued to bring fresh eyes to the editing of these early drafts when I no longer could see the trees in the forest.

I am equally grateful to Mike Roemer and Bryan Shepherd for providing an invaluable sounding board for my arguments both while we were in graduate school and after. Bryan, in particular, helped shape many of my thoughts on the eventual direction I took on the survey analysis. He also made key suggestions on the visual appearance of the charts in the book. More than this, however, the friendship of both Mike and Bryan has been more valuable to me and the project than I can put into words.

Beyond all those that I have acknowledged, this book ultimately would not have been possible without my wife, Emily. Both literally and figuratively, she is my inspiration. For our children, Amelie and Wesley, thank you for always believing that researching and writing this book was somehow hip and cool even when many days it seemed anything but. One day I hope you grow to appreciate this book not as my own personal accomplishment but an important exploration and testament to your Filipino American heritage. Last, but not least, I would like to thank Howard, my Mom (1940–1998), and my Dad, without whom none of this would have been possible. I only wish you all were still with us to share in the joy of seeing this book in print.

ABBREVIATIONS

ANCOP Answering the Cry of the Poor

CBCP Catholic Bishops Conference of the Philippines

CFC Couples for Christ

CFC-FFL Couples for Christ Foundations for Family Life

CLP Christian Life Program

FACOST Filipino American Council of South Texas

FAMH Filipino Association of Metropolitan Houston

Gabriela General Assembly Binding (Women) for Reform, Integrity, Equality, and Action

GK Gawad Kalinga

LNP Ang Ligaya ng Panginoon (Joy of the Lord)

NaFFAA National Federation of Filipino American Associations

PAMAT Philippine American Masons Association of Texas

PCCI People Caring for the Community, Inc.

SANDIWA National Convention of Filipino Apostolates

SAVE Stand Against Violence Everyone

SIGA Serving in God's Army

SLRM San Lorenzo Ruiz de Manila

Ta Tagalog

FAITH, FAMILY, AND FILIPINO AMERICAN COMMUNITY LIFE

CHAPTER 1

FAITHFULLY FILIPINO
AND AMERICAN

Shortly after 8 A.M. on a muggy Saturday morning in Houston, Texas, Dan, a first-generation Filipino American Catholic in his late thirties, urged his family to get ready.[1] The night prior, at their weekly household Couples for Christ (CFC) prayer meeting, Dan and his wife Lita, also a first-generation Filipino American Catholic in her thirties, invited me to join them the next morning when they were to volunteer at a local soup kitchen called Fishes and Loaves. We had been discussing what it means to them to be Filipino and Catholic. I asked them how their faith impacts their understanding of community. Rather than discuss it at length, Dan suggested it would be easier to just show me. "Be at our house tomorrow around 8:30 . . . you can join us and then we can talk some more."

When I arrived at the Cruz household, Lita explained to me that they were a little exhausted from a long workweek and were hard pressed to get things done. "We only have a precious few hours of every weekend to get chores done and spend quality time with our three children." Nonetheless, Lita and Dan appeared energized and eager to volunteer despite the constraints on time that come with work and family. They believe that their efforts at the soup kitchen make a real difference. Like many of the hundred sixty-plus first-generation Filipino American Catholics interviewed over the course of this study, Dan and Lita see their community life as an extension of their Catholic faith. "It isn't easy," Lita suggested, "everyone is tired, barely moving, and all of us could use a few more hours of sleep, but this is what God asks of us for our fellow brothers and sisters."

Quoting their conversations on biblical scripture from the night before, Dan insisted that there is a connection between the message of the Gospels and the significance of their own community volunteering. "Our service [to the community] is a heartfelt reflection on the role of Christian families in God's plan for humanity and it sticks with you the whole week long." As parents of three young children, ages seven through eleven, Dan and Lita hope that this vision of

Christian community will rub off on their kids. Explaining this, Dan suggested that volunteering at the soup kitchen is "a special way of teaching our children compassion for others." He believes that the work exposes the kids to the "other realities of life." Agreeing, Lita offered that this "is not something they will learn in school."

Once we arrived at Fishes and Loaves, the Cruz family unloaded the van and helped other volunteers from various backgrounds prepare the day's meal. It was not exactly a home-cooked meal but it was warm and made with loving intentions. Returning to our conversation from the previous night, I asked Dan again how he sees his faith in the context of building or engaging community. After a short pause, Dan stated, "It is here [at Fishes and Loaves] that we have a real chance to build God's community through love and service."

Questioning Dan further, I asked him what this sense of community has to do with being Catholic or Filipino. Laughing, Dan joked, "Aren't all Filipinos Catholic?" On a more serious note, Dan explained that he was just kidding. "Seriously, most of us are [Catholic], but that doesn't mean that we all practice our faith." Giving her own thoughts, Lita stated, "We are doing his [God's] work here [at Fishes and Loaves] by reminding each other that all of us, served or serving, are children of the one Father no matter how poor or sinful. This is not something uniquely Filipino. We are all brothers and sisters in Christ who must strive to nurture his Church, our family, and the fellowship of God's kingdom here on Earth." After cleaning up after lunch, the Cruz family packed up the van and headed off. On the drive home, Dan and Lita talked to their children about the day, hoping that they had learned a valuable lesson.

On another occasion on the other side of town, I spoke with Lyn, a first-generation Filipina American Catholic in her early sixties, about her views on faith and community. Lyn had been standing in her kitchen for hours making *hopia*, a Filipino pastry made of green mongo (mung) beans. Like my time with the Cruz family, it was a busy Saturday for Lyn as she prepared well over fifty pastries for the San Lorenzo Center's fundraiser to be held that night at 8 P.M. According to Lyn, the San Lorenzo Center, named for the first canonized Filipino Catholic saint, San Lorenzo Ruiz de Manila, is the only independent Filipino American community center in Houston. When I asked Lyn about the center, she told me that it is important to her as a first-generation Filipina. "It's a place of our own where Filipinos can get together to share our faith, culture, and food." Laughing a bit, Lyn also commented that San Lorenzo is special because "I can dance with Federico [her husband] and our friends all night long."

Talking to Lyn, it became clear that San Lorenzo is only a small part of her rich community life. Like the Cruzes, she is active in a host of Filipino American groups and activities in addition to her parish church. However, this does not seem to be enough for Lyn. She told me that she does not have the time to get involved in her community as much as she would like, "I just don't have any time to do anything else, there is so much more I would like to do." For Lyn, watching her grandchildren, caring for her own house, attending prayer meetings, and singing in the church choir take up a lot of her time. When I asked Lyn about making time to bake and help out with the San Lorenzo fundraiser, she suggested, "I do what I can to help, it isn't much . . . I don't volunteer or anything like that."

As we continued to talk, our conversation was interrupted several times by the ringing of the telephone in the kitchen. Lyn was unable to pick it up while in the heat of cooking, but each time the phone rang she stopped her thoughts and listened to the message as it was being recorded. At first the calls posed a bit of a distraction to our interview, but as I listened more intently, the nature of these calls became increasingly important to our conversation.

One call was from Gary. The message was brief and was simply an inquiry as to what he and his wife should bring to the fundraiser that night. Another call, a bit more formal, was from a representative or volunteer for the Catholic Archdiocese of Houston-Galveston calling to remind Lyn, although not by name, to vote in the coming election: "I am calling you, as a good Catholic, to remind you that the coming election is an important one. The issues of immigration and gay marriage are central to the teaching of the Church. . . . The future of the country depends on your vote. The ability of the Church to attend to the poor, many of whom are immigrants, depends on you. The future of the family, a union sanctified by God as a model of community, is being threatened in the coming election. Please vote, it is your civic right and your duty as a Catholic." Looking at Lyn for an explanation, she stated this was the first time she had ever received a call like this from the archdiocese. Somewhat surprised, she offered, "I usually vote, but every year people are telling me that the issues are more and more important." Lyn then told me, "Father has been preaching about these issues a lot this year."

Inquiring further, I asked Lyn if her priest had ever asked her to vote for a certain candidate. "Oh no," Lyn replied, "Father José reminds us what is important to the Church and all of us as Catholics . . . who we vote for is up to us." Taking out the last batch of hopia, Lyn left me with one final thought before she excused herself to get ready for the fundraiser. "Religion and politics is tricky for us Filipinos, but we all try to do what God would ask of us, especially when it comes to the sanctity of the family."

INTRODUCTION

These brief snapshots of life and community represent a typical Saturday for many Filipino American Catholics who have immigrated to the United States since 1965. They reveal what it means to be Filipino, American, and Catholic. Their stories also offer a glimpse of the often hidden but vital relationships between religion and community in the lives of new immigrants. Drawing further attention to the importance of these relationships, this book analyzes the powerful influence of culture, specifically Catholicism, in motivating and shaping Filipino American community life through consciously held beliefs and commitments centered on the sanctity of the family.[2] It argues that through these beliefs and commitments, Filipino Americans not only have the potential to reshape American Catholicism but are also building communities that impact American civic life in the process.

Scholars have long been puzzled by the fact that American Catholicism is devoted to messages of community and provides numerous opportunities for its parishioners to get involved, but does not necessarily lead them to volunteer or participate in other forms of civic engagement at rates higher or even comparable to that of American Protestants.[3] However, in exploring this puzzle, few scholars have studied what these patterns mean for the civic life of new Catholic immigrants. This book demonstrates how cultural forces not only shape the parish and community life of Filipino American Catholic immigrants but also compel them to take action on family issues such as poverty and abortion that extend well beyond any one parish and the Filipino American community itself. Both the Cruzes and Lyn, throughout our conversations, emphasized the importance of family to them as Filipinos and as Catholics. Dan and Lita, for example, make concerted efforts to bring their immediate family together and educate their children about the importance of community. They see themselves, their children, and those that they serve at Fishes and Loaves as God's children. Their civic life is viewed as a spiritual obligation that extends the needs of their own personal family to a greater good and a larger understanding of family. Although there are certainly differences between the Cruzes' and Lyn's idealization of this broader sacred family and the reality of their own mundane familial situations, their faith in action is seen as a means to build God's kingdom. They are driven by this sacred vision, but also struggle with the complications of very earthly realities as they try to bring it about in their own homes and community.

Most Americans would suggest that Lyn is civically active; however, she does not use these terms to describe herself or her efforts. Lyn does not think of herself as a volunteer or a model citizen but as a good Catholic woman trying to do what is best for her family and the community. At the center of this community are her immediate family, her prayer group, the parish church, and the San Lorenzo Ruiz de Manila Center—among others. For Lyn, these overlapping community circles are her family both literally and figuratively, with little or no distinction made among them. Baking and helping out with the San Lorenzo fundraiser is not seen by Lyn as community building but as an extension of her care for a larger family. The same love and attention she puts into cooking hopia for her own immediate family is simply extended to others. Lyn's efforts, both in the community and in her home for her biological family, are an important part of her broader cultural understandings of what it means to be a Filipina (woman), a mother, a *lola* (Ta, grandmother), and a Catholic.

When Lyn refers to her parish priest as "Father," it is not just a gesture of respect; she views him as the center of her community and the head of a broader Catholic family. Lyn sees her priest as a direct intercessory with the Holy Family, connecting an earthly family to the divine. Like many families, however, some form of conflict is normative—not everyone agrees all the time or even most of the time. Filipino American individual and collective interests across communities and associations can and do lead to conflict. At the center lies the Catholic Church. Both revered and subject to intense criticism, the Catholic Church and its priests are often placed in the precarious position of directly and indirectly mediating individual and community relations. For the Cruzes and Lyn, their understanding of a universal Catholic family draws them together as brothers and sisters, but for others in this study, the Catholic Church and its clergy can be a point of contention.

At the heart of this book are intimate accounts of the civic lives of first-generation Filipino American Catholics and the ways in which they think and feel faith matters to all things civic. Their stories provide unique insights into the role of religion in new immigrant civic life. They reveal both the possible benefits and drawbacks of being religious. Understanding this and building on previous scholarship, this book approaches the intersection of religion and civic life with the understanding that people in religious groups and institutions experience many of the same constraints and opportunities as those in nonreligious associations and institutions.[4] Both religious and secular institutions have their own special cultures in which people may struggle to find their place, conform, or seek their own paths and identities. The cultures of the people themselves also matter and can have just as powerful an influence on these institutions. In some cases, this can result in competing forces within these institutions, while in others, the two may converge or facilitate each other in a more dialectical relationship.[5] Yet it is not so much whether Catholicism is good or bad for building community or facilitating American civic life as it is a matter of understanding its impact on individuals and groups. This requires a more grounded exploration of what new Catholic immigrants actually do civically.

Few works have explored the role of Catholicism in new immigrant civic life with an eye on culture. Even fewer have done so looking specifically at Filipino Americans, one of the largest immigrant populations in the country and the second largest source of Catholic immigration.[6] Where previous scholarship has stressed the importance of religious institutions as purveyors of social capital for new immigrant civic life, I join a small but growing number of scholars who suggest that cultural meanings and moral obligations are equally important.[7]

Throughout this book, the words and experiences of Filipino Americans like the Cruz family and Lyn demonstrate how cultural frameworks can shape understandings of the family and animate Catholic immigrant moral commitments to community.[8] Revealing more than Filipino American Catholic community lives, their discourses and the snapshots of their community activities engage the larger question of how religion can, if at all, facilitate the civic life of its newest inhabitants and citizens. Their stories also allow us to compare on a broader level how immigrants attempt to build community through the mobilization of cultural resources within a national context that has not always been welcoming. As the United States continues to diversify racially, ethnically, and religiously, these questions are just as relevant today as they were in the past.

HISTORIC CONCERNS OVER CATHOLIC IMMIGRANT ASSIMILATION

From the late nineteenth through the early twentieth centuries, successive waves of immigration to the United States elevated the American Catholic Church to the largest single religious denomination in the country.[9] Today, new waves of Catholic immigrants are once again transforming the American racial and religious landscape and propelling Catholicism back to the same position. In the last decade alone, immigration has accounted for roughly three-quarters of the population growth in the United States, and much of this growth has been Catholic.[10] Only two prior decades, from 1900 to 1910 and from 1990 to 2000, exceed this growth in the number of immigrants. Today, the United States is home to more immigrants than at any point in its history. As with past immigrant waves, debates and nativists' concerns surrounding new immigrants shape the environment in which they seek citizenship, the spaces in which they forge new or amalgamated identities, and the context in which they develop their own sense of community. This environment is important to our understanding of the opportunities and constraints placed on new immigrant populations.[11] It is also of particular importance to the study of Catholic immigrants today, many of whom are coming from a political and cultural context in which they were a majority in their country of origin to one in which they are both religious and racial minorities.

Historically, the growth of Catholic immigrant populations challenged the cultural and civic dominance of the white colonial Protestant establishment. From 1820 to 1930, for example, roughly four and half million Irish Catholics entered the United States along with large waves of Germans, Poles, and Italians. Many native-born Americans feared that this numeric growth would somehow lead to the papacy taking over the country. Amidst these concerns and others, national anti-immigration legislation was passed that lengthened the time it took to become a citizen. Catholic churches were vandalized, lay and clergy members were killed, and a host of social sanctions privatized schools, social clubs, and civic associations so that Catholics could not join or participate.[12]

Several political groups such as the Order of the Star Spangled Banner, which eventually became the American Know Nothing Party in 1854, mobilized fears against immigrants and stated that Americans must rule America. Mounting successful political campaigns built on this platform, the party claimed that Protestantism emphasized individualism and supported democracy, while Catholicism emphasized hierarchical authoritarianism and placed the priest-hood as an intercessory between God and the governance of society.[13] These widespread concerns fueled additional questions over the assimilability of Cath-olic immigrants and the degree to which they were free from so-called Catholic rule to contribute to a democratic American society.

The Civil War provided a brief lull in the American immigration debate, but by the late 1800s through the turn of the century, this changed. From 1900 to 1910, the United States experienced one of the largest influxes of immigrants in its history. Xenophobia once again ran wild amid the rise of the American Eugen-ics movement and nativists' protests against those who identified themselves as hyphenated Americans.[14] Anti-Catholic sentiments also reemerged, influencing the passage of literacy laws that prevented newly arriving immigrants, specifi-cally the Italians, from voting. Where earlier nativists' concerns were directed toward Irish Catholics, during this period they were largely imposed on Italian Catholics and Eastern European Jews.

In California, concerns also grew over increased Filipino Catholic immi-gration following the United States' violent acquisition of the Philippines as a colony after the Spanish-American War.[15] Although Filipinos were technically citizens after the war, they were widely demonized not so much for their Catholic faith as for their race and ethnicity. Given that Filipino immigrants were once colonial subjects, their racialization differed from that of other Asian immigrant groups entering the state. Filipinos were not simply racialized minorities in a largely white American context, but colonized nationals who were subject to these processes within their homeland even prior to migration. The 1903 United States census of the Philippines, for example, divided the Filipino population into two general categories—Christian or Civilized Tribes and Non-Christian or Wild Tribes, which included Chinese and other so-called foreign elements in the Filipino races.[16] Once in the United States, Filipinos' increasing presence in agri-cultural labor led to fears that they were taking away jobs from native-born labor-ers. This further complicated the ways in which they were received in American communities. Anti-Filipino outbursts erupted throughout California.[17] Build-ing on these fears and pseudo-scientific eugenic justifications of white suprem-acy, anti-miscegenation laws were enacted prohibiting Filipinos and other new immigrants from marrying whites.[18] Like other racialized groups entering the United States, Filipinos found their rights in the country to be severely limited by discriminatory and segregating practices and policies.[19] Throughout the 1920s, the United States also passed a series of laws that limited immigration through the establishment of national origins quotas. In 1934, the Tydings-McDuffie Act answered the specific call for Filipino exclusion by granting the Philippines grad-ual independence over a twelve-year period, thereby stripping all Filipinos of their American citizenship by 1946.

During this period (1920–1940s), it became painfully clear who was welcome and who was not. This inhospitable environment severely limited Catholics' access to American civil society and in many cases prevented them from running for public office. It also relegated them to Catholic ghettos that confined their social memberships and participation to their own racial/ethnic groups and the American Catholic Church.[20] While for some this environment, coupled with their experiences of racism within the American Catholic Church itself, led them to convert to Protestantism or become nonreligious, for others it fostered an American Catholic identity across racial/ethnic groups.[21] In time, this gave way to a Catholic subculture that would eventually build institutions, religious and secular, that somewhat mirrored those they were cut off from in the larger society.[22]

Throughout the twentieth century, the social status of Catholics dramatically improved. The establishment of Catholic charities, schools, and universities, together with increased ownership of businesses by an emerging Catholic middle class, raised their average education and economic levels significantly.[23] By 1900, for example, the American Catholic Church supported over eight hundred charitable institutions and educated an estimated one million children in parochial schools across the nation without tuition fees, even though most Catholics were still working class.[24] The New Deal (1933–1936) also provided a unique opportunity for Catholics to get involved in social activism, as many saw Roosevelt's social reforms as a way they could be both good Catholics and good Americans.[25] Irish and Italian Catholics, as well as others from European decent, were now commonly accepted as white.[26] This was not the case, however, for Filipinos and others who still faced intense racial and ethnic discrimination.

In general, anti-Catholic rhetoric dissipated as American Catholics demonstrated their loyalty to the country time and again through their home efforts and military service in World Wars I and II, the Korean War, and Vietnam. During this period Catholics increasingly joined the ranks of the middle class, became members of civic organizations outside of their parishes, and gained high-profile public positions. In 1956, for example, William J. Brennan Jr. withstood pressing attacks from Senator Joseph McCarthy over his Catholic faith to become a Justice of the Supreme Court. That same year, Senator John F. Kennedy was selected to run as vice president by presidential nominee Adlai Stevenson, but they eventually lost to the Eisenhower ticket. Four years later Kennedy was elected as the thirty-fifth president of the United States.

Kennedy won despite widespread concerns over his Catholic background. It was an indication that anti-Catholic sentiments were still present, but it was also a sign that these fears had largely lost their power to shape public policy or dissuade Catholics from entering the American civic sphere. In 1962, two years after Kennedy's election to office, the spirit of Vatican II further encouraged Catholics, particularly women, to engage civic life by joining civic associations and entering the political sphere to vote or take action on issues of social justice.[27] Vatican

II also called for an end to organizing national ethnic parishes to bring about greater unity in the Church. Catholics were encouraged to celebrate their ethnic and racial differences but also to come together as a singular Church.[28] American Catholics, immigrant or not, were called upon to be civically and culturally integrated under this new spirit. This had a tremendous impact on newly arriving Catholic immigrants to the United States such as Filipinos, who initially found themselves lost in an American Catholicism that was not completely familiar or fully supportive of their specific cultural needs and practices. However, despite essentially ending national parishes based on ethnic origins, other Vatican II reforms such as the vernacular mass actually provided a powerful means by which the Church could increasingly reach out to ethnic groups such as Latinos through Spanish-language services.

Kennedy's presidency was cut short by assassination, but one of his last acts as president was to propose a series of major immigration reforms to Congress that would end race and national origin quotas. As the grandson of Irish Catholic immigrants himself, immigration was a primary concern of Kennedy and his brothers. In 1957 the Anti-Defamation League had approached John F. Kennedy, then the junior Senator from Massachusetts, to write about the contribution of immigrants to the United States and act as a voice for policy change. The resulting book, *A Nation of Immigrants*, extolled the historic benefits of immigration to the nation and highlighted immigrants' importance to the future of American democracy. Returning to the historical writings of the French aristocrat Alexis de Tocqueville, who visited the United States in the early 1800s, as so many scholars and social pundits have done and continue to do, Kennedy asserted that de Tocqueville's America was a society of immigrants built by peoples of widely diverse racial, ethnic, socioeconomic, and religious backgrounds.[29] Both de Tocqueville and Kennedy believed that immigrants, including Catholics, not only fortify the fabric of American life but the freedom and longevity of the nation's civic sphere.

In 1965, President Johnson signed the 1965 Immigration Act into law. The passage of the legislation led to a dramatic shift in the American racial and religious landscape. From 1965 to 1970 the foreign-born population doubled and then doubled again between 1970 and 1990. These new immigrants, post-1965, were and are markedly different from prior immigrant waves. They are racially and ethnically more varied, come from a greater variety of countries, and bring with them a multitude of linguistic and cultural forms that are either new or little known.[30] Yet for all their diversity, the shift in countries of origin from Europe in prior waves to Asia, Africa, and South and Central America today has resulted in a massive Catholic immigration from Mexico and the Philippines that rivals that of the Irish and Italians a hundred years ago. Although Latino immigrants today have been largely racialized as a menace while Asian immigrants have been characterized as a model minority, both of these new immigrant groups find themselves in the midst of controversy and intense national debate over immigration policy.

Contemporary Questions about Catholic Immigrant Assimilation

Today debate once again surrounds immigration policy as people question, among other things, whether the continued growth of the foreign-born population will cause lower wages and worsen conditions for American-born workers or reduce incentives for some industries to modernize.[31] In addition to these concerns and amid growing fears after September 11 that immigrants pose a national security risk, issues have also been raised over the assimilability of new immigrants.[32] Political scientists such as Samuel Huntington contend that issues of assimilation are more pressing for new immigrants today than they were in the past, in large part because of the influx of Latino immigrants.[33] He suggests that Latinos are hostile to becoming American, both literally as citizens and culturally. Given Latinos' proximity to the border and the strength of their cultural and political ties to their countries of origin, some, like Huntington, have also asserted that Latinos pose a threat to national security.

What has been raised as a particular concern is Latinos' common linguistic bond in Spanish, which some scholars and social pundits claim may eventually threaten the dominance of the English language in the United States.[34] However, these fears have not been raised solely against immigrants from Latin America. For the last decade Filipino nurses, a large percentage of whom are first-generation immigrants, have been monitored and restricted from speaking Tagalog, the national language of the Philippines, by English-only codes in California hospitals. Faced with harassment and discrimination, many of their complaints have resulted in lawsuits.[35] Within the Filipino community these incidents are not seen as something new, but as part of a long history of discrimination that has made them feel unwelcomed despite being active and contributing citizens.[36]

During much of the nineteenth and early twentieth centuries, the United States was often thought of, at least metaphorically, as a melting pot—a social experiment in which immigrants would lose what made them ethnic by slowly adopting mainstream values, norms, beliefs, and practices. The reality today, and even then for that matter, is far more complex. The classical assimilation paradigm has increasingly been challenged particularly in how we understand the processes of immigrant acculturation, structural adaptation, and incorporation.[37] While contemporary theorists who support the more general assimilation framework still hold to the idea that new immigrants will become less ethnic the further generationally they are removed from their ancestral homeland, they also suggest that immigrants do not lose their culture but rather mainstream society absorbs it over time.[38] Those who support the segmented assimilation perspective, on the other hand, suggest that there are multiple trajectories that shape and inform the assimilation process—a case in which immigrants may become more ethnic in regards to some cultural practices such as religion and more mainstream in other cultural practices at the same time.[39]

This certainly appears to be the case historically for Catholic immigrants such as the Irish and Italians, but in the case of Filipinos and other new immigrants from the global South, their race and ethnicity have presented and continue to present other barriers to their access to American civil society. Filipinos do not necessarily need to give up being Catholic to become American—Catholics are widely seen as Americans today. However, in a post-Vatican II assimilationist Catholicism, one that no longer supports ethnic parishes, Filipino Catholics may be asked to give up or deemphasize their ethnic practices to become American Catholics. [40] Conservative Catholics warn that after Vatican II, American Catholics are being asked to give up their subcultural identities for an American one that on many levels may be in conflict with their more traditional religious commitments and the ways in which they understand their Catholic faith. [41] Beyond this, the fact remains that racism based simply on the color of people's skin or their pronunciation of the English language can still present barriers to American civic life. This is particularly problematic for new Asian immigrants such as Filipinos, who often feel trapped between images as an Asian model minority and physical features that lead to their portrayal as foreign despite being citizens or native-born. [42] As a so-called model minority they are often seen as capable of overcoming socioeconomic disadvantages through certain ethnic and cultural traits that predispose them to be successful. However, these images are often overinflated and disregard their actual socioeconomic status and struggles. Likewise, given the history of their racialization in the United States, Asian immigrants such as Filipinos have also been seen as forever foreign and hence perceived to be somehow less engaged with American society, regardless of their level of so-called assimilation. [43] It is a complex and troubling paradox.

The central questions over assimilation today are not so much whether immigrants will become more or less ethnic or even whether they will be incorporated into American society, but the degree to which the current environment will impact their incorporation and the terms and conditions under which it occurs. [44] Although an increasing number of scholars have begun to address questions about the assimilation of new immigrants in terms of their economic or sociocultural incorporation, fewer have studied how immigrants define and engage community—a matter of civic incorporation. [45] Several scholars have explored the role ethnic enclaves and institutions play in immigrant civic life, but their findings have not been conclusive. [46] Some find that ethnic enclaves limit civic incorporation by further isolating immigrants from the wider society, while others suggest that they provide a host of physical and psychological resources that immigrants can mobilize as they find their paths to incorporation. [47] Where many scholars are in agreement is that religious institutions often stand at the center of these processes. [48] The religiosity of new immigrants matters. Where religion was once ignored in immigration studies, today scholars are increasingly forced to take it into serious consideration as a major influence on new immigrants' ability to access and be incorporated into American civic life. Despite this trend, numerous questions remain over the general role of religious denominations in American civil society, and hence questions still persist over the extent denominations impact the lives and community efforts of newly arriving immigrants.

IMMIGRATION AND THE PUZZLE OF CATHOLIC CIVIC LIFE

Some scholars have declared that Catholic civic life in the United States is a puzzle.[49] Catholic institutions and teachings continue to foster a more communitarian ethic, and American Catholics appear, for the most part, to be receiving these messages.[50] Mounting empirical evidence suggests, however, that there is little difference between the way Catholics and people of other religious traditions participate in American civic life.[51] This is a paradox. Why are American Catholics no more or less likely to be civically engaged than other Christians, given such an emphasis by the Catholic Church on communitarian messages and social works?[52] Some scholars suggest that priests have been given more leeway in changing the organizational culture of their parishes and hence differences between Catholics and Protestants churches are no longer absolute.[53] Others suggest that in becoming more middle class or assimilating over time, American Catholics have given up what was distinctive about their Catholic faith and adopted more Protestant traits.[54] Still others suggest that the average size of most Catholic parishes results in less social capital being generated for civic life compared to other Christian denominations. In other words, despite historical characterizations of Catholicism as a "friend of the poor" or exemplifying a community-centered ethic, these scholars suggest that being Catholic may, in some cases, actually discourage civic participation relative to other Christian traditions.[55]

Sydney Verba and his colleagues, for example, suggest that being Protestant of any denomination promotes participation in civic life, while being Catholic is a hindrance due to the hierarchical and less democratic structure of the Catholic Church.[56] Likewise, comparing predominately Catholic and Protestant nations, Pui-Yan Lam finds that Catholics are less likely to be members of voluntary associations than Protestants, and Catholic nations have lower membership rates in these types of associations compared to Protestant nations, including the United States.[57] Echoing long-standing arguments about Catholics' ability to acquire civic skills, these studies highlight the fact that despite changes in Catholic culture since Vatican II, the locus of moral authority within the Church remains highly centralized. Catholic parishes also remain rather large, and the number of priests available to attend to these parishes is dwindling.[58] This situation may be the result of the Church's historical attempts to establish an encompassing set of institutions that could insulate a Catholic subculture from American xenophobia rather than build bridges to the wider public sphere.[59]

Given this reality, some scholars question the extent to which Catholic parishes still fit the congregational template.[60] Others find that despite structural concerns about the American Catholic Church and its ability to mobilize people beyond collectivist conceptions of moral authority, churches in Chicago, particularly those with a significant number of Filipino American parishioners, deviate from these patterns and place considerable value on individual freedom.[61] This is more than coincidental, as I will argue. Although all of the questions raised above are compelling and warrant further study in their own right, few scholars, if any, have fully considered these issues in light of recent Catholic immigration—the most dynamic force in American Catholicism today.[62]

Immigration was and continues to be the source of growth and vitality in the American Catholic Church. Historically, Irish, Polish, and Italian immigration made the Church the largest religious denomination in the nation. Today, immigration from Mexico and the Philippines, among others, is doing the same. Immigrants' ethnicity, as was the case with earlier waves of immigration, reinforces American Catholicism as much as it does their own ethnic identity—and this is not necessarily bad for the United States.[63] Historically, at least based on the respected nineteenth-century observations of Alexis de Tocqueville, the reinforcement of an ethnic Catholic identity was not always seen as anti-democratic but vital to the ability of Catholic immigrants to build and engage the American civic sphere. Although his comments about Irish Catholic immigrants predate the most substantial waves of later immigration, I suggest that de Tocqueville's words are just as relevant today in describing newly arriving Catholic immigrants as they were then. "These Catholics show great fidelity to the observations of their religion and are full of ardor and zeal for their beliefs; however, they form the most republican and most democratic class that exists in the United States.... I think that it is wrong to regard the Catholic religion as a natural enemy of democracy. Among the different Christian doctrines, Catholicism seems to me on the contrary one of the most favorable to equality of conditions."[64] Today the Irish, Poles, and Italians are considered just as American as anyone else, but given current debates and popular opinion, this is not necessarily the case for newly arriving Catholic immigrants from the global South.

Scholars and social pundits alike are once again questioning the contributions and place of Catholic immigrants in America. Where the Catholic Church is seen by some scholars as a transnational, multiethnic institution that can encompass a host of possibilities for immigrant social and civic incorporation, others question not only whether Catholic immigrants can become American but also the degree to which the Church can facilitate the process.[65] For the latter, it is not so much the content of religious beliefs that concerns scholars as the way religious life is structured and practiced. Some scholars suggest that the Catholic Church benefits more from immigration than the immigrants benefit from Catholicism. David Lopez, for example, suggests that in the case of Mexican Catholics there is very little that the American Catholic Church does today to advance their socio-economic success compared to prior immigrant waves.[66] He also points out that, unlike the Irish or Italians, Mexicans are sorely underrepresented in everything from enrollment in parish schools to the priesthood and the hierarchy of the Church itself. Given that other studies do not fully support these claims, considerable debate remains.[67]

The Italian-Mexican immigrant comparison has rightly drawn increasing theoretical discussion. However, in highlighting the fact that both represent the great low-wage labor migrations of their time and were/are vital to the future of the American Catholic Church, these studies have largely ignored other Catholic immigrants. At two and a half million people and growing, Asian American Catholics are an important part of the demographic transformation of American Catholicism.[68] One of the Asian American groups having the greatest influence is Filipino Americans. Although numerically smaller than the Mexican immigrant population today or the Irish and Italian waves of the last two centuries, Filipino immigrants hold the distinction of not only being former colonial subjects but also being an important part of both eras of the country's greatest increases in immigration. Their numeric growth over the last decade is also one of the central reasons why Asians have for the first time in recent history collectively surpassed the influx of Latino/Hispanic immigrants moving to the United States.[69] As a result, Asian immigration now exceeds that of Latinos.

Filipinos are more than just one of the many immigrant groups whose religious and civic life we should be studying today. Like Mexicans, their sheer size alone begs further study, if for no other reason than to understand what their numeric growth means for the future of American religious and civic life. This is not to say that other populations are not important; they are. However, to put things into perspective, we know more collectively about the religious and civic life of Korean and Japanese Americans than that of Filipinos, whose population is larger than both of these groups combined. We must understand how Filipino Catholicism differs from American Catholicism in practice and beliefs. We must also question the potential impact these differences may have on American Catholicism itself. Equally important, and central to the arguments of this book, we must question, regardless of their numeric size, how Filipinos' religious life impacts their civic life in the larger context of the puzzle of American Catholic civic life.

FILIPINO CATHOLICS IN AMERICA AFTER 1965

Despite the fact that Filipinos have lived in the United States for over two hundred years—they are one of the oldest Asian immigrant groups in the country—it was not until 1898, after the United States' violent acquisition of the Philippines from Spain, that Filipinos first came in significant numbers.[70] From the turn of the nineteenth century through the mid-1920s, Filipino migration steadily grew. The Great Depression and the passage of the Tydings-McDuffie Act in 1935 effectively brought an end to major Filipino immigration, as American xenophobia and racism halted their immigration into the country.[71] Thirty years later, the 1965 Immigration Act raised the immigration quota for Filipinos and other Asians to 20,000, a dramatic increase from the meager 50 a year legislated previously.[72] After 1965, the number of Filipinos migrating to the United States dramatically increased.[73] However, as some scholars have noted, the 1965 Immigration Act is not the sole reason why so many Filipinos have come and continue to come to the United States. The unique military, economic, and cultural ties forged with the Philippines throughout its history as an American colony and then as an ally today have also shaped these flows.[74]

Today, the foreign-born Filipino American population is almost two million people (1.7 million) or a little over 4 percent of all the foreign-born population in the nation, and this estimate does not include the nearly 280,000 unauthorized Filipino immigrants living in the country as of 2010.[75] Of the adult Filipino American population, 69 percent is foreign-born, and an estimated 53 percent of the overall Filipino American community is foreign-born.[76] From 2000 to 2010, the Filipino American community grew by roughly 44 percent, compared to only 39 percent growth in the Chinese American community, currently the largest Asian American community.[77] Given these gains, Filipinos could become the largest Asian American community in the near future.[78] Although the rapid increase of Filipino immigrants has slowed somewhat from its pace in the 1990s, roughly 25 percent of all Filipinos, the majority of whom are women, arrived in 2000 or later.[79]

Women are an important part of the Filipino diaspora both culturally and economically. Nearly one in every four employed immigrant Filipinas, for example, worked as a registered nurse in 2008.[80] Overall, as of 2008, Filipinas were more likely to participate in the civilian labor force than all other foreign-born women. Filipino men, by comparison, participated less in the civilian labor force than all other foreign-born men.[81] Regardless of employment but obviously linked to the nation's economy, between 2000 and 2008, the number of Filipino immigrants in three states, California, Illinois, and New York, grew by 25,000 or more. Despite the fact that California remains Filipinos' number one migration destination, their presence has increased around the country, especially in Nevada, Florida, and Texas, where their population has grown anywhere from 77 percent to 142 percent between 2000 and 2010.[82] Unlike prior waves of Filipino immigrants before 1965, Filipino immigrants today are not primarily low-wage laborers but, by and large, are educated professionals and tend to be doing better socioeconomically than many immigrant populations.

As was the case historically, Filipino immigrants today constitute a rather diverse population. They come from over 7,000 islands (the exact number depending on the tide, as many Filipinos will jokingly tell you), and bring with them a multitude of cultural and religious practices, not to mention a host of regional linguistic and provincial differences. From Tagalogs and Ilocanos to Bicolanos and Cebuanos, to name a few ethnic/regional groups, Filipinos are not a singular people, but like earlier waves of Italian immigrants represent diverse communities from the same nation.

Religiously, as was noted earlier, the Philippines is the second largest source of Catholic immigration to the United States. Although clearly not all Filipinos are Catholic, Catholicism has been one of, if not the single, most culturally pervasive influences in the Philippines over the last four hundred years.[83] Today, 86 percent of Filipinos in the Philippines claim to be Catholic—over sixty-one million adherents and growing.[84] The Catholic Church reports that nearly two million Catholics (1.7 million) are baptized every year in the Philippines, more than the combined totals of France, Spain, Italy, and Poland. At the present rate of baptisms, the Filipino Catholic population could grow to upward of ninety million in 2025, and by 2050 this total could reach one hundred and thirty-nine million, making the Philippines home to one of the largest Catholic populations on the planet.[85]

In terms of religious practice and the importance of Catholicism to Filipinos in the Philippines, more than half of all adult Filipinos report attending church at least once every week, if not more. The pope is still widely considered one of the most trusted and idolized figures in the country, and Philippine Catholicism stands as one of the most traditional and conservative adherents to a traditional form of Catholicism. Compared to the more liberal views of Catholics in nations such as Ireland, Germany, Spain, Poland, Italy, and the United States, Filipinos reported in 2002 that they would like the next pope to be less open to change in the Church, to oppose priests getting married, and to be more focused on religious issues rather than what life is like for the ordinary person.[86] Given these views and the cultural prevalence of Catholicism in the Philippines, being Filipino has historically become synonymous with being Catholic. It is an ethnically fused religious identity that is forged in childhood and carried on throughout life. Philippine citizens, as some scholars have pointed out, are expected not only to be law-abiding people but also God-fearing Catholics who are taught to see the Church as a "fourth branch of government."[87] Filipino Catholics are unique in this respect among all other Asian Christians.[88]

In migration, Catholicism remains important to Filipinos as both a resource and cause for solidarity.[89] Every year over a million temporary workers leave the Philippines to work overseas in an estimated 190 countries. They join roughly nine million Filipinos (8.7 million) who have already left the Philippines, making them one of the largest migrant populations in the world.[90] Of the numerous destinations for Filipinos in migration, the United States remains among the top draws. By most accounts, although subject to considerable theoretical debate, they are a people in diaspora.[91] Although Filipino migrants have a home to return to, most do not return permanently.[92] For many Filipinos, home is thus as much a place that is dear to their hearts and heritage as it is the physical location in which they reside.

Ironically, where Filipinos were once the target of Spanish and American colonial proselytizing, today Filipino Catholics join a growing number of formerly colonized people in the global South who are proselytizing back to the heart of these empires and heralding that their former colonial rulers have lost their way. As several scholars have noted, these more "southern" manifestations of Christianity, including a charismatic variety of Filipino Catholicism, are not only markedly more theologically conservative but are also compelling several social developments internationally that may impact both the way Christianity is identified or defined and the way in which global sociocultural relations are structured.[93]

Filipinos in the American diaspora are no exception to these patterns. Although comparable statistics to the Social Weather Survey cited above do not fully exist for Filipino American religiosity, the United States Conference of Catholic Bishops estimates that roughly 83 percent of Filipino Americans are Catholic.[94] Other survey estimates suggest that the number of Filipino American Catholics overall, both foreign-born and native-born, is closer to 65 percent of the community, but still a strong majority.[95] Ethnographic accounts of Filipino Americans likewise suggest that many Filipinos are just as religiously active in the United States as they are in the Philippines and are equally conservative or traditional in their Catholic practice.[96] By and large, they go to mass every Sunday, if not more often, and still ardently celebrate their special devotional practices both in their daily lives and around major religious holidays. Many Filipinos, for example, are just as active in venerating their Philippine provincial saints in the United States through lay-led novenas as they were in their hometowns. Traditions such as Simbang Gabi (Ta), which celebrates the nine days leading up to Christmas, are also still celebrated annually and are increasingly visible in parishes across America.

Religion continues to have a tremendous impact on Filipino American civic life, as well. Research on the religious practices of Filipino Americans in San Francisco, for example, suggests that their faith provides a key lens through which they view their civic engagement and their integration into American life.[97] Although these studies do not focus exclusively on Catholics, they suggests that the development of *kamashan* (Ta), or a sense of togetherness in and through religious institutions, urges Filipino Americans to convert this energy into a sense of civic unity and community action or *bayanihan* (Ta)—a matter of bonding and bridging capital.[98] Beyond these important resources, the meanings and moral obligations that Filipino Americans attach to various forms of community participation are equally important and are not fully explained by these capital-only approaches.

Like other immigrant Christians coming to the United States from various parts of the global South, Filipinos are more conservative than native-born American Christians. Their culturally conservative understandings of issues such as abortion and the moral commitments they engender, for example, shape and influence the ways in which they engage civic life. However, unlike many of these other conservative Christian groups immigrating from the global South, Filipinos by and large, do not live in ethnic enclaves, nor do they worship in independent ethnic churches that only serve their own ethnic communities. Today, unlike prior historical waves of Filipino migration, there is no discernible pattern to Filipino residential settlement.[99] Filipino Catholics, for the most part, worship in large multiracial/multiethnic parishes that serve various populations of a host of backgrounds, immigrant or not. Although this certainly does not mean that by their sheer size and scope Filipino Catholics have a greater impact on American civic life through their religious life, it does suggest, as I will argue in subsequent chapters, that through these more diverse contacts, structures, and opportunities there is greater potential to have a more far-reaching impact beyond their own ethnic community than groups who live solely in ethnic enclaves and whose houses of worship only serve their own ethnic populations.

Despite the distinctive characteristics outlined above and the fact that Filipino American Catholics are an important part of American demographic changes, they are surprisingly one of the least studied. As many Filipino scholars lament, Filipino Americans are all but an "invisible and silent minority" whose increasing presence has been sorely neglected in immigration and historical studies; they are the "forgotten Asian Americans."[100] Although Filipino American studies as a discipline continues to try and rectify this, few have explored the impact of Catholicism on Filipino American community life outside of using Catholic churches as sites for recruiting samples for study. Among those that have explored Filipino American religiosity, none has done so with an eye on cultural frameworks and the understanding that religion can both facilitate and present certain barriers to the formation and engagement of an immigrant community.[101] I explore these issues in the coming chapters by offering a complementary and comparative work outside of the typical California context of most Filipino American studies. In doing so, this book demonstrates how Filipino Americans have the potential to reshape American Catholicism beyond their large presence in California and are currently impacting American civil society more broadly through communities built on faith and family.

STUDYING FIRST-GENERATION FILIPINO AMERICAN CATHOLICS

My research is based primarily on ethnographic data collected in the Houston Filipino American community with extensive analysis of St. Catherine's Catholic Church (pseudonym), the San Lorenzo Ruiz de Manila Center, and a host of religious and secular associations over a six-year period.[102] St. Catherine's Catholic Church is one of, if not the largest Filipino American Catholic congregation in Houston. It is located in a lower- to middle-class socioeconomic area of southwest Houston. The area is highly diverse and predominately nonwhite. However, members of St. Catherine's do not necessarily live within the geographic jurisdiction of the parish but come from across Houston to attend and serve this specific parish. The San Lorenzo Ruiz de Manila Center is likewise located in southwest Houston but outside St. Catherine's parish in a remote part of the adjacent county. The center is the only independent Filipino American center in Houston outside of community center spaces located on church properties in various parishes.

Among a host of religious and secular groups, I studied two Filipino American ethnic associations, an umbrella institution that attempts to unite various Filipino groups, and several religious fellowships/prayer groups. Extensive time was spent studying two specific religious fellowships—Bibingka (pseudonym), named for a Filipino sweet cake, and Couples for Christ (CFC).[103] Although CFC is registered with St. Catherine's parish, it stands, like Bibingka, largely outside of its authority and control. Bibingka and CFC were selected specifically as cases that shared similar attributes but on varying levels. CFC household units, the formal sites for fellowship meetings, like Bibingka, are composed of roughly twenty-five people or fewer per group. However, CFC is a rather large international organization. In Houston, CFC has twelve household units to just one for Bibingka.[104]

In addition to conducting a detailed ethnographic study in each of these settings, I interviewed over 160 first-generation Filipino Americans over six years. I also surveyed over 200 first-generation Filipino Americans at St. Catherine's about issues ranging from religious and community participation to views on abortion and the Church's role in the community. The survey was conducted during a general public event on the anniversary of Philippine independence. Face-to-face interviews lasted anywhere from one to four hours and were often followed up with email or phone conversations. In addition to these interviews, I conducted several focus groups over this period. Likewise, I monitored and engaged Filipino American community listservs and on-line groups.[105] Triangulating this unique and original data collection, I situate it in the context of an extensive review of secondary literature on immigrant religious and civic life, including comparative census data about the wider United States Filipino American population.

WHY HOUSTON?

Houston has experienced one of the largest and most diverse influxes of immigrants to the United States since 1965. From 1960 to 1997, for example, the Houston foreign-born population increased by roughly 20 percent and continues to rise today.[106] As an emerging gateway city, Houston poses a unique case for study. Unlike other historical destinations for immigrants such as New York or San Francisco, Houston is almost exclusively a new immigrant destination—one that other scholars have rightly highlighted as an exemplar for studying religion and post-1965 immigration.[107]

Houston also represents a fairly new Filipino community.[108] Today, the Filipino American population in Harris and Fort Bend counties, Houston and its surrounding suburbs, is roughly 39,492 people and is growing at a rapid rate.[109] Houston joins other emerging metropolitan areas such as Las Vegas that have at least the same size foreign-born Filipino population or larger.[110] The growth of the Filipino population in these areas has been large enough that products and media that were once marketed exclusively to California, New York, or Chicago are now widely available. The Filipino Channel (TFC), which streams the latest news and programming from the Philippines, for example, only became available in Houston in the last five years. This can be attributed directly to the growth of Houston's Filipino population during this period and the expansion of the Texas Medical Center. The Texas Medical Center is the largest medical center in the world, with over fifty medicine-related institutions, fifteen hospitals, and three medical schools. The majority of Filipino American Houstonians are professionals, specifically medical professionals, and hence, as the Texas Medical Center has grown so has the Filipino American community.

Findings from the Houston Area Survey suggest that Filipino Houstonians are well educated, with over 78 percent holding college degrees.[111] They have also established over 1,203 businesses, many of them health related, and employ nearly 8,000 people with connections to other Filipino American companies on the West Coast.[112] Unlike the West Coast, Houston lacks the historical foundations of pre-1965 Filipino immigration, including the establishment of "Manila towns." While the age of the Manila towns, for the most part, has come and gone with the passing of many prior waves of first-generation immigrants, these historical roots provide a context for new Filipino immigrants on the West Coast that are not present in Houston.[113] The linkages with the past that exist in the Houston situation are more fluid and in many cases come as an inheritance brought to the area from other regions of the country or directly from the Philippines. Of the families and young couples that formed the core of my snowball sample, the majority resettled in Houston from either the East or West Coast, and all others entered the country through Houston to be reunited with family and friends. As a less established community, Houston serves as an excellent case for studying post-1965 immigrant civic life and the role religion plays in building community.[114]

BOOK OVERVIEW

To further explore the central arguments of this study, namely, that Filipino immigrants have the potential to reshape American Catholicism and are impacting American civil society through their Catholic faith, this book is organized into eight chapters. The first two chapters, including the present one, provide an overview of where Filipino Americans fit into the context of recent American immigration, Catholicism, and theories about American civic life. The remainder of the book is divided between chapters exploring how Filipino Americans define and build community and chapters analyzing how they navigate and engage it.

Chapter 2, "Catholic Culture and Filipino Families," discusses the historical influence of Catholic cultural frameworks on Filipino American understandings of family and community. It then theorizes their impact on Filipinos in immigration to the United States as they forge new communities. Chapter 3, "Community of Communities," maps out the Filipino American community of Houston by exploring Filipinos' sense of faith and family in the context of cross-cutting memberships in community, religious, and personal associations and groups. It provides a thick description of the community and outlines how each of these overlapping circles influences Filipino Americans' passive and active involvement in civic life as well as the way they define community.

Chapter 4, "Communities in Conflict," examines how Filipino American interests within several communities and associations can lead to conflict and contentious politics. Highlighting two specific cases, the split of the Houston Bicolano association and the splintering of Couples for Christ over the Gawad Kalinga project/movement,[115] the chapter demonstrates how the Catholic Church and its priests, particularly its Filipino priests, often directly or indirectly mediate individual and community relations both at the local and international level. In some cases, the Church is reluctantly drawn into these situations and in others it is a willing participant. Chapter 5, "Building Centers of Community," focuses on the centrality of the Catholic Church in the Filipino American community and the struggle of Filipinos to build their own community centers outside of the Church. It reveals how first-generation Filipino Americans overwhelmingly believe that the Catholic Church is and should be the center of their community but also want to carve out a sense of independence from its authority through Filipino institutions such as the San Lorenzo Ruiz de Manila center.

Chapter 6, "Caring for Community," moves from how Filipino Americans define community to how they engage with it. It argues that despite contention among groups and associations, Catholic familial frameworks motivate Filipino Americans to engage their community members as brothers and sisters through informal helping and formal volunteering. Whether it comes in the form of assisting a neighbor or volunteering at a community health fair, the chapter illustrates how this sense of a universal Catholic family extends Filipino American care for the community beyond other Filipinos and Catholics to embrace a wider vision community.

Chapter 7, "Protecting Family and Life," builds on the previous discussions to argue that Catholic familial frameworks not only shape Filipino American views on family values, gay marriage, and abortion but also compel them to take action on these issues. Providing an immigrant perspective on American civil society, the chapter explores how first-generation Filipino Americans view the role of Catholicism in United States politics. It also explores how they view their own impact on American politics as they engage issues such as the right to life. Chapter 8, "Growing Presence and Potential Impacts," argues that Filipino Americans not only have the potential to reshape American Catholicism but are already doing so. Additionally, it concludes that Filipino immigrants are presently establishing new communities or building on older established ones that impact American civic life as they act on their Catholic faith with a cultural and institutional focus on the sanctity of the family.

CHAPTER 2

CATHOLIC CULTURE AND FILIPINO FAMILIES

On the 110th anniversary of the Philippine Declaration of Independence from Spain, hundreds of Filipino Americans gathered to celebrate a thanksgiving mass at St. Catherine's Catholic Church in Houston.[1] The service was led by St. Catherine's resident first-generation Filipino American priest, Monsignor Father José. Those in attendance, also largely first-generation Filipino immigrants, wore brightly colored *barongs* and *baro't saya* (Ta) or Maria Claras, the traditional formal shirts and dresses worn by Filipinos on special occasions. Coming from all over Houston and neighboring cities, they represented Filipinos from nearly every Philippine region and province that has immigrated to the United States since 1965, and the vast cultural diversity among them.

The annual Independence thanksgiving mass, which is followed by food, traditional dances, and singing at the fellowship hall, is the largest single gathering of Filipinos in the city each year. It is also a rare opportunity for Father José, a respected leader among many Filipino Americans, to address the entire community. At the beginning of his homily, Father José, speaking in Tagalog, proclaimed, *Ang hindi marunong lumingon sa kayang pinanggalingan ay hindi makararating sa kanyang paroroona*—loosely translated as, "Those who do not know how to look back at their past or where they came from will not reach their destination." It is a well-known Filipino idiom, one that Father José used to discuss his hopes for the future of the Filipino American community and the importance of remembering the past.

Later that day, I asked Edwin, a Filipino American engineer in his late fifties, what he thought Father José meant by the idiom. "Father wants us to remember where we came from and who we are as Filipinos and Catholics." Continuing, Edwin stated, "I believe in the saying, 'when in Rome, do as the Romans do.' I am proud of my Filipino heritage, but by the same token, I want to be as American as the person next door. In the Philippines we are all Catholic but not all of us practice like we should. Here in America we can also lose our way and forget what is important, too."

Questioning Edwin further, I asked him to explain what is important to him as a Filipino. "Faith and family, it's that simple." Continuing our conversation, I asked Edwin how this is different from any other American. Pausing, he answered my question with a measure of hesitancy, "Look, no offense, but we Filipinos have a unique understanding of these things that are just not part of American culture. I mean you say faith is important, but where does it show? You still allow abortion! You talk a lot about family values, but why do you put your parents in retirement homes? This doesn't make any sense to us. It is just not how we are wired. Our faith and our families are our life, and that's how it always has been. I know you read that article in *Filipinas Magazine* on Filipino values 101; it really is that simple." The article that Edwin mentioned, which, I had indeed read, was written by France Viana after a seminar promoting business and product marketing to Filipino Americans.[2] Although brief, the article summarizes the thoughts of many Filipinos I talked to after mass.

In December of 2003, the Asian Business Association in partnership with Wells Fargo Bank, *Filipinas Magazine*, IW Group, Inter Trend Communication, and Dae Advertising organized a seminar for prominent businesses in California entitled *The Growing Importance of the US Asian Market: Focus on Filipino Americans, the Best Kept Secret.* The seminar was put together at the request of local business groups to help non-Filipinos understand Filipino culture and gain better access to a growing but untapped American ethnic market. Glossing over many of the intricacies of Filipino culture, France Viana, who helped lead the seminar, suggested that to become a quick expert on Filipino culture all you have to do is remember four key elements—family, face, faith, and fiesta. Among the four Fs, Viana stated, "If there is one value universal to the Filipino, it is family." However, Filipino families, as Viana pointed out, extend well beyond biological relatives.

Overseas Filipino Workers, as an example, are expected to take care of those they leave behind when they migrate to America. It is a moral duty, one that is intimately tied to Catholicism and familial practices such as godparenting, as we will see, that serve as an equally powerful influence on Filipino values. Godparents, in these cases, may or may not be biological relatives. Hence, religiously sanctioned family obligations can extend rather broadly and encompass a host of individuals and groups. This extended family is what Filipinos have historically called their *barangay*, Tagalog for a confederation of groups that compose the extended family, and it is one of the key foundations of all Filipino social relations.[3]

After highlighting the important relationship between Filipinos and their extended family, Viana then summarized the impact Spanish colonial history has had on the Philippines. "Four hundred years is a very long time to spend in the convent . . . no wonder we haven't quite shaken the habit, if you forgive the pun."[4] Continuing, she concluded, "Faith is the 400-pound gorilla in the room of the Filipino social structure. At least externally, we faithfully observe all Catholic holy days, rituals, and feast days mixed with our own folk rituals. The Catholic Church is a big influence not only on our spiritual life but in our politics and economic affairs." Viana made it clear that among all the forces that shape the Filipino community and their daily lives, Catholicism stands side by side with the family at the center. She went on to state that if you want do business with Filipinos or just contact the community in general, the best route is through their churches—and most Filipino Americans interviewed, such as Edwin, agree.

FOUNDATIONS OF FILIPINO COMMUNITY

If we are to truly understand the present context in which first-generation Filipino Americans build and engage community, we must explore their past. Filipino American scholar Royal Morales once poignantly stated, "The promise of Philipino American Studies, is just that, a promise . . . it is an unfinished agenda."[5] Part of this unfinished agenda, I would contend, is bringing Catholicism and family back into our theoretical and analytical discussions.[6] Doing so requires us to consider the historical importance of these forces on Filipinos in the Philippines and then in the American diaspora. Rather than providing an exhaustive chronological history, this chapter briefly outlines themes in the historical relationships that developed over time between Catholicism, Filipino families, and the Filipino community. Clarifying these relationships helps to contextualize the ways in which Filipino Americans in Houston are not only building and engaging their community but are influencing American Catholicism and American civic life more generally in the process. The chapter also defines my use of cultural frameworks and specifies the role Catholicism plays in motivating or deterring Filipino American community life through consciously held beliefs and commitments centered on the sanctity of the family.

HISTORICIZING FILIPINO FAITH AND FAMILY

Throughout Spanish rule of the Philippines (1521–1898), there was no separation of church and state.[7] Both custom and law gave direct authority to the Catholic Church in order to support the broader aims of the Spanish Crown.[8] The first contact most Filipinos had with both Spain and Christianity came through the *encomenderos* or military prefects and the priests that followed them during tax collection. Despite their associations with the encomenderos, priests were often the only advocates of the people against the Crown and the harsh treatment of the military.[9] When most Filipinos had nowhere else to turn, parish priests, where available, served as their sole counselors and confidants in matters of the state. They were also instrumental in raising a class of indigenous elites that eventually stood as yet another buffer between the state and local peoples. However, this did not lead to an increase in the number of native clergy or those in positions of authority within the Church itself.[10]

Over three and half centuries of Spanish rule, Filipinos grew into a devoutly Catholic population.[11] They ardently practiced their religious devotionals at home and celebrated religious holidays with their extended familial clans. Given the shortage of priests in the islands, coupled with the Church's refusal to raise a native Filipino clergy, the average Filipino did not see a priest more than two or three times a year, if that.[12] Attempting to address this problem, priests organized confraternities of lay people, particularly women, to help meet the religious needs of Filipino Catholics. It was the hope of the Church that this would keep religious devotion alive in the absence of the priests, which it did do to a certain extent.[13]

Before the Spanish arrived, Filipino society revolved around barangays, confederations of extended families.[14] Socialization into these barangays, oriented toward collective decision making, geared Filipinos to think about their clans before themselves.[15] When Spaniards colonized the Philippines, they quickly realized that any successful governance would need to address the power of these barangays. Between 1565 and 1570, when the Church first began to aggressively evangelize in the Philippines, it is estimated that only one hundred baptisms were carried out, mostly among women. By 1583, well after the conquistador Miguel López de Legazpi had established permanent Spanish settlements in the Islands, there were still fewer than 100,000 baptized Filipinos. From 1586, conversions rapidly increased, nearly doubling to 200,000 baptisms when *datus* (Ta), local leaders, encouraged their barangays to seek out priests because they believed baptism could cure physical ailments.[16] During this time the Church grew, because becoming Catholic was perceived by Filipinos to be literally healthy for the family.

The institutionalization of godparents further linked barangays to each other and to the Church over time. Church law and tradition required that godparents be assigned and present at baptisms and confirmations—it was a contractual obligation between the godparents and the godchild.[17] Should anything happen to the parents, godparents were to assume responsibility for their godchild's economic well-being and moral education. Even though the notion of godparents existed in the barangay well before Spanish colonization, the Church used this system to serve Spain.[18] According to the Crown, every Filipino had to belong to a barangay. Although Filipinos could change barangays whenever they moved, a baptized person could not move from a local village that was under religious jurisdiction to another lacking it, nor could he or she change barangays within the same community. Spain also split up traditionally powerful barangays, fearing that datus could regain their precolonial authority and challenge the state.[19] Hence, the Philippines were largely divided along existing barangay lines, with the exception of the most powerful or larger barangays that were broken up. Under this new system, any problems that developed between barangays were referred to the Church as a representative of the state. This did not end competition or infighting by any means, but it provided a central authority for adjudication. It also provided a religious rhetoric through which alliances could be made and problems could be mitigated.[20] For some Filipinos, this drew them closer to the Church, while for others it drove them away.

When opposition to Spanish rule arose in the late 1890s, most Filipinos were not anti-religious or even anti-Catholic, but rather anti-Church and anti-clerical. They sought changes in authority and Church structure that would make Catholicism institutionally their own.[21] From 1898 to 1909, after the Philippine revolution for independence from Spain and after the United States had violently taken control of the Islands during the Spanish American War, the Philippines experienced a radical transformation both religiously and civically. American colonial rule brought with it new civic and cultural influences, including the legal separation of church and state.[22] It also opened the door for Protestant evangelization in the Philippines on a scale that was not possible under Spanish Catholic rule.

The introduction of Protestantism to the Philippines by United States missionaries inadvertently served as a catalyst for a massive reform movement in the Catholic Church that would eventually help Catholicism retain its position as the dominate religion of Filipinos.[23] In 1906, the Catholic Church sent in the Redemptorists, the Benedictine Sisters, the Congregations of San José, and the Missionaries of the Immaculate Heart to create a new image for the Church.[24] Frank Laubach, a well-known Protestant American missionary at the time, noted that the influx of these new highly trained priests and nuns reinvigorated Catholic schools with young, vibrant scholars and sparked a "Catholic Counter Reformation."[25] This reformation changed the approach the Church took toward the Philippines, particularly in its civic scope and outreach to the community. It also led to the training of an indigenous clergy that would finally make the Catholic Church a Filipino institution in the Philippines.

Almost a century later, this Catholic renaissance was solidified by the crucial role the Church played in the nonviolent toppling of the Marcos regime during the People Power Movement. The Church openly endorsed Corazon "Cory" Aquino, the widow of slain Marcos opposition leader Benigno Aquino.[26] In fact, Cardinal Sin, the Catholic archbishop of the Philippines at the time, called Cory a Filipina Joan of Arc and a messenger of God in the face of unjust rule.[27] The Catholic impact on the 1986 People Power Movement against Marcos, also known as the EDSA 1 Revolution, was not just a matter of institutional support, however, but also an expression of faith.[28] As hundreds of thousands of Filipinos crowded the streets, hoisting images of the Virgin Mary and Santa Niño, the infant Jesus, into the air, singing hymns, and praying the rosary, Marcos's troops were emotionally moved to join the crowd, and Marcos subsequently fled the country.[29] Today, in part as a result of EDSA 1, the Catholic Church plays just as vital a role in Philippine religious and community life as it did during the latter part of Spanish rule. As the number of Catholics continues to grow in the Philippines, the nation is also on the brink of becoming the largest English-speaking Catholic country in the world and the third largest Catholic nation. The end result, as many scholars have suggested, is that the Philippines figures to be an important part of the future of global Catholicism.[30] Although widespread rumors and corruption lead many Filipinos to question the role of religion in contemporary Philippine politics, Catholicism overwhelmingly remains one of the most salient forces in the nation and a major influence on its diaspora communities.

Contextualizing Filipino Faith and Family in the American Diaspora

During the first decade of the twentieth century, the first wave of Filipino immigrants to the United States, the *pensionados*, arrived by the thousands to work in the fields of Hawaii and California. Catholicism played a central role in their survival and efforts to construct communities.[31] However, the realities of American racism both within and outside the Catholic Church pushed many Filipinos to seek out other sources of community.[32] Fearing that Filipinos were converting to Protestantism, but not willing to integrate their churches, several American archdioceses facilitated the formation of Catholic clubs outside of the Church. Echoing the approach of the Church during Spanish rule of the Philippines, the American Catholic Church turned to its laity to foster Filipino religiosity.[33]

Throughout the 1920s, in places such as Seattle and San Francisco these clubs, as well as regional associations, supplied employment bulletins and contacts, aid to the sick, legal support for discharged servicemen, and financial support for all Filipinos in need. They also provided scholarships for young men to attend college.[34] By 1956, many Filipinos who had grown increasingly frustrated with their treatment in the American Catholic Church began to mobilize priests in the Philippines on their behalf.[35] Archbishop Egidio Vagnozzi, the apostolic delegate to the Philippines at the time, for example, wrote the Sacred Consistorial Congregation in Rome to complain that Filipino Americans were largely shut out from "Irish churches" in the United States, but little changed as a result of his letter. Filipinos were still perceived as too foreign by the American Catholic Church, despite gains both in citizenship and native births. As a result of this, and compounded by heightened scapegoating by the general public during a depressed American economy, Filipinos continued to face intense racial discrimination both within and outside the Church for several decades.

After the passage of the 1965 Immigration Act, the number of Filipinos, particularly women, immigrating to the United States dramatically increased. The increased presence of Filipinas had a tremendous impact on the Filipino

American community and continues to shape it today. Given the centrality and cultural importance of Filipinas in the home, particularly in the raising of children, coupled with the fact that women tend to be more religious than men, Filipinas not only united and solidified Filipino American family life but also brought and continue to bring a renewed sense of religious vitality. They have also in many cases served as the voice of change within the Catholic Church. Filipinas such as Naomi Castillo in San Francisco, for example, have rallied Church leadership to address the pressing concerns of those who feel ostracized and neglected.[36] This lay leadership, as will be discussed in subsequent chapters, is one of several ways Filipino immigrants, both women and men, are challenging the Church and bringing about changes in American Catholicism.

In the late 1980s, the Assembly for Filipino Catholic Affairs of the Archdiocese of San Francisco, of which Castillo was a key member, brought Filipino leaders together from different parishes to set goals and share their experiences in the Church. Among the most common complaints many Filipino Americans noted was that Catholicism in America was too businesslike, with strict rectory hours and priests often requiring appointments to see parishioners.[37] They also noted there were no statues in many churches, few devotional services, and a strict registration policy that required Catholics to stay primarily in one parish. Responding to the complaints of the assembly, as well as the complaints of other Asian ethnic groups, the American Catholic Church held a series of hearings from 1989 to 1990.[38] From these hearings, the United States Conference of Catholic Bishops issued a report entitled *A Catholic Response to the Asian Presence*.[39]

A landmark statement, the report sought to publicly acknowledge the increasing presence of Asians in American Catholic parishes and highlight the rich diversity of culture, tradition, and religious practices they bring to the Church. The Church admitted that it had long neglected the voices of Asian American Catholics, who in the past had been subject to discrimination and unwelcoming "coldness" in their parishes.[40] Looking at Filipinos specifically, the report lamented the abuses that the Church brought on the Philippines during Spanish colonial rule.[41] It also emphasized that in a post-EDSA 1 Philippines, the Church had revitalized itself and taken stronger roots in the hearts of Filipinos. Coming full circle, the report, largely based on Castillo's initial *Introduction to Filipino Ministry* and her *Pastoral Plan for Filipino Ministry*, outlines how parishes can better serve the needs of Filipino Americans in their parishes.[42] Calling on parishes to be more open to Filipino personal needs and traditional celebrations, many Filipino Americans took the report as a sign that the Church was changing.

In September of 2001, ten years later and largely overshadowed by the terrorist attacks of that same month, twenty-four archdiocesan directors and coordinators of the Filipino Catholic Ministry gathered to form the Filipino American Catholic Ministries Council.[43] It was the first national organization formed to respond to the growing needs of Filipino American pastoral ministers. Largely developed to improve communication and coordination among lay ministers, the council was also created to discuss national issues facing Filipino American Catholics and advocate for appropriate and sensitive responses to those issues. Four years later, in June 2005, the Chapel of San Lorenzo Ruiz in New York opened as the official national Filipino American Church for the Filipino Apostolate. A monumental accomplishment, the chapel highlights the continued growth of Filipino American population in the United States and the Church's recognition of their importance to the future of American Catholicism.[44]

Today, Filipino Catholicism is practiced as strongly within the Church as outside it. Filipinos not only have a voice in the institutions that once pushed them away but are a vital part of what is keeping the Church alive. This is an important point, as other scholars have noted in the case of Filipino immigrants in San Francisco.[45] The number of Filipino Americans attending masses in San Francisco and around the country fills pews that were once vacant. Likewise, Filipino priests serving in these parishes are replacing an aging American priesthood that struggles to recruit new priests. Hence, both in the pews and from the pulpit, Filipinos are a vital part of their parishes.

For many first-generation Filipino Americans, their parish church is the center of their community. Historically, American xenophobia forced Filipino immigrants to carve out civic spaces within the Church because they had relatively few outlets beyond their parishes and their own regional associations. Today this is not the case, given Filipino immigrants' relatively high socioeconomic status and their continued integration into mixed racial/ethnic neighborhoods across the country. However, with a long historical memory of a more unwelcoming past, coupled with a desire to continue and strengthen the Catholic faith they bring with them from the Philippines, the Catholic Church remains a trusted foundation of Filipino communities in the diaspora. Their priests, Filipino or not, are likewise seen as the leaders of these communities. Religiously revered but also subject to intense scrutiny, as was the case historically in the Philippines, these priests often mediate individual Filipino and communitywide relations, including those among Filipino American regional and ethnic associations and groups. While this draws many Filipinos together through a common faith bond, for others the Church can be seen as a source of community conflict.

Outside their parish churches, Filipinos continue to celebrate their faith in their homes, associations, and familial clans, just as they did historically. As in the past, a unique Filipino and Catholic understanding of family sits at the center of this religiosity. When many first-generation Filipino Americans get together in their home devotional and prayer groups, they often say *pupunta tayo sa barangay*—"let's attend the barangay" or *magbarangay tayo ngaying gabi*—"let's barangay tonight." Most of the people attending these devotionals are not biological family, but they are bound to each other as Filipinos, often from the same region in the Philippines, as well as through their Catholic faith. They are brothers and sisters in diaspora who serve as godparents to each other's children and stand side by side the biological family through times of celebration and despair.

Both in the Philippines and in the American diaspora, the Catholic Church and the family remain the foundations of the Filipino community. Exploring the relationship between these two institutions is important to our understanding of how first-generation Filipino Americans not only establish communities but engage them. However, understanding these institutional dynamics is not enough; we must also analyze the underlying cultural frameworks that animate these institutions and the people in them. Doing so requires that we outline the differences and similarities between Filipino cultural understandings of Catholicism and the understandings of native-born American Catholics. Likewise, we must also investigate the degree to which Filipino Catholic beliefs and practices are similar or different from the conservative practice and beliefs of other immigrants coming to the United States from the global South. In answering these questions, we can better assess not only the potential that Filipino American immigrants present for reshaping American Catholicism but also the impact this potential has on American civic life, given long-standing questions surrounding the puzzle of American Catholic civic life more generally.

MOTIVATIONS, MORAL COMMITMENTS, AND CULTURAL FRAMEWORKS

Throughout the social sciences, cultural theorizing remains a virtuoso affair.[46] Although highly sophisticated and offering us a wealth of insights, the nature and definition of culture itself are still the subject of widespread debate. Some theorists view culture as cohesive and a highly integrated force that binds people together and constrains their behavior.[47] Others see it as more fragmentary and subjective—as a toolkit of resources or repertoires for social action.[48] Across this spectrum, few studies agree on the nature and definition of culture, and even fewer build on the assumptions of one another. The result is that cultural theorizing has not provided us with a complete or convincing account of people's motivations for social action.[49] Doing so requires an operationalization of culture that allows us to understand how culture can provide the normative ends toward which people act.[50] It must also account for the powerful influence cultural frameworks have in motivating this action through consciously held beliefs and moral commitments.[51]

Cultural frameworks are knowledge structures that are both modular and transposable. They shape and bias our cognition by mediating and giving form to our experiences.[52] Through them social life is rendered meaningful. They structure cultural memory and provide motivations that compel us to act. In doing so, cultural frameworks not only pattern our behavior but equally constitute who we are and how we see ourselves and others. This can happen consciously or unconsciously in a more taken-for-granted process. We may not, for example, always be immediately aware why certain symbols or metaphors resonate with us. Likewise, we may not be fully cognizant of the more embedded social patterns, routines, and rituals that animate our daily lives.[53]

Every social system, structure, and institution is defined and made meaningful by a host of cultural frameworks. Whether it is a nation, a church, or a family, each of these social orders shares certain rules and cultural understandings regarding family and community which can shape individuals' lives and actions. Understanding this, I join other cultural theorists who suggest that we need to continue focusing our analytical attention on how cultural frameworks are acquired, modified, and spread.[54] We must also focus on the context in which these processes occur. People are not only rational calculators and purveyors of social capital but also cultural and moral beings whose beliefs and commitments constitute and direct their social actions.[55]

For some people or in certain circumstances, culture can be consciously mobilized for strategic action. For others or under differing circumstances, culture may be tightly organized around national identities or religious traditions and hence manifested in similar ways across domains and situations.[56] Either is plausible and equally probable. It is important to note that people's beliefs and moral commitments are not necessarily religious, but they are centered on intrinsic motivations about the nature of what is a right or wrong course of action in a given situation or context. They permeate all facets of society from our socialization into cultural norms to our identities and the capacities within which we understand our own social actions. They find expression within people as an emotive resonance that binds people together through the experience of their own cultural understandings. People act on these cultural frameworks because they feel morally bound to do so.[57] However, this does not mean that people do not have agency in navigating these complexities.

A society is made up of a countless number overlapping and competing social orders. It is up to people to craft their place within them. Individuals and groups may choose to appropriate all of the cultural frameworks found within a given social order, adopt only some of them, or none of them at all. On a larger societal scale, individuals and groups may choose to appropriate cultural frameworks from multiple social orders which, in turn, get emphasized differently depending on the context or situation of their social action. Complicating matters, people may not choose these paths as consciously held strategic actions but follow their hearts—a matter of doing what feels right. Hence, the internalized cultural frameworks people carry within themselves may not match the social orders in which they are embedded and with which they interact externally. This can lead to conflict between groups and individuals both within a single social order and across multiple orders.

Understanding the historical importance of the Catholic Church and family or broader barangay to Filipinos, in the following pages I specify a series of cultural frameworks within each institution that can serve as both the locus and motivation for their social actions. Although each is discussed independently, considerable overlap exists between them. Each, in many cases, facilitates the others, but they can also stand alone as independent forces that animate their own set of moral commitments.

SPECIFYING CATHOLIC FAMILIAL FRAMEWORKS

Catholicism is self-professedly profamily. This is not to say that other religious traditions are not, but this is a point of emphasis where we can begin to understand how Catholic positions on contraception, abortion, charity, and welfare all stem from cultural frameworks that promote familial obligations by extending the family beyond the biological. The individual, the biological family, and the community are all seen as integral parts of a singular Catholic family that constitutes the core of the Catholic social order.[58] In the catechism of the Catholic Church, family is seen as the "original cell of social life" and the center of community. It is the duty of every citizen and the political community itself to honor the family, to assist it, and to ensure its' freedom and protection.[59] When the family is threatened or the political community contradicts the values of the Church, the catechism states, "A citizen is obliged in conscience not to follow the directives of civil authorities when they are contrary to the demands of the moral order, to the fundamental rights of persons or the teachings of the Gospel."[60] Hence, any social actions within this order are not conceived and carried out solely in the context of self-interest. The doctrine mobilizes Catholics by connecting their beliefs and commitments to broader communal interests, because an action is viewed as the right thing to do or what God would ask of them. In doing so, it also compels people to share their resources as a family and protect the sanctity of that family.

Looking more closely at Catholic theology and devotional practice, we see that the Holy Family serves as a divine model from which Catholic familial frameworks are derived.[61] The doctrine of the Trinity establishes God as a supreme Father who not only created humanity as his children but is ultimately the head of a larger divine family, from Jesus as Son to a host of saints and disciples who are reflections of his Holy Spirit. God, as this ultimate father figure, is seen as judge and divine ruler of creation, which is in effect his household. Within this celestial household, Jesus is seen as God's obedient son. These same familial relations are also echoed in the Catholic understandings of the Holy Family of Mary, Joseph, and Jesus. On a broader level, the dynamic of a father, a mother, and a child also serve as a model of traditional Christian views for Catholics' own families.

Unlike Protestant denominations, however, Mary has been elevated within Catholicism to a divine status as the Queen of Heaven. She serves in a vital intercessory role for Catholics in the larger scope of the divine family. This unique role, as a divine woman, is without equal in the more masculine underpinnings of Protestant theology. Nevertheless, as in Protestantism, Joseph serves as the quintessential model of a devoted husband and father.[62] This is important. Beyond the theology, these cultural frameworks animate gendered models for Catholics, both men and women, that act as guides in their daily understandings of themselves in society. They provide religious motivations for their social actions. This is particularly true for Catholic women, who may find powerful justification and legitimacy for their social actions through the model of Mary and through Marian devotions.[63] Given the outwardly patriarchal nature of the Catholic Church, this is an important point in understanding the role of women in the parish and any struggles they face in mobilizing their voices within the Church.

Liturgically, the Catholic Church reifies the family by dramatizing the Holy Family in its devotional practices and nomenclature. Priests and nuns are often referred to as father and sister, respectively. Fellow parishioners embrace each other during mass as brothers and sisters in Christ. And godparents and friends alike stand side by side with biological parents as part of a larger understanding of Catholic family.[64] Institutionally, priests serve as fathers of their parishes in more than just name. As Alexis de Tocqueville noted in his historical observations of American Catholicism in the early nineteenth century, "Among Catholics, religious society is composed of only two elements: priests and people. The priest alone rises above the faithful; everything is equal below him."[65] The same can be said today. The priest is the moral authority of his parish. He can command a wealth of material and human resources. However, while a priest may convey or even promote Catholic understandings of the Holy Family that reinforce his own position of authority, he does not necessarily take power directly from his parishioners. It is cultural frameworks that compel parishioners to cede this power to him. Likewise, it is these same cultural frameworks that compel Catholics to seek out their priests for Communion or for advice and absolution through confession.

A priest's power to consecrate the Host in Communion or sit as an intercessory between God and parishioners during confession is derived from cultural frameworks operating at two levels. At one level, a priest's training gives him mastery over a wide range of "explicit and implicit techniques" which enable him to perform his duties.[66] At a second level, the priest has been elevated to a position of reverence by ordination, which makes it possible for him to transform bread and wine into the body and blood of Jesus as well as confer penance for sinners.[67] Although a priest alone holds this authority, Catholics, both women and men, can and do appropriate resources within Catholicism independent of a priest's authority to facilitate their own identities, paths, and understandings of the Catholic family.

Catholic familial frameworks should not be seen strictly as Church laws that constrain Catholics' power, agency, and resources but also viewed as more implied assumptions that guide their behavior.[68] Despite the fact that the Catholic Church is one of the largest transnational institutions in the world, with a rigid hierarchical administration and a universal set of transposable institutionalized cultural frameworks, Catholics can and do find motivations for their social action from a host of overlapping or competing cultural sources.[69] Given the immense cultural diversity and varied experiences Catholics bring to any parish, how they were raised or where they were raised also shapes what it means for them to be a good citizen and a good Catholic.

FILIPINO FAMILIAL FRAMEWORKS

As was discussed at the beginning of this chapter, prior to Spanish conquest of the Philippines in the sixteenth century and prior to the introduction of Catholicism in the Islands, Filipino society revolved around the barangay—a confederation of extended families and groups. At the heart of these barangays was the nuclear family, which extended bilaterally through marriage and coparenting.[70] Marriage was not simply a matter of love but often an alliance between families and groups. However, women were not merely married off as commodities for economic or political gain. Filipinas in precolonial Philippine society were fairly equal to men. Unlike what would follow under Spanish colonial rule, Filipino women before colonization could own and inherit land, engage in commerce, and even become the datu or chieftain of their barangay.[71]

Within their nuclear families, women were also respected as near equals to men and given the exclusive rights to make important decisions about the naming, raising, and future marital arrangements and choices of their children.[72] Filipinas were more than the bearers of children. They were also the bearers of culture and vital leaders both inside and outside of their homes. This is an important point. Even before Catholic cultural frameworks further sanctified the family and cemented the place of women in Philippine society through its liturgical focus on the Trinity and Holy Family, during and after Spanish rule, both were already culturally important and animated a distinctive social order of their own. As some scholars have pointed out, Filipinos appropriated from Catholicism what they needed to make it their own faith.[73] Hence, these two understandings of family eventually overlapped and became intertwined, with one complementing the other.

Specific Filipino Catholic traditions that arose over time, such as the devotions to Santo Niño (the baby Jesus) and the Virgin of Antipolo, also further sanctified Filipino understandings of family through liturgies that celebrate a Holy Mother and Son. Again, these traditions were essentially precolonial. In the case of the nearly two hundred different regional devotions to Santo Niño that emerged, we can historically retrace how Magellan's attempt to baptize the royal court of the Philippine Island of Cebu in 1521 failed until Queen Juana was presented with a gift statue of the Christ Child—a gesture that had significant cultural resonance.[74] Likewise, some hundred years later, when the newly appointed governor general of Manila arrived at the city he brought with him a statue of the Blessed Virgin, later known as the Virgin of Antipolo. It was carved out of dark hardwood in Mexico, and unlike more traditional Spanish Marian art, physically looked more like the average Filipina. This sacred image of a more indigenous Holy Mother eventually became the iconic Virgin of the Philippines. Through a series of historical and now mythical events that are hard to retrace, the image was lost, sent back to Mexico, and was nearly destroyed several times over a hundred-year period. When it eventually returned permanently to the Philippines, the statue was celebrated and enshrined as Our Lady of Peace and Good Voyage. Beyond this, other Marian celebrations that emerged, such as Flores de Mayo and Salubong at Easter, gave further sanctification to existing Filipino understanding of family, and of motherhood specifically.[75]

Precolonial Filipino familial values saturated every facet of Philippine culture. They were also instilled in Filipino youth and reinforced throughout adulthood. Socialization into the barangay, as we might expect, was oriented toward teaching the value of a greater communal good. Through the enactment of cultural frameworks that placed value on cooperation and sharing, Filipinos were obligated to think less about their own self-interests and needs. Absolute loyalty to the barangay was not simply a matter of ritual oath but one forged in deeds. This is not to say that individual achievement was discouraged, but Filipinos' true worth was measured by what they did for their family, not themselves. Here again, family is not simply the nuclear family but the extended barangay. Little to no distinction was made between members of the biological and extended barangay family. Group interests took precedent. The result was the establishment of tightly bound groups that often struggled with one another for power and status—a matter of competition between groups versus individual pursuits.[76]

Precolonial Filipino practices such as coparenting, which later became known as the *compadrazco* system under Spanish rule, ritually and contractually bound members of the barangay to each other as the *comadres* and *copadres*—extended mothers and fathers of each other's children. More than positions of honor or familial and group alliances, comadres and copadres were required to assume their extended children's moral upbringing or financial security should their biological parents die or become unable to do so for some reason. The introduction of Catholicism to the Philippines reinforced these practices by requiring godparents to be present and legally sign sponsorship for children at baptisms and confirmations. Likewise, Catholic communal frameworks were not simply imposed on a Philippine cultural tabula rasa but appropriated by Filipinos as an extension of their own cultural understandings of sharing in the precolonial family.[77] Through both ritual and law, Catholic churches literally and figuratively became houses of worship that further entrenched the barangay family as the model of Filipino community.[78]

Today the extended family remains the heart and institutional foundation of Philippine society. Parents, especially mothers, still exert a great deal of influence on their own biological children's attitudes, values, and cultural understandings.[79] However, adults more generally are also expected to support these same roles in their interactions with the larger extended family and their children.[80] As was the case historically, contemporary Filipino children are socialized to respect and obey older members of the family—biologically related or not.[81] Specific Filipino familial frameworks centered on obedience, shame, and communal obligations ensure this is the case.

Children are raised with an understanding that a sense of face, one of the four F's of Filipino culture according to France Viana in *Filipinas Magazine*, is an important mechanism of self-control that must insure that shame or *hiya* (Ta) is not brought to the extended family through individual actions.[82] This value is instilled in children within an internalized cultural framework that places them in debt to their parents and the larger barangay through a sense of gratitude and respect for everything that has been done for them. This sense of reciprocity or debt of gratitude, *utang na loob* (Ta), is not something that can be repaid but is a lifelong obligation that compels Filipinos to continually make sacrifices for the greater good of the family.[83] It compels Filipinos to think less about themselves through a sense of mutual obligation and cooperation—*pakikisama* (Ta).[84] Outward and more symbolic gestures of these obligations can be seen in the Filipino practice of *mano* or *mano po* (Ta), in which respect for elders is demonstrated by touching their hand to your bowed forehead. It is also manifest in the cultural and economic relationship of Filipinos in the diaspora to their families in the Philippines, who are deeply aware of the income and resource differentials that exist between them.

The diaspora continues to challenge the Filipino family today much as it did historically. It is estimated that by 2030 the proportion of intact family households in the Philippines will be roughly 78 percent, a decline from 83 percent since the 1970s.[85] This prognosis is based on the continual migration of Filipinos overseas and the unwelcome but economically driven growth of transnational families. This has been particularly difficult for Filipinas (women) around the world, as Rhacel Salazar Parrenas's work on the global Filipino diaspora continues to highlight.[86] It has also been difficult on youth, of whom an estimated nine million are growing up without at least one parent due to migration.[87] What keeps Filipino families together beyond necessity are the aforementioned cultural frameworks that bind them. Catholicism and faith more generally also matter, as we might expect. Studies of Filipino youth, for example, find that families that pray together are able to stay together, and their children are less likely to ever smoke, drink, use drugs, or have premarital sex.[88]

In the United States, at least after 1965, Filipinos have had more successes in bridging these divides and issues than in the Philippines, largely due to their higher socioeconomic status. This has been particularly true for Filipinas.

Reprising their precolonial status, Filipina Americans have risen side by side with men as important leaders in their communities. Likewise, Filipinas are just as likely today to be the *ilaw ng tahanan* (Ta) or nurturers of the family as they are its breadwinners or *haligi ng tahana* (Ta). Beyond sex and gender roles, a barangay mentality still exists in the American diaspora, and nuclear families continue to expand both within the United States and through transnational linkages to the Philippines. Compared to other Filipino diaspora communities, Filipino American families in general have largely remained more intact through successive waves of chain migration. Obligations to these extended families, however, remains well vested in the cultural frameworks outlined above and continue to be fostered by Filipino Americans' Catholic faith and practices both within and outside their parish churches. This is not to say that diaspora does not present a host of challenges to Filipino families in America; it does. In fact, 64 percent of Filipino Americans state that the strength of their family ties was better in the Philippines than in the United States.[89] Despite this, or perhaps because of it, Filipino Americans today are just as compelled to think more communally, for the barangay, as they were historically in the Philippines.

Evidence of the powerful commitments the barangay instills in the contemporary Filipino diaspora can be seen in the numerous ethnic and regional associations Filipinos establish in their new destinations. These organizations are important transnational linkages between Filipino diaspora communities and the cultural contexts and providences they migrate from. They are a matter of pride that distinguish Filipinos from one another in the diaspora and engage them in the politics and concerns of their specific regional homelands. Likewise, the proliferation of these organizations is an important means by which Filipinos from various ethnic and regional backgrounds can resist being homogenized in their new country into one catchall Filipino American category.[90] Although membership in these groups is certainly not required, there is considerable social pressure to join and participate, considering the fact that these organizations have historically been some of the few spaces where immigrants, particularly men, could gain social standing and positions of leadership within their diaspora communities.

Beyond this, the power of these commitments to the barangay can also be seen in the numerous *balikbayan* boxes (Ta), care packages of assorted goods, or the amount of remittances Filipinos in diaspora send home to the Philippines each year. In 2007, for example, Filipinos overseas sent home an estimated fifteen billion dollars (United States currency equivalence) in remittances—over 10 percent of the Philippine gross national product for that year.[91] As discussed at the beginning of this chapter, France Viana points out that remittance are essentially a moral duty. However, these obligations to family and the broader barangay, particularly through remittance, are not without tensions and can entail very personal and emotional costs.[92]

A SUMMATIVE EXAMPLE

Further illustrating the complexity of the dynamic cultural forces that orient Filipino Catholic lives, we might take the example of Imee, who was interviewed throughout the course of this study. Imee is a first-generation Filipina nurse in her late thirties. She is married with three children and has an extensive extended family living both here in the United States and in the Philippines. Imee is also a comadre for three children living in Houston and five back in the Philippines. Although Imee earns a respectable wage as a nurse, and her husband is also employed as a nurse, making them an upper-middle class family of five, their familial obligations are taxing.

Imee told me that her family is rather small by Filipino standards and that there is always a great deal of pressure on her to have more children. She loves her children, but told me that she does not want any more. "This is a real ethical bind . . . we know as Catholics that we should not use contraception but we do sometimes." Continuing, she stated, "I am pro-life; I was even part of a peaceful march to end abortion last year, but I can't afford more children so we use contraception sometimes—it's cheating I suppose." Discussing this further, she explained, "When you really think about it, I am a mother of eleven and all of them need me, not just my biological kids but especially the ones in the Philippines." Imee is clearly bound to her family but she is also torn between the official teachings of the Catholic Church, which compel her to participate in social protests against abortion on one level and suggest she not use contraception on the other.

Imee sends remittances home to the Philippines every month in addition to numerous yearly balikbayan boxes for her immediate relatives. She is often torn in deciding who gets what and how much. Each decision is fraught with anxiety, and can be met with disappointment or even suspicion from those back home. In Houston, Imee also gives money to her parish church every week and has been one of the church's more generous sponsors in helping to raise funds for a new chapel. When I ask Imee how she budgets her philanthropy, she laughed and stated, "I give to a host of causes, and when I don't have the money, I'm usually pretty good about raising it." Continuing, I asked Imee how she prioritizes her remittances and the financial needs of the causes she supports; she stated, "They are all equal, well sort of, if you are talking about the new chapel versus my family—obviously they are both important. Both have been there for me when I needed them. I am indebted to them for this. I just have to work harder to make sure everybody has what they need to survive; ultimately we are one big Catholic family." For Imee, her parish church is an extension of her family and has been there for her through difficult times. As Imee explained, she has gone to her parish priest for advice about her son who has been in trouble lately. "Father always knows what to do." She has also gone to her parish priest for liturgical advice for her home devotional prayer group.

As the former vice president of a Filipino American ethnic or regional association, Imee has likewise sought her priest's advice for how to deal with interper-
sonal conflicts during the group's elections. However, Imee admitted this has not
always gone well. "Sometimes I think he is flat out wrong when it comes to our
associations. . . . Father is Filipino and knows how things are with us, but I think
he takes sides and this has been a problem." Continuing, she explained that her
priest is from the same region of the Philippines as herself. As he was a spiritual
advisor for the regional association for which she was president, Imee expressed
concern over his role in community affairs: "I am not sure if his allegiance is to
the parish, our hometown, or both. . . . For myself I am often torn between what
is right for the Church and best for our association." Although Imee has not
always agreed with her priest, the Church is the center of her community, and her
Catholic faith stands side by side with her extended family as an intimate force
that animates her social life.

Conclusion

Imee is only one individual, but her personal decisions and thoughts do not
vary much from other first-generation Filipino Americans interviewed. Where
they do, the context of these decisions remains the same. It is within the
complementary and competing cultural frameworks outlined in this chapter
that Filipinos at both the micro level of the individual and macro level of the
barangay build their senses of community. It is also within these forces, as will
become more apparent in the coming chapters, that they engage this sense of
community and find motivations for their civic lives. The end of fourteen years
of Philippine Congressional debate in August of 2012 over the Reproductive
Health Bill, which would mandate sex education in public schools and sub-
sidize contraceptives for the poor, is a prime example of both the micro and
macro level struggles of Filipinos within these cultural forces. Like Imee, Filipino Catholics in the Philippines remain divided and have struggled for years
with their support of the bill, which would ostensibly improve conditions of
the poor by reducing high birth rates, but has also received staunch condemnation from the Catholic Church. Although the bill has not been passed into law,
the movement of the bill forward out of debate has caused archbishops such as
Angel N. Lagdameo to publically exclaim, "May God have mercy on our Congress."[93] With such strong words, it is no wonder that devout Filipino Catholics
feel torn over this and other related issues.

Despite the fact that the Catholic Church has a well-established patriarchal
hierarchy, Filipinas such as Imee do have a strong voice in their parishes. She is
one of many men and women who represent a growing lay movement within
the larger Catholic Church. Through the voicing of concerns and a mobilization
of fellow parishioners, this laity, Filipino or not, is playing an important role in

the reshaping of American Catholicism. Likewise, with a focus on the sanctity of the family, new immigrants from the global South, such as Filipinos, are also demonstrating the potential to impact American civic life through their faith in action. Both within the Church hierarchy and in the pews, Filipino immigrants are pushing both their own and broader communities to enact policies that protect their cultural understandings of family on issues such as abortion. Far from being civically inept due to their Catholic faith or limited by their status as immigrants, first-generation Filipino Americans are providing several possible answers to the question of where immigrants fit in or are impacting American civic life.

Before delving into these issues more fully, the next chapter outlines the complexities of the Filipino American community of Houston. It analyzes how Filipino immigrants' sense of faith and family in the context of cross-cutting memberships in ethnic, religious, and personal associations and groups shapes the ways in which they build community. Providing a "thick description" of the broader contours of the community, the chapter explains how each of these overlapping circles can influence Filipino Americans' passive and active involvement in civic life as well as the ways in which they define community.[94]

CHAPTER 3

COMMUNITY OF
COMMUNITIES

"Shhhhhh . . . be quiet, don't say anything; he's coming already, get ready to sing," shouted Reyna, a first-generation Filipina American and the organizer of the party. As we all crouched down, Stan Estrada, a first-generation Filipino American and the guest of honor, entered the restaurant with his first-generation Filipina American wife Cheryl. The crowd met them with a rousing "Surprise" followed by a loud round of "Happy Birthday" or *Maligayang bati* (Ta), sung by some in English and others in Tagalog. The occasion was Stan's sixtieth birthday. The celebration also marked his official early retirement from a long career in the energy field. The small Mediterranean restaurant was packed with some fifty-plus people, both Filipino and non-Filipino. Affectionately known as Tito (Ta, Uncle) Stan by friends and family alike, some attendees came to celebrate Stan's birthday. Others also came to honor a man they believe has had a profound impact on their lives and their community.

As people began to take their seats and wait for further directions on how to proceed to the buffet, the room revealed itself to be more than a simple birthday party. It was a coming together of a vast set of social networks in which Stan is only one of its key members. The seating arrangement in the restaurant was completely open. However, many people clustered around tables of their family, closest friends, and the groups or associations that are most important to them. At one end of the room sat Stan's family, biological or otherwise. These are his closest friends, his children and their children, his godchildren and their children, and those with whom he has shared some of the most important and intimate moments of his adult life. We might call this Stan's barangay, but it is also something more. In the middle of this group, bridging Stan's familial circle and crossing it, were members of Bibingka. This is Stan's weekly prayer and fellowship group. The couples in Bibingka have been together for over forty years. From their early years of adjusting to life in America to the raising of their children and the birth of grandchildren, these couples have been a vital part of what Stan considers to be his family and community.

Behind Bibingka sat members of Stan's Catholic church, St. Catherine's. Some of these parishioners knew Stan from their fellowship at the church. Others had worked with him on various parish activities. Next to his fellow parishioners sat members of the Texas Association of Mapua Alumni, of which Stan is a member, as well as members of the Texas alumni of the University of Santo Thomas, where Cheryl went to college.[1] Beyond this, the tables were a mix of people and groups. At one table sat members of the Our Lady of Lourdes prayer group and members of Couples for Christ (CFC), another Catholic renewal group with which Stan and Cheryl recently got involved. Next to them was a table with members from the Knights of Rizal, Philippine American Masons Association of Texas (PAMAT), the Tagalog Association of Texas, the Bicol USA Association, the Asian Pacific American Heritage Association, the Philippine Nurses Association of Metropolitan Houston, and the Filipino American Council of South Texas (FACOST).

Stan and Cheryl are members of many of these groups, as are other people who were sitting at other tables. While I could only make note of groups and individuals I knew in the crowd, the party was probably even more diverse than I could ascertain. As people worked their way through the buffet line and began to eat, at Cheryl's urging, it was a clear reminder of how central food is to any Filipino gathering.[2] People were enjoying their meal and waiting for the PowerPoint presentation that was being cued up by Stan's two sons. The room was festive and echoed with laughter. Casual conversation and in some cases intense debate, on everything from the current state of politics in the Philippines to the curious absence of Filipino food at the party, could be overheard. On one table various business cards and brochures from different groups and companies competed for space. On another table, a sizable display provided literature for Gawad Kalinga, a housing project for the poor in the Philippines.[3]

"Again, can I have your attention?" Jack, Stan's Filipino godson and a close family friend exclaimed. As he attempted to quiet the crowd, he directed everyone's attention to the projection screen. After a somewhat tearful and at times comedic retelling of Stan's life in pictures and words, Stan's friends and family took turns offering insights and adoration for a rich sixty years. Stan's older son thanked his father for "lessons hard learned" and for inspiring him to "to seek out an education and make a life of my own." His youngest son first thanked his older brother for taking the heat off of him, then thanked his father for showing him "how to be a good man and a man of faith and devotion." This theme carried over to many other speeches, including one by a white woman who thanked Stan for introducing her to the "real meaning" of being a Catholic. "Without Stan I would have never become a Catholic. Without his leadership and model, I would not know what it means to know God and live a meaningful life engaged in the

Catholic community." For this woman, Stan is not simply Filipino, but first and foremost a Catholic who had provided her guidance during an important time in her life. Like other non-Filipinos who made similar statements during their own speeches, she highlighted the fact that Filipino Catholics like Stan are impacting the lives of people across their parishes, immigrant or not and Filipino or not.

Breaking the serious tone for a moment, Cheryl attempted to embarrass Stan a bit before her own speech by calling out a belly dancer for a birthday stroll. Stan, loving every minute, played along, even getting Cheryl to duel with the dancer for his affection. As the dance ended, Cheryl began to talk about her husband as more than just a life partner. She explained how Stan is an inspiration and model communitarian by pointing out all the groups with which he is involved and the extraordinary sense of compassion and dedication he has shown in "putting his faith in action." Whether it is raising money for scholarships, educating kids in catechism classes, or helping out a neighbor or fellow member of the parish, Cheryl outlined Stan's accomplishments in rich detail. Continuing, she noted, "His faith has moved me, too. It has allowed me to explore my own mission in life, to get involved in my community knowing that I had a partner who would support me in every cause I saw fit." As the night came to an end, it was clear that Stan is a community leader, although he would not say so himself. Standing side by side with Cheryl, he offered a concluding show of appreciation for the party and modestly suggested that his life to that point had been wonderful but not as extraordinary as some suggested.

More Than a Party

Underlying the celebration of Stan's sixtieth year of life and his retirement from fulltime employment was a celebration of his civic life. It was also an acknowledgement of the Catholic faith that has spurred him into community service and tied him into a rather complex set of social networks. Although the birthday party was not a large public event but a more intimate and private affair, the crowd gathered at Stan's party represented a gathering of communities, groups, and associations, Filipino or otherwise, that was as vast as the Philippine Islands themselves. Stan and Cheryl are clearly well respected by many individuals and groups that were in attendance, not just for their service to these communities but also for their faith and inspiration. Yet upon further inspection they were not really unique among other members of the crowd.

Stan and Cheryl are devoted Catholics who attend their parish church weekly, if not more often. They are members of a religious prayer group, active alumni and supporters of their alma maters, members of several Filipino American ethnic associations, and devoted to their extended families. For many first-generation Filipino Americans interviewed, being involved in all these groups and activities is not uncommon. "This is the Filipino way," commented Reyna when I talked with her about this. She suggested that "Filipinos value community . . . we are hyper involved in everything and the Church nurtures this spirit." When I asked her how she manages her involvement in all these groups, Reyna told me, "Not well, I mean I think we spin our wheels a lot trying to find our way, but it helps if you have a map."

The map that Reyna refers to is not a physical map but a more holistic mental image of the vast connective networks and forces that make up the Filipino American community in Houston. Reyna uses this image and her own cultural understandings and experiences, both consciously and unconsciously, to navigate its complexity. In some situations or contexts, Reyna, or any other first-generation Filipino American, may strategically use this image to accomplish a certain aim or community project. In other situations and contexts, Filipinos may set out on a certain path that feels right or appropriate, not consciously recognizing the forces that guide them. This chapter attempts to reconstruct this community image by highlighting some of the key groups, networks, and forces that form the foundations of community for first-generation Filipino Americans in Houston. It then analyzes the ways in which first-generation Filipino Americans not only define community across and within these overlapping and competing forces but also how they build a sense of community that motivates their civic commitments to each other and the broader Houston community.

Emergence of the Filipino American Community in Houston

Prior to the 1960s, the Houston Filipino American community was virtually nonexistent. However, with changes in immigration legislation in 1965 and an increasing need for professionals in the Houston labor force, the Filipino immigrant population grew rather quickly. This was particularly true in and around the emerging Texas Medical Center. Filipino nurses and doctors came to Houston en masse throughout the late 1960s and gained recognition as some of the city's top medical professionals.[4] In fact, Susan, a first-generation Filipina interviewed as part of this study, was honored during that time as the "Outstanding Nurse of the Year" by M. D. Anderson Hospital. As the Filipino American community began to grow, the need for professional and community organizations grew, as well. Unlike more established Filipino American communities in California that had historically been built up over multiple decades of immigration and community organizing, Filipino Houstonians started almost at square one in the 1960s. With the exception of the Catholic Church and Catholic clubs, no institutional infrastructures existed for first-generation Filipino Americans to build upon.

It is said that wherever two or more Filipino immigrants get together they form a club or association.[5] Historically, regional and provincial differences among first-generation Filipino immigrants have indeed shaped their community ties, their social networks, their extend families, and the organizations that form the very foundations of their community. Although regional loyalties have often been high-lighted as a source of contentious politics among Filipino immigrants, in Houston, at least during the early 1960s and 1970s, there were not enough Filipinos from any given region for this to occur on a large scale.[6] Filipinos came together across regional and provincial lines to build the early Filipino Houston community.[7]

The first Filipino organization, the Philippines Association of Texas, was formed in 1963. Six years later, and after a considerable growth in the population, the Filipino Association of Metropolitan Houston (FAMH) was formed. These associations were open to all Filipinos no matter what region of the Philippines they came from. In 1972, Mayor Welch, recognizing the growth and importance of the Filipino American community to Houston, signed the Philippine Inde-pendence Day Proclamation at a ceremony with members of FAMH. This was the first time the Filipino American community had been recognized officially and collectively by the city. In 1979, another pan-Filipino association, the Filipino American Society of Texas, was formed and was quickly followed by the forma-tion of the Philippine Nurses Association of Metropolitan Houston in 1980. By this point, the number of associations began to multiply exponentially with the growth of the Filipino American population. As one first-generation Filipino American community leader described it, "Back then our community organiza-tions multiplied faster than rabbits." With the growth of the Filipino community also came an increase in the number of more ethnic and regional associations. By 1998, for example, the number of Filipino American associations, many of which were more provincial in nature, was estimated to be around thirty-five. Today, that number has more than doubled to seventy-eight.[8]

From their early historical beginnings to the present, Filipino ethnic and regional associations have been a "space of their own." They are an arena in which many first-generation Filipino Americans feel comfortable voicing their grievances and advocating on behalf of their specific regional and provincial communities. For Filipino immigrants prior to 1965, these associations were a major political outlet when the exclusionary conditions of a pre–civil rights movement America had cut off access to traditional political parties and organi-zations.[9] Today they constitute the overwhelming majority of the organizations and institutions that make up the Filipino American community in Houston. Despite decade-old pleas for unity, these associations remain largely regional. They are barangays in diaspora that strengthen a sense of home and identity.[10] They link the Filipino American community transnationally to the Philippines by region and ethnic group, but not necessarily across them. Describing this fact, the Filipino American social pundit Perry Diaz suggests, "When the Filipino diaspora started in the mid-1900s, the 'barangay mentality' was kept alive in the new settlements of Filipinos around the world. Wary of the influence of their new non-Filipino political leaders, they band themselves into 'barangays.' They didn't call their groups 'barangay.' They were probably not even aware that what they were doing was similar to what their forefathers did more than 2,000 years ago along the coastlines of the Philippine archipelago."[11] Today, at least in Houston, not much has changed.

The Filipino community in Houston is essentially a community of communities. Drawing further attention to this, Butch, a first-generation Filipino American in his mid-fifties, noted, "I think that for the first-generation of Filipino immigrants, unity within the broader Filipino community will be difficult to achieve." Continuing, he stated:

> They all came from various regions and provinces in the Philippines which were separated in terms of geography, and each have their history, language, means of communication, culture, and traditions. Everyone has strong attachments to their families, town mates, schoolmates, and province-mates and thus usually tend to associate with the same people where they came from. They have unity within their own smaller groups but they seem not to be able to find a common bond that cuts across their differences and gives them a genuine feeling that they truly belong to the larger Fil-Am [Filipino American] community . . . That explains why there are so many small associations. Umbrella organizations unifying the smaller associations have been formed, but a strong rallying objective to unify them has been unsuccessful thus far . . . we can only hope for the best.

Butch provides a measure of insight into the regional and cultural reasons why there are so many Filipino associations in Houston. He suggests that a shared ethnic background and speaking a common regional language/dialect can draw Filipinos together into small groups but also prevents them from uniting across them. Acknowledging this, however, Butch remains rather optimistic. He points to a measure of hope that umbrella organizations such as the Filipino American Council of South Texas (FACOST), the successor of the Council of Philippine-American Organizations started in 1984, can bring about unity and further connect the Filipino American community to the wider city.

This is not to say that first-generation Filipino Americans are not active in the wider Houston community or are unwilling to become Americans. They are well connected to Houston but not necessarily through their ethnic associations. This by no means suggests that these associations are anti-American or anti-assimilationist. At any given Filipino American associational meeting, one is just as likely to find Filipinos singing the American national anthem as the Philippine national anthem. Planning relief benefits for their extended families both in the United States and the Philippines, as well as speaking a host of regional languages in addition to English, every meeting is a testament to transnational lives. In these associations, many first-generation Filipino Americans express an equal pride in their Philippine heritage and their United States citizenship—a sense of being Filipino and American simultaneously. However, the purpose of these groups is essentially Filipino for Filipinos. It is in other organizational settings that the Filipino American community in Houston extends beyond these regional or provincial lines and connects first-generation Filipinos more fully with other groups and populations in the city.

MAPPING THE FILIPINO AMERICAN IMMIGRANT COMMUNITY OF HOUSTON

Returning to Stan's birthday party as a point of reference, Figure 1 maps some of the complex forces and organizations that make up the Filipino American community in Houston. It is an oversimplification of what is obviously much more complicated and dynamic, but it serves as a general snapshot to guide discussion about the wider community. At the center of Figure 1 is Stan or any other first-generation Filipino American Catholic. He is linked institutionally to three overlapping and competing community circles. These include the wider community which encompasses all Houston residents, Filipino or not; the Filipino community which encompasses all Filipino regional and ethnic groups; and what can be described as the Catholic universe which encompasses the Catholic Church as well as the groups and institutions associated with it or with Catholicism more generally. Underlying these community circles is a series of more informal networks, particularly among women, that are not represented in the figure. As several scholars remind us, these types of networks often go unseen but are highly specialized and often contested resources that permeate the spaces between more formal organizations and institutions.[12] Together, each community circle and the networks between them have their own loci of authority and exert a different set of influences on first-generation Filipino Americans and other Filipino Americans in general.

Looking first at the somewhat fluid boundaries of the Filipino community, we can see that attendees of Stan's party, including Stan himself, belong to a host of regional, ethnic, and professional organizations that are exclusively Filipino. Highlighted within this grouping is the Filipino American Council of South Texas (FACOST), an umbrella organization that attempts to coordinate over forty Filipino organizations and associations in the region. Among these groups is Bicol USA, Ilocano Club of Metropolitan Houston, Pangasinan Association of Texas, Visaya Mindanao association, and the Tagalog Association of Texas, to name a few. Together, both the groups within the jurisdiction of FACOST and those who have not joined its alliance constitute the overwhelming majority of associational memberships for first-generation Filipino Americans interviewed. Yet these institutions are only part of a more complex picture. Filipinos at Stan's party, including Stan himself, are also members of groups such as the Asian Pacific American Heritage Association or the Asian Chamber of Congress, which link first-generation Filipinos to the wider Houston Asian American community (see Figure 1). Beyond this, but not outlined in Figure 1, first-generation Filipino

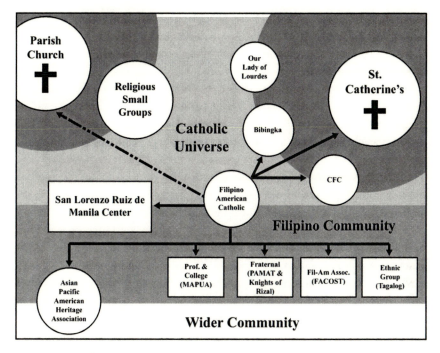

Figure 1 Map of the Filipino American Community of Houston. *Source:* Figure created by Stephen M. Cherry.

Americans may additionally be members of organizations such as the YMCA that further link them to the broader Houston community.

As we focus next on the Catholic universe, we see that Figure 1 highlights the importance of the Catholic Church and more general Catholic organizations to first-generation Filipino Americans in Houston. Included among these institutions is the San Lorenzo Ruiz de Manila Community Center. Although the San Lorenzo Center is independent from the Church—in fact, the only independent Filipino community center in Houston—it is also a Catholic social space for Filipinos and is named after the first canonized saint in the Philippines. Although the San Lorenzo Center has had a rather contentious relationship with St. Catherine's over the years, its members are overwhelmingly still devoted Catholic parishioners and are ardent supporters of the church.[13]

St. Catherine's has one of, if not the largest first-generation Filipino American congregation in the city of Houston, but it is not the only Catholic church with a sizable Filipino population. Although first-generation Filipino Americans may be registered with the parish closest to where they live, they may also frequently attend other parishes depending on the time of year, the call of a friend, or host of other reasons. Part of the draw to these churches is the increasing presence of Filipino American priests and other Filipino congregants. Another part of the draw is the cultural and spiritual importance of Catholicism itself. In the

Philippines, Filipinos, on average, attend church weekly if not more than once a week, but are accustomed to visiting whatever church they like without registering. In the American diaspora this tradition remains the same, much to the dismay of Church leaders.

At St. Catherine's, Monsignor Father José is a charismatic leader who draws Filipinos and others from around the city to weekly mass. Many of the members of St. Catherine's do not actually live in the parish, as we might expect, but drive anywhere from forty-five minutes to several hours to attend mass. According to Father José, "Many of the Filipinos that attend mass are registered with St. Catherine's but not all." Continuing, Father José expressed a certain amount of frustration. "You will notice that our records show that Filipinos are about 40 percent of the congregation but it is really closer to 50 percent . . . we just cannot get them to register because their old ways in the Philippines are too hard to break." While first-generation Filipino Americans make up the largest ethnic group at the church, St. Catherine's is not a Filipino parish but a very multiethnic/multiracial congregation. Understanding this, Father José does not cater more to Filipinos but actually works very hard to insure that each group is equally represented in all church councils and affairs. "This is an American Catholic church [St. Catherine's], we come from every background but we must practice the same religion . . . yes, many of the parishioners are Filipino, but this is not a Filipino church."

Although St. Catherine's hosts a monthly Filipino mass and sponsors a number of traditional Filipino religious celebrations, it cannot possibly accommodate all the rich regional devotionals and practices that first-generation Filipinos bring with them from the Philippines, nor does Father José want to. "We support Filipino traditions, but the church is for everyone." Continuing, he told me, "If we celebrated every novena and devotional for every ethnic group in the parish we would never have time for mass. We must practice the basics of an American Catholicism that appeals to the faith of all. We encourage every group to explore their own cultural practices, but we only have so much space and so much time. We obviously do try to support and nurture these groups but our focus must be on the larger church body." Turning once again to Stan's party and Figure 1 as a point of reference, we can see that these practices find their full expression in home devotional and prayer groups.

These groups are an important part of first-generation Filipino American religiosity in Houston. Groups such as Our Lady of Lourdes and Couples for Christ, of which Stan and the attendees at his party are members, represent only two of the nearly twenty-five Filipino religious groups that are officially registered with St. Catherine's parish. Among these includes several Marian groups such as the Legion of Mary and other Filipino specific fellowships such as Lord's Flock Charismatic Community and Totus Tuus, to name a couple. Other groups such as Bibingka are not registered at St. Catherine's and can span several parishes despite their relatively small size. Outside of their obvious religious significance, in many ways these groups serve as an alternative Filipino spiritual space to the more political orientations of the Filipino American associations described earlier. They are likewise evidence of a growing lay movement, Filipino or not, within the larger Church.

When you ask Filipinos how they would classify these more religious associations, the answers often suggest a link between Filipino American understandings of family and community. Vanessa, for example, emphatically answered the question by stating, "This [CFC] is my home." Expressing a similar sentiment, Angie, a first-generation Filipina American member of another home devotional group, offered, "Bibingka is my community. These are my brothers and sister; they are my family." This theme resonated throughout interviews with first-generation Filipino Americans in Houston. However, these sentiments are not necessarily unique to Filipinos. It is estimated that roughly 40 percent of Americans are members of a small group and 60 percent of those are affiliated in some way with a house of worship.[14]

Since Vatican II, American Catholics have been encouraged to join small groups and fellowships. In fact, the *aggiornamento* or spirit of "bringing the Church up to date" during Vatican II, built on the strength of lay leadership in the United States and not only encourages lay movements but has helped the Church see the benefit of establishing these groups.[15] Historically this should not be a surprise, especially in the case of first-generation immigrants, for whom these smaller groups often facilitated the spaces between home, community, and the Church itself.[16] Today, although many of these groups are registered with a parish and priests visit or participate in them from time to time, the Church has little authority or control over them outside of the more normative moral commitments it engenders among the participants as Catholics.

Many Church leaders target these groups as a way to get people more involved in the wider activities of the church.[17] Others question whether the inward focus of these groups will ultimately deter from church life and service to the parish community.[18] As Father Roberto, another first-generation Filipino American priest from another Houston parish, St. Stephen's stated, "When you usually go to observe Couples for Christ they use the buildings here but most of them are not members of the parish, they just use it. They do something like use the Catholic Church but their loyalty is not in the church, and the pastor has no hold over them. For example, in Knights of Columbus, pastors are holding them because they are really Catholic; the Catholics Women's League, the Legion of Mary are also really Catholic, but this Couples for Christ have their own identity." Although Father José at St. Catherine's does not share this assessment of CFC or any of the other prayer groups in his parish, Father Roberto's sharp criticism is an indication that there is a certain amount of debate over these groups among the clergy in Houston. This was evident throughout discussions with other Catholic clergy and parish staff in Houston. However, the fact that Filipinos have built alternative religious groups and organizations outside the control of the Church should not be surprising. At least historically, the home has always been a major center of Filipino religious practice, either by choice or during periodic waves of exclusion from institutional resources under Spanish rule and in response to American racism both within and outside the Catholic Church.

Through home prayer groups and devotionals, Filipinos forge an important, more personalized, resource for their community life that transcends parish and national boundaries. Thus, despite the intimacy shared in these groups, their focus is not always inward. Couples for Christ, as an example, is a rather large international organization. In Houston, CFC comprises roughly twelve households of twenty-five people or fewer, compared to just one household of the same size for groups such as Bibingka. By its size alone, CFC is unique in its scope and in the spread of its transnational networks. Both of these groups, CFC and Bibingka, as is the case with other devotional groups examined, remain deeply linked to their parish churches and their larger communities.[19]

Trying to define Filipino American prayer groups and home devotionals is difficult. Unlike the religious groups studied by many scholars of American civil society, the groups in this study often cross parish lines and draw from members across multiple zip codes.[20] Although their structure involves a relatively high degree of formal organization, with goals, agendas, and lesson plans, a high level of informality and flexibility often leaves power in these groups relatively diffuse and broadly democratic with no one leader in charge.[21] Some groups, such as CFC, have elected household leaders, both men and women, but even in these situations meetings are often moved from house to house, thereby distributing authority and responsibility. Other groups such as Bibingka claim to have no leaders at all, although they are sometimes led by Sister Diana, the Filipina wife of the first-generation Filipino American Permanent Deacon of St. Catherine's.

At a more general level, these groups are equal parts Filipino regional or provincial devotional, family support, and Bible study. At the same time, they can also serve as a network of interlocking women's groups, men's groups, couples' groups, and general therapy or self-help groups for first-generation immigrants in the diaspora. As Adler, a member of Bibingka in his late fifties, pointed out, "When I came to Houston this group became my home, my support in hard times, and a family that I look forward to seeing every Friday night. . . . They really understand me as a Filipino."

Considering Adler's words, Filipino American devotional groups are also an important space where ethnicity can be reproduced. In any given prayer group, the access to a common language and traditional Filipino food is a means by which being Catholic and being Filipino are conjoined. Ritually, the service and fellowship found in these groups provide a cohesive point around which faith is made relevant to Filipino lives. Hymns are sung in Tagalog and accompanied by guitar and tambourine, people proclaim their faith with charismatic zeal, and the Bible is interpreted through purely Filipino lenses. This carries with it a heartfelt expression of how these Filipinos see the world and feel their faith. As Adler explained, "I don't have to tell them what I mean, they know; they understand because they are Filipino."

Religious artwork in the homes where these groups meet also reflects the icons of faith, such as Our Lady of Antipolo or Santo Niño, that Filipinos most identify with in the Philippines and upon which their devotion is often centered. While in many American Catholic churches these icons and statues are missing, in Filipino American home devotionals and prayer groups they are on full display, playing to the pageantry and vibrancy that is Philippine Catholicism. These images also serve as models of empowerment, particularly for Filipinas, who turn to Marian images and devotionals for comfort and legitimacy in their community endeavors. Doctrinally these groups are essentially no different from other Christians immigrating from the global South. They are socially conservative, in many cases charismatic, and represent a part of a larger trend that is reshaping the American religious landscape through their lay leadership and diverse religious practices. Although the specific Filipino groups in this study are not performing exorcisms in their homes, like some Christians immigrating from the global South, they do believe in the power of supernatural forces and divine intervention. The members of Bibingka, for example, are actively trying to bring about the spiritual and physical healing of one of its members who is terminally ill through prayer, a laying on of hands, and the ritual use of holy water and other sacred objects. These are not beliefs and practices widely held by most native-born American Catholics. With this in mind, these groups are just as important, if not more, to the Filipino American community as secular Filipino ethnic associations and organizations. Likewise, they are an important part of the dynamic changes occurring in American Catholicism today.

BRINGING THE MAP TOGETHER

Reviewing the broader holistic map presented in the previous pages, it makes intuitive sense that each of these cross-cutting memberships can passively and actively shape first-generation Filipino Americans' civic outlooks and the ways in which they attempt to build community across these groups.[22] Highlighting this, we might take the examples of Jimmy and Fred, both first-generation Filipino American Catholics in their early sixties who have taken differing paths through similar religious and secular organizations in Houston. Jimmy was once an active Mason but stopped attending his local Masonic lodge after joining Couples for Christ. "The fellowship among the [Masonic] brothers was unequal to anything, but upon becoming a new Catholic through CFC I learned how Masonry was historically an anti-Catholic group." Lamenting this situation, as tears welled up in his eyes, Jimmy stated, "It was a painful break . . . I was a former Master. I loved, still love my brothers." Jimmy sees his sacrifice as a necessary part of being re-catechized and building community within the Catholic universe.

Fred, on the other hand, a founding member and former Master of PAMAT (Philippine American Masons of Texas), believes that his involvement in his devotional group Bibingka and his life as a faithful Catholic does not require this sacrifice.[23] "There is nothing anti-Catholic about PAMAT . . . in fact, we even have priests who join our fellowship." Continuing, Fred emphasized how on numerous occasions, including various Filipino religious celebrations, PAMAT has worked side by side with St. Catherine's, his parish church. Clearly, Jimmy and Fred have taken different paths through their community in Houston. While mapping out these overlapping and competing circles allows us to better understand some of the key groups and forces that impact these routes, it does not fully answer how first-generation Filipinos in Houston actually define community, nor does it elucidate where or in what context they gain their greatest senses of community.

Defining Community with Faith and a Sense of Purpose

Asking any first-generation Filipino American in Houston to locate or even define community is not an easy task. The question of "How do you define community?" or "What do you consider to be your community?" is often met with a certain amount of confusion. Highlighting this, Jane, a first-generation Filipina American accountant asked, "What do you mean by community, my church, my associations, where I live . . . do you mean Filipinos in Houston?" Rather than answering the question, many Filipinos wanted me to define what I meant by community before they answered. When I did not define it, either in English or Tagalog, I found that the location in which I asked the question usually framed their responses. Explaining this, John, a first-generation Filipino American retail manager in his late fifties emphasized, "For us Filipinos, community is found wherever two or three are gathered together whose activities range from simple interactions to worshiping the Lord together."

Like the transnational lives of first-generation Filipino Americans in San Diego to which previous scholars have drawn attention, Filipinos in Houston carry their homes in their heart and build their communities wherever they gather.[24] Their communities have no fixed geographic boundaries. They are just as connected to their regional provinces in the Philippines as the American suburbs in which they physically reside. Although a single Filipino organization or association may provide a bridge that can link some of these transnational divides, most Filipino immigrants in Houston are members of multiple associations, as was already discussed. It is across these organizations and forces that Filipinos build their senses of community. Discussing this, Keith, a first-generation Filipino American choir director in his mid-forties, explained, "I believe that you can be a member of more than one community. I offer myself as an example. I am a member of several groups, the Church, etcetera, and each is a community but they do overlap . . . it is a community of communities." As we have seen, the Filipino American community in Houston is indeed a community of communities, but this is not necessarily unique to them.

Most scholars agree that people in general, not just immigrants, are influenced by the community in which they live or were raised, but few recognize that they are simultaneously members of multiple communities that function in varying degrees of harmony or discord with each other.[25] This produces a host of competing forces that shape their public and civic life. It also influences how people define and build their senses of community. Not all of these forces, however, are equal. Some forces and institutions are more influential than others. For most of the first-generation Filipino Americans interviewed, family is considered the basic building block of community. Drawing attention to this, Dora, a first-generation Filipina American civic leader in her late fifties, stated, "Our extended family is our first ring of community and each ring overlaps with that of another. . . . Somewhere in every gathering of Filipinos you know someone is bound to be your tito [uncle] or tita [aunt], your kuya [older brother] or ate [big sister], blood or not." Continuing, she explained, "We are family and yes, families do fight, but there's a difference between fighting with your brother than someone messing with your brother . . . there's a bond there that cannot be broken. We are Filipino brothers and sisters and we are Catholics in Christ. I really think the connection is in our families, we are all one Catholic family." Family is clearly the foundation on which Dora sees the Filipino American community being built, but she also draws attention to Catholicism as an equally powerful force that connects Filipinos and groups in Houston.

Drawing on survey findings, Figure 2 illustrates that first-generation Filipino American Catholics surveyed in Houston gain their sense of community from a wide range of religious and secular sources.[26] Twenty-eight percent indicated that other Filipinos greatly contribute to their sense of community, the second largest source according to survey results, but they also suggested that their places of employment or work did not.[27] Religious institutions, such as the Catholic Church and prayer groups, ranked as the most important contributors to respondents' overall sense of community. In fact, 78 percent of first-generation Filipino Americans surveyed in Houston consider their local parish church to be the greatest contributor to their sense of community.[28] This is not surprising; many Filipino immigrants operate within the Philippine notion of the *poblacion* (Ta) or town plaza, wherein the church is seen as the center of the plaza and hence the center of their community.[29]

Despite the cultural diversity across Filipino ethnic and provincial groups, the varieties of religious expression they practice are not essentially a cause for strife but rather part of the united mission of the Catholic Church itself. Looking at the

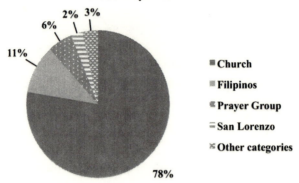

Most important

- Church
- Filipinos
- Prayer Group
- San Lorenzo
- Other categories

2% 3%
6%
11%
78%

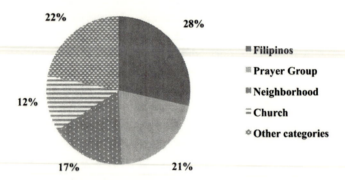

Second most important

- Filipinos
- Prayer Group
- Neighborhood
- Church
- Other categories

22% 28%
12%
17% 21%

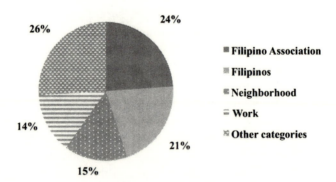

Third most important

- Filipino Association
- Filipinos
- Neighborhood
- Work
- Other categories

24% 26%
14%
15% 21%

Figure 2 Most Important Contributors to First-Generation Filipino Americans' Sense of Community in Houston. *Source:* The Houston Filipino American Survey 2010; see Methodological Appendix for further details.

Percent of total importance points

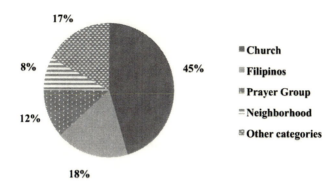

- Church
- Filipinos
- Prayer Group
- Neighborhood
- Other categories

Figure 2 (*continued*) Most Important Contributors to First-Generation Filipino Americans' Sense of Community in Houston. *Source:* The Houston Filipino American Survey 2010; see Methodological Appendix for further details.

mission statement of St. Catherine's, for example, this is made even clearer: "As a parish we strive to be a community of disciples faithful to the teachings of Our Lord Jesus. . . . We strive to be sensitive and responsive to the longings and needs of our diverse cultural groups to give praise and worship to God in their own language and tradition."[30] This mission statement is not just given in words but is also realized through Father José's ardent attempts to make sure every group in the parish is represented on the parish council and is made to feel that they are a valued and empowered part of the parish.

Although conflict does occur, and certainly not every group agrees or feels equally valued, most of the first-generation Filipino Americans interviewed suggested that their Catholic parish provides a certain amount of "structure" to their sense and understanding of community. As Delia, a first-generation Filipina nurse in her early forties, explained, "The parish is not perfect by any stretch of the imagination and I would imagine that some people think we Filipinos get certain privileges because of our size and because Father [José] is Filipino, but that is not true." Continuing, she suggested, "Real community is found in the parish. We have one vision plus there are certain rules that govern the community and a certain culture. Part of this is centered on the fact that if you go against it, like have an abortion, you may not be a part of it anymore. So I look at it as what's important is to follow the culture of the Catholic community and the same beliefs." Delia sees the central teachings of the Church and her Catholic faith as the foundation of her community. She also suggests these unified beliefs may not all be practiced in the same way. "We all practice in our own unique way, but that does not mean we are not a community or that we do not share in our love of the Church."

The Church, as we have seen, encourages its various ethnic groups to form their own devotional and prayer groups to further their own culturally specified religious expressions. It is the Church's hope that these devotional groups register with their parishes. Those that do are often given space to meet in Church buildings, given opportunities to hold specific masses or devotionals for their regional saints and patrons, and are brought together throughout the year to celebrate in parish-wide events such as Flores de Mayo, which unifies various Marian groups. Those that are not registered are not necessarily frowned upon but are not always given access to the same resources. In either case, these groups are important to the Filipino American community.

Survey results indicate that religious devotional and prayer groups are the third largest contributor to first-generation Filipino Americans' sense of community in Houston (see Figure 2). Given the historical importance of these groups to Filipinos both in the Philippines and in the American diaspora, this should not be a surprise. Most of the Filipino immigrants interviewed see these groups as a holistic part of their larger vision of the Catholic community. Highlighting this, Jimmy pointed out, "A community is people who share the same values, standards, morals, and beliefs. Couples for Christ is not a society but a community. Being a member of CFC has helped me define the gray areas that divide society and community." Making a clear distinction between society and community, much as the classical social theorist Ferdinand Toennies would, Jimmy points to his own sense of community as intimately centered around a smaller collective who share certain morals and religious beliefs.[31] Although CFC is not a society per se, for Jimmy, the group redefines community by comparison and leads him to see that there is a spiritual relationship between the two. It defines the "gray areas," as Jimmy puts it, between his idea of community, other communities, and society more generally.

Agreeing with Jimmy, Keith, also a member of CFC interviewed while attending a Friday prayer meeting, stated, "Being a member of CFC has brought me a sense of community on how early Christians may have been like—where people share things as it should be within a community to better others who are less fortunate for [than] you, spiritually, mentally, emotionally, and even financially. I have been protected and prayed for by members of this community [CFC] and I know that this is what I want my children and my children's children to experience. To me is the epitome of a community—communal worship and partaking of the Lord in the Holy Mass wherever you may be."

Adding to our conversation, Tony, another member of CFC, explained, "Being involved in CFC made me see things from a different perspective, I should say, from a Catholic perspective. Though I see myself as a member of my family, my most immediate community, I am also a member of several other communities—my place of work, CFC, the parish, the society at large, my mother country and the whole world . . . Somehow, it is through CFC that I see things in a wider perspective." Continuing, Tony pointed out that it is not just being Catholic or a member of CFC that matters but holding a true spiritual commitment. "As you get deeper into the life of community, especially when it's organized like CFC, you notice that, just like any other community, there will be diplomatic and political struggles that people will want more power than others. Some people want more control—that's human nature. You notice that the more spiritually mature and more exposed ones to God's love will be able to overlook these and see the true meaning of community that gives support and nourishment to the souls that need it the most." This spirit of community that Tony describes is not a matter of being Catholic in name only but also being "spiritually mature," as he puts it, and practicing one's faith. These sentiments resonated throughout conversations with members of CFC and were likewise shared by many members of other Filipino American devotionals and prayer groups interviewed. Gail, a first-generation Filipina American member of Lord's Flock, for example, stated, "Before I joined a devotional group, community was just people living together in the same area or something like that but now I see it as something more . . . it is more about putting our faith in action than just calling ourselves brothers and sisters."

Ultimately, community for first-generation Filipino Americans is not about place so much as it is about purpose. Across all the interviews presented in this chapter, first-generation Filipino Americans consistently point to intimate bonds such as religion and family as the sources that draw them together and form the foundations of their understandings of community. While in some cases these are idealized visions of how first-generation Filipino Americans want their community to be versus its more mundane realities, they see their daily efforts and interactions as important to bringing these visions to fruition. More than holding them together through name or membership, these bonds are forged through collective actions and mutual dependencies that weave their lives into the fabric of this vision of community. In order for this to occur, first-generation Filipino Americans suggest that people must truly share a common definition of what community is. Likewise, they state that people must share a common purpose or understanding of what their role is within community as they struggle to make these ideal communities a reality.

Further highlighting this, we might take the examples of four first-generation Filipino American Catholics from various backgrounds interviewed during the study. Sally, a first-generation Filipina American in her late thirties and a member of FACOST, suggested, "A community can be diverse, with people coming from different faiths and different places, but they must believe in one vision or mission, like a family—that is the heart of any community." Sally, although she is Catholic, emphasized that community does not require people to be of the same faith but they must share a singule vision or mission. Expressing much the same assessment but from a different point of view, Nell, a first-generation Filipina parishioner at St. Catherine's, stated, "Community is a group of people united in a mission. . . . They must be one in mind and heart in certain things such as their faith and understanding of family." Once again, much like Sally, faith and family come to the forefront of Nell's conversation, as does an emphasis on the singularity of purpose for community.

Unlike Sally and Nell, Adler, a first-generation Filipino American member of Bibingka, pointed specifically to his own home devotional group as the source of his vision of community. "Community is a group of people bound by a common purpose and interest, like our prayer group. . . . A prayer group is a smaller community." Although Adler specified Bibingka as his community, like Sally and Nell he suggested that any community, no matter what size, must be bound by a common purpose. Vanessa, a first-generation Filipina nurse interviewed at Stan's party, expressed the same thought. "Community is a group of people sharing the same mission and vision, the same faith and the same goal. . . . [It] can be anywhere you share the same vision."

CONCLUSION

The diversity and complexity that make up the Filipino American community in Houston is virtually boundless. Their community is not a singular entity for a singular people but multiple communities drawn from thousands of islands and a host of regional and cultural differences. This point has been overlooked far too often or, in some cases, has been minimized by scholars, particularly those who conduct survey research. Scholars who work with secondary data are often forced to lump the diversity described in this chapter within a single Filipino American category or, even worse, collapse them into a larger pan-Asian American category.[32] Even among studies that have analyzed Filipinos' religious and civic life as part of a larger Asian American Catholic subcategory using national datasets have largely not been able to explore the various characteristics that distinguish the Filipino community from other Asian Catholic communities or those communities from each other. Whether they are coming from Vietnam, Korea, or the Philippines, for example, each group, regardless of country of origin, is not only diverse within itself, both socioeconomically and culturally, but has had a historically unique relationship with Catholicism.[33] As a result, each Asian American Catholic group may attach different cultural meanings to community and civic life that cannot be understood under the umbrella of a pan-Asian American category, no matter how you define it.

Filipino Americans are unique among Asian American immigrants and are even unique among other Asian American Catholic immigrants. Unlike many Asian Catholics immigrating to the United States from Vietnam or Korea, for example, Filipinos are coming from a nation in which Catholics are the overwhelming majority and have been for hundreds of years. Filipino Catholics are not moving from a majority religious status in the Philippines to a minority status in the United States, nor are they moving from minority to majority religious status.[34] As Catholics emigrating from a Catholic nation, they join the American Catholic

Church, alongside other immigrants from Latin America, as a growing part of the single largest denomination in their new nation. In terms of outward religious status, nothing has changed for these Filipinos. However, they are immigrating from a post-EDSA 1 Philippines in which the Catholic Church and a charismatic variety of liberation theology played a prominent role in the ousting of Ferdinand Marcos and continue to be seen as major forces shaping Philippine civil society today. The Catholic Church is not the symbolic fourth branch of government in the United States, as it is in the Philippines. The relationship of Catholicism to American civil society is different. Nonetheless, given the cultural prevalence of Catholicism in the Philippines and the fact that being Filipino is almost synonymous with being Catholic, this majority status is not drastically challenged in immigration to America, and hence, Filipinos remain actively Catholic.[35]

Although the immigration process can certainly lead to increased religious participation for new immigrants, given the alienation inherent in their transitions, Filipinos in the diaspora are by all indications just as religious in the United States as they were in the Philippines and more so than the average Americans, among whom only 59 percent state religion is important to them.[36] With this in mind, it should not come as a surprise that Filipinos in America continue to see the Catholic Church as the center of their communities and civic lives. Add to this the fact that Philippine Catholicism stands as one of the most traditional and conservative forms of Catholicism in the world, especially compared to the more liberal views of American Catholics, making it more akin to the charismatic practices and beliefs of Evangelical Christians in the global South, and it should also come as no surprise that Filipinos have the potential to be one of the most dynamic sources of change shaping the future of American Catholicism.[37]

Filipino Catholics, such as Stan discussed in this chapter, are already impacting the lives of many people of various backgrounds across their parishes, not just Filipino immigrants. They are also bringing about changes within their parishes through their leadership as priests and various lay voices both within and outside the Church. Lay-led prayer groups, such as Bibingka and Couples for Christ, represent part of these dynamic forces, but are only a few examples of the complexity and diversity that has been largely underexplored or lost in previous studies of Asian American Catholics' civic lives. Also lost are the vibrant connections these diverse Filipino communities maintain with their homeland and the importance of their Catholic faith in building communities in the diaspora. As the Philippines is poised to surpass the United States as the largest English-speaking Catholic nation and is quickly becoming one of a very few sources American parishes can count on for newly ordained priests, these transnational linkages cannot be ignored.

Not unlike many other new immigrants, the first-generation Filipino Americans described in this chapter live transnational lives. They are rooted in Houston but forever linked to the Philippines and their friends and family wherever the diaspora has taken them. They carry their homes in their hearts and build community across geographic lines. At the center of this community are the Catholic Church and a common faith. Although Filipino Americans like Sally and Adler or Nell and Vanessa have taken different routes in building their senses of community, they share a unique Catholic and Filipino vision of faith and family. For them, community is found wherever Filipinos are gathered with a purpose and deep spiritual commitments. Although these are largely idealized visions of community, they nonetheless drive first-generation Filipino Americans as they attempt to build community in the diaspora. This is not to say that there are no differences between Filipino Americans' idealized visions of how good Catholics, Filipino or not, should interact with one another versus the realities of the contentiousness of their community politics. There are numerous differences. Some may hold, for example, that Filipino culture is to blame for the divisiveness among groups, while others may suggest that Catholicism is the force that brings the community together. In reality, the situation is much more complicated. These two sets of cultures are just as intertwined as the Filipino Catholic identity itself.

Conflict, as will be made clear in the next chapter, is an ever-present part of the Filipino American community in Houston. Although this is perhaps no different from the struggles of other new immigrants, the role that Catholicism plays in immigrant community affairs, particularly at the institutional level, is unique among American religious traditions. Whereas many new immigrants who immigrate to the United States from the global South or elsewhere establish ethnic or regionally specific independent churches, Filipino Catholic immigrants, like other Catholic immigrants, build their new spiritual homes within established American parishes that are increasingly racially and ethnically diverse. The days in which the Catholic Church fostered ethnic parishes are long gone and have been replaced by a push to mold American parishes from its growing diversity. As a result, the Catholic Church is often at the center of community conflicts, but not necessarily the cause. Given the myriad associations, groups, and forces presented in this chapter that constitute the Filipino American community in Houston, both individual and collective interests across them can and most certainly do lead to contentious politicking.

Despite—or perhaps in some cases as a result of—the common Catholic faith shared among the majority of first-generation Filipino Americans, the Catholic Church and its priests, particularly its Filipino priests such as Father José, are often placed in the precarious position of directly and indirectly mediating individual and community relations. Not everyone agrees with the results of these mediations nor do they share a unified understanding of what the role of the Church should be in community affairs. The next chapter charts the complexity of these conflicts and chronicles the history of several specific cases. It details how the Church is involved in these conflicts at both the local and international level and explores how first-generation Filipino Americans perceive this involvement through the lens of their own cultural understandings of faith, family, and community.

CHAPTER 4

COMMUNITIES IN CONFLICT

It was eleven o'clock at night, and for members of Bibingka, all of whom are first-generation Filipino Americans, their Friday night fellowship had really just gotten started. They had been praying the Rosary, singing, and sharing their thoughts on scripture for over three hours. As the final prayer closed with a resounding, "Amen" and one last song was sung, they all made their way to the kitchen to prepare "a little midnight snack," as Janis put it. More like an extravagant buffet, the kitchen was filled with dish after succulent dish of Filipino cuisine, including Jun's famous *pancit* (Ta) noodles.[1] Taking the last few dishes out of the oven and microwave, the members of Bibingka gathered around a large breakfast table adjacent to the kitchen. "Let us bow our heads and give thanks." After making the sign of the cross and blessing the food, they began to pass the dishes around the table. Some took their seats at the table and began eating. Others stood and ate throughout the kitchen or sat around the coffee table in the living room.

Energized from their fellowship, the group began to talk more casually over food, and loudly at that. While it was difficult to keep up with all the discussions, furiously floating in and out of Tagalog and English at the same time, some form of community politics appeared to be on everyone's mind at our end of the table. Rose, for example, asked the group, "Have you heard that Bicol has split again?" Responding, Lyn stated, "It's not a surprise . . . with the election and everything else that is going on you knew it was bound to happen, right?" She then explained, "It is not like it is the first time it has happened and it probably won't be the last either." As other members gave their own thoughts while some remained rather silent, Janis, clearly upset, questioned, "Why can't we get our community affairs together? It's embarrassing and just makes me sick."

Interjecting, but curiously laughing, Stan announced, "Well those Filipino Lions have gone off and split again too!" Continuing, Stan stated, "I am not even sure how many of them there are now? Hey you guys, how many Filipino Lions make up a pride? No one knows because there aren't enough of them left in any one group to fill this den!" Almost everyone laughed but I felt as if I had missed an inside joke. I understood the intentionality of the joke and its cleaver play on words. I certainly knew a great deal about the history of contentious politics in the Filipino American community in Houston, yet I also knew from interviews with members of Bibingka that many of them were currently involved in some of the very groups they were laughing about or groups and associations such as Philippine American Masons Association of Texas (PAMAT) and the Tagalog Association of Texas that are very similar to them.

As we continued to talk about community politics, Cheryl stopped her own conversation and stated, "[Our] associations have not made a dent in society at large." Disagreeing with Cheryl, Ernesto interjected, "Our groups, like PAMAT, can and do make a difference." Agreeing with this statement but raising her own complaint, Janis told me, "I really admire a lot of Filipinos and their associations because they do a lot for the Filipino community but I expect more from them." Janis went on to explain that she feels as though the Filipino community could do so much more, "but politics always gets in the way."

Clearly, not everyone in the group that was a part of the discussion agreed with the relative success or impact Filipino associations have made or are making in the community, but most seemed to be concerned about unity on some level. Chiming in on our discussion, Adler explained, "You see, with Filipinos there is political talk, there is whole lot of organizing, and then maybe a little action." He then stated, "We have so many associations, like Cheryl said, but it's always a matter of unity talk and we never have unity, at least not in most of the Fil-Am associations; nothing but our faith really brings us together."

When I asked if there is a difference between Bibingka or devotional groups in general and more secular Filipino associations, everyone sitting near me responded with an emphatic "Yes." Explaining the differences they perceived, one by one the members of the group told me that even among prayer groups Bibingka is somewhat different. Janis, for example, suggested, "We are so much more casual than others but that does not mean we don't work just as hard." She then suggested one of the big differences lies in the fact that Bibingka does not have elections. Agreeing, Angie stated, "That's the real difference between us and the other Fil-Am groups." Continuing, she suggested that, "Whenever there are elections in any of the groups someone's bound to get mad . . . it's a leadership issue; they all want to be in charge and split when they lose the elections."

Throughout the night everyone shared their own opinion on politics in the Filipino community. While some members of the group were clearly more guarded in their conversation, others were willing to lay everything on the table, metaphorically speaking. Across these conversations most of the members of the group pointed to problems with the structure of electoral politics or raised concerns over leadership and the role of the Church in community affairs. When I asked if elections are problematic in other prayer groups and faith organizations, Jake and others told me that indeed sometimes it is. Highlighting this, Cheryl pointed out, "CFC is in trouble . . . they may end up splitting, too, but then again the Vatican might hold them together." Responding to Cheryl, Jake tried to sum up the evening's discussion in one sentence before everyone started to pack up their food and dishes for the drive home. "Religion and politics is a funny thing for us Filipinos, sometimes it makes things better and sometimes the [Catholic] Church can really mess it up." Not everyone agreed.

SITUATING FILIPINO AMERICAN COMMUNITY POLITICS

Over the six years of this study, the original Filipino American Lions group in Houston, a member of the national Lions Club, split five times. The group split so many times and so frequently that Stan was not the only first-generation Filipino interviewed that made jokes or had something to say about the situation. However, the Lions groups were not the only ones to split. During this time the Bicolano association also split into two groups after just reuniting as one group just prior to the start of this study. Likewise, the Philippine American Masons Association of Texas (PAMAT), one of the few original groups in Houston that had not broken up since its inception, split into two groups over a disputed election. And Couples for Christ (CFC), which again is a larger international Filipino Catholic organization, split into three organizations globally, resulting in two groups with multiple chapters or households locally in Houston.[2]

Today, countless other groups and associations, secular or religious, have either split after their annual elections or continue to engage in very intense and public politicking. Secular groups and associations have faced quite a few more challenges than religious groups, given their structure and the frequency of their elections, but splits among religious groups have at times been equally contentious. Local Houston Filipino American newspapers and online blogs lament these splits in their editorials and often raise sincere pleas for unity among the groups. One such editorial in the *Manila-Headline*, the largest Filipino paper in print locally and across Texas, called for the community to adopt a new paradigm at the turn of the New Year. Describing the community as he sees it, the columnist Ben Ongoco joked, but with all sincerity stated, "Filipinos can outdo the atomic physicists in splitting isotopes. They always divide their organizations. Here in Houston, there are two Bohol organizations, so with Pangasinan, and lately Bicol. There are even four Filipino-dominated Lions clubs. As I was telling the Lions district governor, it is now tight to support four clubs. They know that if the Filipino organization has some human behavioral problems, they will be going to split. Sometimes, it is because of a bruised ego. Ego trips, they say."[3] As an influential and active community leader in addition to being a columnist for the paper, Ben was highly criticized by many Filipinos for his editorial.

Discussing the community's response to the column, Ben later suggested, echoing his own words from the editorial, "I really thought I was above and beyond those problems until I realized that I am in the loop and a part of the problem. . . . At least I try, but they just don't get it." Continuing, he expressed how frustrated he was that little has changed since he came to Houston. He also noted how tired he is of watching groups split. "We must find a solution or will remain forever lethargic . . . maybe it's your turn to help us, you're the social scientist with the PhD." Despite the fact that many, if not most, of the numerous Filipino American associations and groups that make up the community remain intact in one form or another after these splits, the problems members of Bibingka shared about associational elections and leadership in general are clearly very real concerns for the wider community.

At the same time, this contentious politicking is not unique to Filipinos living in Texas, as we might expect. On some level it is culturally driven and has changed very little over the centuries. Part of the problem, particularly in diaspora, stems from the fact that Filipino American associations often appoint or elect as many officers as possible in order to try and recognize as many people in the community as they can. Although this is largely a way of gaining status in the community, or as was the case in the past, a way to counter racist exclusion from mainstream American society, the growing number of Filipinos in these communities today means that everyone cannot be recognized, and thus the number of groups continues to proliferate, as does the contention around elected positions within them. This does not mean, however, that Filipinos do not want the political climate in their communities to change. In fact, as Bedo, a member of the Filipino Council of South Texas (FACOST) in his late thirties told me, "The fact remains that other cultures can put aside their differences and form a viable collective. While there may be in-fighting amongst other nationalities, such as the Koreans, Vietnamese, Greeks, Italians, etcetera, etcetera . . . they are still able to get together as a group and provide a unified front and lobby for their needs. Filipinos on the other hand, form groups upon groups, associations upon associations, and continually fight amongst each other. We have no unity." For Bedo, the problems facing the community are uniquely Filipino. "Our ways, our politics, and the business we conduct in these groups is just counterproductive, but I guess that is who we are . . . it's cultural." Although scholarship on other new immigrant communities would disagree with Bedo, suggesting that contentious politics is more normative than not, Bedo's concerns for his own community are legitimate nonetheless and are shared by many first-generation Filipino Americans in Houston and elsewhere.[4]

Pointing to this fact, Perry Diaz, a Filipino social pundit who has written editorials for numerous papers both here in the United States and the Philippines, editorialized in his online column, "Filipino-American political leaders are more interested in protecting their little turfs. . . . Leaders need to rise above the pettiness of "barangay politics" and think outside of the box, and free themselves from political bondage. This mindset has been our biggest drawback. We should push each other up; instead, we are pulling each other down and the whole community loses. The community needs to get its act together. We have a choice: political enlightenment or perpetual political bondage."[5] Drawing further attention to these issues, Ray Colorado, editor and publisher of an online community page in Houston, suggested, like Diaz, that the Filipino community needs to address its associational problems if it is going to grow or mature politically.

Recognizing that Filipino groups and associations are the foundations of the community, Ray called on them to change. "The practice of political maturity must begin with our community organizations, for they are the smallest unit of our political involvement . . . We must break away from the 'pioneer syndrome' and be aware of it presence as a political disease keeping us politically immature."[6] By "pioneer syndrome," what Ray meant and many other first-generation Filipino Americans interviewed described is a situation in which Filipino American associations and groups split over issues of pride and recognition. When Filipinos form a new association or group, they often recruit new members on the promise that there will be many programs and activities designed to benefit the Filipino American community at large. As the new association grows, top leadership positions are rotated among a small founding group of pioneers. When new members join, they are not granted access to these positions despite working just as diligently. Overlooked or given little credit, these new members leave to start associations of their own. This was largely the case observed throughout the years of this study. However, in some cases new members did or do make head way in these associations.

When this occurs, or when pioneers lose key leadership positions, the pioneers often rally the original members and start another association with the aim of not only recouping a sense of face but outshining or even crushing their former association. This is what many first-generation Filipinos interviewed describe as a "crab mentality." It is paramount to a crab pulling down its peer as it makes its way to the top of the bucket. Together, a crab mentality and the pioneer syndrome present real barriers to building community among first-generation Filipinos in Houston and elsewhere. As Ray pointed out, "These two patterns of breakup are too common among Pinoy [Filipino] communities such that we have too many organizations in every city."[7] Continuing, he questioned, "Today, who really cares about induction of officers? The officers of course, but those same individuals may have been elected a dozen times. The question is, is attending many meetings to organize induction of officers worth sacrificing personal health, family time, and church time?" What ultimately matters to first-generation Filipino Americans, according to Ray, is being with family, maintaining one's religious faith, and seeking a balance among numerous obligations. But this is not to the exclusion of an active civic life. As Ray emphatically pointed out,

"It is not true that Filipinos are losing their civic consciousness . . . far from it, but they have raised the standards for wise use of their time."[8] For some Filipino Americans interviewed, this desire for balance has led to apathy. For others, it has led to a deepening in religious life or a turn to the Church for guidance in community affairs.

Highlighting this, Marlena, a Filipina nurse in her early fifties, told me while working at a blood drive during a community fair that she is a member of several Filipino American associations but not really very involved. "I don't even have time to go to their annual induction balls . . . I guess I am a member in name only." Similar to the people political scientist Robert Putnam describes as metaphorically and literally "bowling alone" despite being members of bowling leagues, Marlena pays her dues but is not physically present in her associations.[9] When I asked Marlena why this is the case, she stated, "I moved to the U.S. in the 1970s. It is sad but I have seen the crab mentality among Filipinos. I have seen it in the Fil-Am association that is why there is always a split in the Fil-Am Associations here . . . I guess you see it more in civic organizations rather than religious organizations . . . this is why I stopped attending them and now devote my time to CFC." Many of the first-generation Filipino Americans interviewed, like Marlena, have retreated somewhat from associational life. Although they still pay their dues or attend an occasional fundraiser, they have grown tired of a lack of unity across Filipino associations.

Agreeing with Marlena, Gloria, a Filipina nurse who was also working at the blood drive, stated, "I have given up on our associations . . . they're good for nothing and just can't seem to ever move beyond their own egos and regional spats." Continuing, she suggested she attends meetings and votes in elections sometimes but has turned to other sources to get things accomplished in her community. When I asked her what these sources are, she suggested, like Marlena, that she has turned to religion. She also told me that this is where she believes the answer to "barangay politics" can be found. "They [Filipino associations and groups] really need to remember that they're Catholics first and build from there . . . maybe the Church can keep them out of trouble?" While certainly not everyone interviewed agreed with Marlena and Gloria or the sentiments of members of Bibingka, the Church, welcomed or not, has historically been a major force in Filipino community politics and remains so today.

CHURCHED POLITICS

Every year through the duration of this study, I attended the annual thanksgiving mass at St. Catherine's Catholic Church in celebration of Philippine Independence. As noted in previous chapters, the mass and the formal dinner that follows it are some of the largest annual gatherings of Filipino Americans in Houston. Although the banquet is often better attended than the mass, those who want to be seen or need to be seen for political and community reasons always attend both. Knowing this, Father José often uses the occasion as an opportunity to give his state of the Filipino community address during the homily. The message usually centers on a call for unity and reminds attendees that faith is always more important than politics and personal gain. As a master orator and a crafty lobby-ist, Father José never lays blame on any one group or leader during his homilies but instead talks in more vague community parables and jokes. However, on one occasion, the 108th anniversary of Philippine Independence, Father José's mes-sage and the events during the homily were a bit different. Several community groups had split or were fighting during this time, and Father José used his hom-ily to call the entire community to the table to work things out.

The homily began like those in any other year, or any since, with a general teaching on the virtues of being a good Catholic and loving your neighbor. After talking at length about, "building God's community on faith, hope, and love," Father José asked the leaders of all Filipino groups and associations in attendance to join him at the altar or stand in their pews. He then asked the congregation to applaud them and their efforts in the community before having them return to their seats. What followed was somewhat shocking. Pausing for a moment, Father José stated, "You know we Filipinos are funny, we are good Catholics but we have no real fear of the devil." Father José then questioned the congregation:

Do you know why? Let me tell you a joke. There was once a Filipino who went to hell. He was not all that bad but he did enough to fall out of God's grace and get a one-way ticket south when he died. When he got to hell the devil showed him around. He showed him that every group of people on the planet had its own giant caldron to stew in for eternity. Each caldron was labeled by nation and the caldrons were put in alphabetical order. When the devil asked the Fili-pino to find his national caldron, he said he was not sure if it was listed under "P" or "F." After the devil located the right caldron for him, the Filipino asked the devil why it did not have a heavy lid on it like all of the other cauldrons. The devil said, "Well you see every other nationality would run away and escape if I did not keep a lid on them, but with Filipinos I don't have to worry about that because they always pull each other down.

As nearly everyone in the congregation laughed, the seriousness of the joke was obvious. It was a direct reference to "barangay politics" and it was not really meant to be funny.

After the laughs came to a stop, Father José, said, "In all sincerity, who needs the devil when your own brothers and sisters can pull you back to hell?" Con-tinuing, Father José, perhaps sensing that tensions were building, stated, "We must first and foremost understand that we are children of God who must love each other as one Catholic family. I know you all love God. Through Christ we can do better and we must. . . . As we celebrate our history and culture on this blessed day let us not repeat the mistakes of the past." While Father José did not invite the Church into the political arena, he was clearly challenging the Filipino community and its associations and groups to stop its barangay politicking. It was an open call for unity based on Catholic morality and a broader sense of family. For Father José, the contentiousness of Filipino American politics may be culturally Filipino, something that he has observed among Filipinos both in the Philippines and here in the United States, but it is not indicative of his view of the culture of Catholicism nor does not fit within his vision of how good Catholics, Filipino or not, should interact with one another.

Although some Filipino Americans I spoke with after the mass only remembered the joke, stating that "Father always tells the best jokes," others took the message as an invitation to mediate community disputes. As Bert, one of the first-generation attendees at the mass stated, "Father is calling on us to work things out. . . . As a true man of God he knows what is best. . . . He [Father José] has helped us in the past and as the shepherd of the parish can guide us." Others were not as receptive and suggested that the Church has no business in community politics, "religion and politics are not a good thing." Explaining this further, one Filipina pointed out, "Look, you just don't understand . . . the Church means well but in the end it only complicates matters." Clearly not everyone agreed on the intentionality of the message, but for better or worse the Church, albeit reluctantly at times, has and continues to mediate community affairs, especially where it sees the issues as matters of faith.

Drawing on two additional examples involving St. Catherine's church and the relationship of the parish and Father José specifically to the Houston Filipino community, this chapter joins the discussions of a growing number of immigrant scholars in assessing the larger role of the Catholic Church in social relations and how these relations impact immigrant community life.[10] The chapter reveals the often unseen role of institutional religion in local immigrant community affairs and explores how the broader international Church, including the Vatican itself, can get involved in immigrant communities affairs and associational politics transnationally. In some situations, as we will see, Filipinos may openly petition the involvement of the Church in its community affairs. In other cases, they may seek to keep it out. Either way, the Church is often placed in the precarious position of directly or indirectly mediating these situations, whether it deems it necessary or whether it has been drawn reluctantly into these conflicts.

Before proceeding, it is important to note that the cases presented in this chapter are not unique but representative of a broader normative pattern of relations between the Filipino community and the Church.[11] As we might expect, not all Filipinos agree with the results of these mediations nor do they share each other's views of what the Church's role should be in community politics. While these cases certainly shed further light on Filipino immigrant and Church relations, it is also important to note that from a more institutional perspective, the way the Church and its priests get involved in or negotiate these disputes has clear implications beyond the Filipino American community itself. They reveal the possible roles the American Catholic Church might take in interacting with other immigrant communities or the parish in general.

Bicol Breakup

Bicolanos, Filipinos from the Bicol (Bikol) region of the Philippines, are one of several large regional ethnic groups that make up the Filipino American community in Houston. Although reliable data on the number of Bicolanos living in Houston do not exist or are complicated by non-Bicolanos being members of Bicol associations, the Bicol community is a major force in the community and continues to grow in size. In fact, Bicolanos in Houston have hosted the Bicol National Association of America convention several times, most recently in 2010, due to this growth and activity. Despite coming from the same region of the Philippines, Bicolanos often get together in smaller groups based on what province of Bicol they come from—Camarines Sur, as an example. Like other Filipino ethnic groups in Houston from other regions, Bicolanos have formed their own specific associations and groups and have also experienced their fair share of barangay politics.

Complicating matters, a disproportionate number of Catholic priests from the Philippines in Houston are Bicolano, including Father José. As a result, these priests often have personal connections and interests in the Bicol American community. It is not uncommon, for example, that Bicol priests get together with fellow Bicolanos at community parties and social gatherings. Likewise, given the fact that the majority of Bicolanos celebrate the feast and novenas for Our Lady of Peñafrancia, Bicol priests often preside over weeklong fiestas honoring Peñafrancia at their parish churches or in smaller gatherings in Bicolano homes.[12] When I asked Father José about his own personal relationship with the Bicol community, he stated, "I do not favor Bicolanos in the parish because I am Bicolano but I do enjoy being with them from time to time because I miss home and I enjoy their company . . . we are friends and I am their spiritual advisor." Knowing that the Bicol community had recently split, I asked Father José if anyone in the community had come to him asking to help mediate the situation. At first Father José stated, "Well not really," but as we continued to talk he suggested, "I was trying to mediate, but it seems like they are already rooted in their groups so I just said let's go, unless they request me to openly support their leaders then, no I do not mediate . . . it's really complicated."

The situation was and is very complicated. Depending on which group you ask, the facts surrounding the split vary, as do their opinions of clergy involvement or what their actual involvement was throughout the conflict. Although I cannot claim that I fully understand everything that transpired, the perspectives that first-generation Bicolanos and Filipino Americans in general shared about the situation are very telling about the complex nature of their continuous community politics. Laying blame and judgments aside, the attempts to retrace the events that led up to the split and afterward are not nearly as important as how first-generation Filipinos perceive the role of the Church in community affairs.

Prior to the official split of the original Bicol group, Bicol USA, Bicolanos had already nearly split over disputed elections several times. In fact, the founders of the group, the pioneers, had largely stopped attending meetings. Describing what happened, Ilene, a fairly new member of the Bicol association explained:

> The pioneers, they already had someone they had groomed, you know that had really worked for the association and it was her turn to become the president. She was vice president I think . . . the new ones had the person they wanted to run but wasn't even at the picnic, the election place, and they waited for her to arrive. They really catered to her, and when she arrived most of the people had left already and she became president. The election was very irreverent and she became president so the other people were disgusted. These were the pioneers, and they left. We were the new batch of officers that came in and we didn't even know what was going on between the two factions . . . we made it work for the first, second, and third years.

Although Bicolano priests often expressed their concerns and relayed their hopes that the group would remain intact throughout this time, they did not get directly involved, to the best of my knowledge, outside of listening to the issues and trying to help each side communicate better with one another.

When I asked Karla, a first-generation Filipina from Bicol and a former president of Bicol USA, about her involvement in the community and her relationship with the Bicolano priests, she said, "They [priests] were our friends. . . . Back then they would come to my house, about twenty of them. We would feed them; it was always a big party." But as Karla continued, she explained that her ability to organize the parties and bring Bicolanos together led to the priests pushing her into politics. "I had never run for office before and was not all that involved officially. I had parties where fifty or sixty people [were] coming in and out of the house. My house was called the party house back then in the early 2000s. That's why they said you should run [for president] because you can put all the Bicolanos together because they trust you, and so I did." For Karla and others interviewed, this is when things began to go wrong within the group. It is also the point at which the Church got more heavily involved.

Karla repeatedly stated that she did not really want to run for president, but felt considerable pressure from Father José and other Bicolano priests. "I said I don't want any more and I just want to be in the background and you know be the secretary and help out." She then explained, "They [priests] said no. We know you are a leader and you can. You know all of these people, the pioneers, and you can bring them together. I just didn't want to. . . . Even the pioneers talked to me and said that we will only rejoin the group again if you run because we trust you. So I did and I won. . . . Mother Mary must have wanted me to lead them." It is important to note that it was not just the Bicolano priests that privately endorsed Karla but the original pioneers, as well. Emphasizing this point, Karla stated, "When I was a member there were already two groups, one the original, the old-timers that started the group had already become inactive and they were all friends of mine, they were my neighbors from back home and I stayed neutral. They encouraged me to run for president to bring the groups together, and I did." The major division, as we might expect, was between the pioneers and the new Bicolanos, but Karla was somewhat new to the group with strong ties to the founding members, new members, and the Bicolano priests. Although priests did not openly endorse her, problems later arose when Father José supposedly privately endorsed another candidate for the next election.

According to members of both current Bicol groups, the national president of Bicol USA, who was the president of the central and only group prior to the split, openly endorsed Gabby Romano for the local chapter during the national convention in Houston. Most of the pioneers were pleased with Gabby's nomination and saw it as a means to continue what they perceived to be a peaceful unity that was built during Karla's term. Describing this, Pinoy, a Bicolano pioneer stated, "I thought it would all work out well this time around . . . she was a sure winner." However, as we might expect, an oppositional candidate, Anna Reyes, did rise and made a strong bid for the presidency because not everyone was pleased with Karla or the pioneers' candidate.

Over the next two weeks Anna made a strong bid for the presidency but also alienated the pioneers in the process. According to one Bicolano I spoke with, "What she [Anna] did was sign up every Tom, Dick, and Harry and Mary that she knew to become a member of the group . . . she invited all her Tagalog and non-Bicolano friends." Continuing, she explained, "You see, there was a loophole in the constitution that if you paid your dues you could vote whether you were from Bicol or not, and she knew she was going to lose." Making it even more complicated, Anna was and is an active member of St. Catherine's and many of the pioneers felt that Father José had endorsed her for the election. Karla, who was very close to Father José, stated that at the time she was out of town with her family when it all happened. "I called Father and told him I was hearing all these rumors from New York and New Jersey, and all over, that you have endorsed somebody and that it is Anna." She then stated that "Father even called the choir the night before the election and told them to vote for her at the picnic."

While it is not clear exactly what happened next, Anna did win the election. When I asked a few members of the choir if Father José had contacted them, they told me that he had not. Despite this, the pioneers believed that he did. Others Bicolanos, including Maricar, a well-respected leader in the wider

Filipino American community in Houston, also felt that Father José had indeed contacted the choir. She explained, "When I got to the picnic the whole choir was there and I asked 'What are you guys doing here?' and they said, 'I am just here to eat, you know this is a picnic, I am here because there is a lot of food.' And they said, 'We were told to come to the picnic by Father and vote for Anna.' Right there, all we did is look at each other and say that I can't believe this is happening. I mean to say that, they won't lie. Not just one person said that but every person you asked." She went on to tell me, "I don't think Ellen got the call but I know Lisa, my comadre, did and so did Sunny, my godchild. . . . I have 172 godchildren, so in some way or another I am connected to everything that goes on because they tell me everything!" When I asked her about Father José's involvement, she said, "He does not admit it, but he knows it. I told him you should not commingle your work with Filipino politics. . . . He's nice but you know, you make mistakes and this was one." Many people interviewed shared this sentiment. When I asked Karla if she ever spoke with Father José about what happened, she told me, "I never spoke with him. I got so mad I stopped going to St. Catherine's, I stopped giving them money. I stopped volunteering. I never said a word about it to him, but he knew . . . we were so close."

Although I was not at the picnic and did not push the issue too far with those interviewed, it was clear that something did go wrong. When I asked Father José about the situation, he stated, "Yeah, it is kinda hard . . . in fact I was thinking about when we had a candidate that was acceptable to both groups. We tried but still the division was there until finally about a year ago when the group officially split. This split tried to get me to identify with the other group, but I ignored their complaints and so then they tried to divide me but luckily I wasn't able to. I was in the middle of both groups. Now they formalized the spilt . . . they are still friends but some of them just are not talking to one another but they all still come here to church." After he explained to me how complicated the matter was, I asked Father José if he thought that the split was good or bad for the community. He suggested, "neither," and went on to say, "one group does their own thing and the other the same. . . . One day they will come back together, I pray." While members of both groups still attend St. Catherine's, as Father José stated, most of the pioneers who supported Gabby now attend mass at St. Joseph's and have formed the Bicolanos of Texas association. The original Bicol group, Bicol USA, has lost its founders and now supposedly has a large number of non-Bicolano members. This group still regularly attends St. Catherine's.

Complicating matters further, when the group officially split, controversy arose over the ownership of the statue of Our Lady of Peñafrancia (Mary) that had been entrusted to the original association. The problem was not resolved to everyone's liking and now, after the purchase of new statues in the Philippines, several statues are in circulation among the two groups. Other issues also arose over where and how to coordinate the celebration of Our Lady of Peñafrancia.

Although Bicol USA, the original group, was and is not a prayer group, the devotees of Our Lady of Peñafrancia depended heavily in the past on the association to coordinate her festival and novenas with parish churches. Prior to the split, the full nine-day novena was celebrated at St. Joseph's, and the final celebration and mass were held at St. Catherine's. After the split, and given the migration of some of the pioneers to St. Joseph's, the final mass is now held in both churches through great coordination between the Bicol clergy in both parishes. Explaining this further, Father José told me, "What happened is, is that they used to have the novena for the nine days there and then the final mass, the celebration here. When they split, they had one there and it continued here. There is now one here during the evening and the one there is in the morning. So a lot of people, especially the non-Bicolanos, they go there in the morning and then they come here in the evening, also the priests. . . . I still hope and pray to see them come back together and celebrate one mass but right now it is difficult because feelings have been hurt."

Although the mass is now held in two parishes and is supported by two different Bicol groups, the splinter group Bicolanos of Texas, composed mostly of pioneers, does not directly sponsor the mass at St. Joseph's. The mass is now sponsored by a new prayer group, the Devotees of Our Lady of Peñafrancia. It is a separate group devoted only to religious practice. When I asked Karla about this new group, she told me, "Most of the members of Devotees of Our Lady of Peñafrancia are members of Bicolanos of Texas." Continuing, she stated that "We learned our lesson and now split the civic from the spiritual and the religious . . . they have not mixed well for us."

Many Bicolanos now attend both masses and celebrations, putting the Church in a somewhat awkward position between them. Although it is not clear whether the Church will continue to be drawn into additional situations in the future, the actions of one parish or one priest can impact others and can even influence national politics, as we have seen. This is not always to the benefit of the community, but is subject to what the Church often deems best. In some cases the Church's involvement can smooth community relations and lead to greater community participation among its parishioners. In other cases, groups and individuals can be made to feel disenfranchised, and this may lead to them participating less in their parishes or community organizations.

Either way, the Church is not the sole and final authority in these community affairs, despite being a respected voice. Filipino laity, particularly women such as Karla and Anna, have a great deal of influence within their parishes despite the more patriarchal nature of Church hierarchy. Their voices are also well respected outside of their parishes, even when they choose not to heed the advice of their local priests. However, this is not always the case. Female or not, although the laity have a great deal of agency within their local parishes, when the larger global Church takes a stance on an issue or intervenes in a particular situation, the

Church's authority can often have an even greater impact on diaspora community relations and is likewise not completely open to lay negotiation. The next example is such a case.

Uncoupling for Christ

In 2007 Couples for Christ (CFC) split into two organizations after several years of very public contentious politicking. The split was highly controversial and impacted many in the global Filipino community, including Filipino Americans living in Houston. Unlike the Bicol associations discussed in the previous pages, CFC is a Catholic renewal group that extends well beyond any one regional group in the Philippines. Prior to the split, CFC was one of the largest, if not the largest Catholic renewal movement coming out of the Philippines. By 2004, for example, CFC had over a million adherents in 160 countries.[13] However, despite the religious nature of the movement, or perhaps as a result of it, as we will see, barangay politics has hampered the organization as much as they have the Bicol associations in Houston. Once again, laying blame and judgments aside, the events leading to the split and after further illustrate the complex relationship that exists between the Catholic Church and Filipino community politics, but on a global scale.

Couples for Christ began in the early 1980s in metro Manila with sixteen couples as part of an outreach to evangelize married couples within the charismatic community Ang Ligaya ng Panginoon's (LNP), Joy of the Lord in Tagalog.[14] Among the pioneering couples of the movement were Frank Padilla and his wife. In 1993, a group led by Padilla severed ties with LNP over differences on how to approach evangelization, and CFC emerged as a new organization out of the split. Through consultation with one another, the members of CFC developed the Christian Life Program (CLP) to recatechize Filipino Catholics. Members of the group felt that Catholicism had become too culturally ingrained for many Filipinos. As one of the early members described it to me, "Catholicism had become more of an identity than a religious practice." Mobilizing as a result of this perceived problem, the CFC pioneers suggested that the Philippines needed a program that could renew people's commitment to God, renew their commitment to their families, and renew their commitment to the Church. Throughout the 1990s Filipino couples around the world, including those interviewed in Houston, joined the movement for these reasons, in addition, perhaps, to an increased turn toward religion given the alienation inherent in the migration process itself.[15]

Although the majority of the first-generation Filipina Americans (women) I spoke with stated that they were religiously active in their parishes and homes prior to joining CFC and were not too concerned about being recatechized, many suggested that there was something missing in their family life. Explaining this, Vera, a Filipina nurse in her mid-forties and longtime member of CFC, told me, "Spirituality was the one thing missing in our family, and CFC was more of a family that could help us grow." Continuing, she stated that she was even afraid of losing her husband. "You know Filipino men. It takes something drastic for them to wake up and notice that something is wrong and Christ is the answer. . . . When you go to Church it's us women who pray and watch over the kids while they smoke and talk politics outside." Many Filipinas shared this sentiment, and the men tended to agree that it was their wives who got them involved with CFC.

Highlighting this, Gerry, a fairly new member of CFC stated, "My wife pushed me to go to our first CLP and I hated it at first but after a few weeks I felt better and realized that I need to change and my marriage would be better for it." Other Filipinos (men) explained that they had been involved in extramarital affairs and that it was not until they got caught that they turned to CFC, in some cases, begrudgingly. Dave, for example, told me, "When my parents found out what I had done and that I was screwing up my marriage, they flew here from the Philippines and took us to our first CLP." Describing what transpired, he then said, "I was so embarrassed, but the Lord works in mysterious ways and look at how happy we are now." Certainly not all of the couples interviewed were in failing marriages prior to joining CFC. Most couples stated they had simply grown stronger after joining CFC, with no prior issues in their marriage. In either case, these examples illustrate the importance of CFC to many first-generation Filipino American Catholics in Houston as a lay ecclesial movement focused on the family. This said, many CFC members also suggested that if it were not for Gawad Kalinga (GK; literally to give care in Tagalog), a social development project within CFC, they would not remain active in the group. "GK is God's gift to humanity through the Philippines. Without it we would lose our purpose as a group." This is both important and problematic, as we will soon see.

By the end of the 1990s CFC had spread well beyond the Philippines or even Houston and was recognized by the Philippine Bishops' Conference as an official evangelization movement within the Church. In 2000 the Vatican, through the Pontifical Council for the Laity, began the process of officially recognized Couples for Christ as one of 122 recognized International Associations of Faithful.[16] Full recognition was decreed in 2005 by the same authority. As a global movement, CFC began to set organization goals beyond the CLP program. CFC established seven pillars or aims. These included: 1) evangelization, 2) pastoral support, 3) family renewal, 4) social renewal or ministries, 5) pro-life ministry, 6) special ministries or projects, and finally 7) Gawad Kalinga. Among the seven pillars, GK quickly spread as a major focal point of CFC members globally, including first-generation Filipino Americans living in Houston.

Gawad Kalinga developed out of a series of social experiments in the early 1990s led by Tony Meloto and a group of likeminded friends. As a group, largely connected to the early pioneers of CFC, they had become increasingly aware of several disruptive behaviors they thought made impoverished conditions in the slums of metro Manila worse. Highlighting issues such as gambling and gang involvement, the group founded Serving in God's Army or SIGA, meaning light or fire in Tagalog, as a rehabilitation program to break the cycle of these conditions.[17] Supported finically by successful and affluent philanthropists in the community, the group began to study the slums. At the same time, members of SIGA along with others from CFC began to organize a series of peer and faith events for their own children. By 1993, the ideas flowing in both programs began to merge.

In 1995, Meloto and CFC, together with Youth for Christ and other members of SIGA, began a series of camps for out-of-school youth in Bagong Silang in Caloocan City, one of the largest slums in metro Manila. After two successful camps, the membership of SIGA rose from just a few to over five hundred.[18] With this success, the group formed the ANCOP foundation—Answering the Cry of the Poor, to serve more youth in the area. By 1998, ANCOP decided that in order to successfully meet the needs of the youth in Bagong Silang it would need to take a more holistic approach to community and literally rebuild the slums. In 1999 ANCOP built its first house for the Adduro family.[19] In 2000, the name Gawad Kalinga was coined to describe the movement, and eleven teams were organized to build a series of homes, soon to be villages, outside of Bagong Silang. Also that year, ANCOP USA was founded as a diaspora extension that could further fund the movement.

In 2001, CFC ministries officially launched Gawad Kalinga. The following year GK also picked up its first major partner. President Gloria Arroyo allocated thirty million pesos, roughly $686,100 United States dollars, to build 1,000 GK homes in Dumaguete City in Negros Oriental.[20] In 2003, GK was formally registered with the Securities and Exchange Commission as the Gawad Kalinga Community Development Foundation Inc. During this same year, GK held its first GK Expo and launched the GK 777 campaign to build 700,000 homes in 7,000 communities in 7 years. What started as a CFC mission quickly expanded to a multisectored partnership that included secular sponsors such as McDonald's, Pepsi and Coke, Proctor & Gamble, Gillette, and Colgate. British millionaire Dylan Wilk began to give generously to the movement during this time and eventually became a fulltime member of its global team. He also married Anna Meloto, the eldest daughter of Tony Meloto. In 2006, Meloto and GK received both the Ramon Magsaysay Award and the Gawad Haydee Yorac Award for their efforts in the Philippines—both prestigious national awards. CFC was GK and GK was CFC. However, it was also clear that two leaders had emerged. Meloto was running GK and gaining national as well as international fame, and Padilla was still the executive director of CFC, which was continuing to spread internationally. Complicating matters, Pfizer, a manufacturer of oral contraceptives and Viagra, partnered with GK to help fund its projects. A controversy erupted, and the Church became involved, as we might expect.

Although the temporal ordering of the events that transpired in 2007 are confusing and subject to opinion, depending on who you ask, it is clear that the rise of these two leaders coupled with a growing GK movement sparked internal tensions and in some cases intense barangay politics. After a series of articles in the *Philippine Daily Inquirer*, the most widely circulated newspaper in the Philippines, praised GK and Meloto's involvement, a series of emails and subsequent editorials a few months later, some of which were published in the *Inquirer*, began to challenge Meloto and question the direction of GK.[21] In February, during the International Council meeting of CFC, Meloto resigned from the body, as did Padilla, and they requested that a third member, Arturo Lagana, also resign. All three key elders or pioneers resigned, leaving only four members on the council. José Tale was appointed executive director, replacing Padilla. On April 8, Easter Sunday, Padilla released a statement about the future of CFC:

> One of the most important reasons for my resignation from the CFC Council, if not the most important, is the continuing tension and conflict between CFC and GK.... Since I will again be misunderstood by some in GK because of this paper, let me say this clearly and unequivocally. For me, GK IS ONE OF THE GREATEST BLESSINGS OF GOD FOR CFC, AND FOR THE WORLD THROUGH CFC. I have consistently extolled GK in all CFC assemblies, whether here or abroad. I am still all-out for GK as one of CFC's 7 pillars, and as our defining work with the poor.... Now here is the basic problem as I see it. GK IS SLIDING AWAY FROM GOD'S PLAN FOR IT.... The question is: is GK fulfilling God's plan for it? In other words, the basic danger is that GK will become a SOCIAL work that has lost its SPIRITUAL foundation (emphasis is original).[22]

Continuing, Padilla questioned Meloto, the direction of GK, and the sponsorship of partners such as Pfizer. "To call Tony or anyone else the founder, father or driving force is to put the person in place of God. Further, it makes GK simply of human and not divine origin. Still further, God is a jealous God and this can put Tony in jeopardy.... Let us not build the cult of any one person.... Do what is right in the Lord. Implement our pro-God/pro-family/pro-poor/pro-life/pro-environment agenda. If partners are not on the same page, simply explain things to them. If they tie their help with aspects that violate our pro-God agenda, then say goodbye to them."[23] After this statement Padilla, who had originally split from LNP to form CFC, initiated the Easter Group as a new group seeking to get back to the evangelical foundations of CFC—the same issue, consequently, that led to the original LNP split in 1993.

In June, Meloto wrote Bishop Reyes of the Diocese of Antipolo apologizing for the International Council's neglect of the bishop as a spiritual advisor. Later that month, Bishops Villagas and Reyes, in addition to Archbishop Lagdameo of the Archdiocese of Jaro, wrote the elders of CFC on behalf of the Catholic Bishops Conference of the Philippines (CBCP), calling on them to mediate their issues, rethink their resignations, and postpone the election of a new council. "Even if it takes several sessions of discussion, let them do it with humility, openness of mind and heart.... Remember they are not doing this for their individual sakes but for the good of CFC."[24] Continuing, the bishops stated, "It appears that certain CFC principles and way of life are giving way to Gawad Kalinga.... The spiritual and pastoral culture of CFC must not be sacrificed for the sake of GK."[25] It was clear that the bishops had sided with Padilla. However, in response, CFC told the bishops that they would move forward with the election after creating a separate GK board. The Easter Group, led by Padilla, claimed that by ignoring the recommendations of the bishops, CFC had disobeyed the Church. In the wake of the much political bantering between the sides and a series of correspondence with the CBCP and the Vatican through Tale, a pro-GK/Meloto council was elected with a four-seat majority.

In August, the *Inquirer* published "Quo Vadis, Couples for Christ?" and Couples for Christ Foundations for Family Life (CFC-FFL), Padilla's Easter restoration group, was officially recognized by Bishop Reyes as "a private association of the faithful" in the Dioceses of Antipolo.[26] The splintering of CFC seemed to be official. At the end of August, the CBCP once again attempted to mediate the dispute through the Episcopal Commission on the Laity but with no success. Meanwhile, in the United States, Padilla was removed as national director, and CFC-USA, a separate legal entity, voted unanimously for a state of "status quo." It, in effect, refused to recognize the split. As several newspapers wrote of the imminent demise of CFC, articles began to surface laying blame in every direction. Many of the articles such as "Crabs and God's Design" and "The Good, the Crab, and the Ugly," for example, pointed to barangay politics.[27] Some pointed to how religion and the Church itself had complicated matters, while others publically outlined which side the Church recognized or supported.

In April of 2008, just one year after Padilla and CFC-FFL announced their split from CFC, the Vatican sent a letter to Tale, the new executive director of CFC, voicing the Church's disapproval of CFC's "overemphasis" on social work through GK as well as GK's partnering practices. Although the letter went on to state, "Your decision to stop receiving this type of funding will help recover the good standing of your association Couples for Christ," suggesting that changes in practice had been made and noted, when the letter went public Filipinos, including those interviewed in Houston, were in shock.[28] As Alfie, a first-generation Filipina member of CFC stated, "The Church should stay out of politics ... since EDSA 1 they think they know what is best, but they only make it worse." Continuing, she suggested, "As a Catholic I must honor what the Church decrees, but what are we going to do now? GK is too important to let die." Complicating matters, bishops throughout the Philippines announced who they supported in the split and even wrote to Filipinos in the diaspora, instructing them what to do. Bishop Cantillas of Maasin, for example, in writing to the chaplains and pastoral workers of the Filipino Communities in Europe, stated, "Not intending to influence your discernment, I wish to share the information that in my diocese I would recognize and welcome the CFC-FFL of Bro. [brother] Frank Padilla."[29] Sides had been taken, and many Filipinos, as was the case in the Bicol case, were in disagreement over what the role of the Church should be in the matter.

In September of 2009, under growing pressure, CFC relinquished its control over the GK board. The same year, the outspoken Archbishop Cruz of Pangasinan instructed his parishes to have nothing to do with Gawad Kalinga—directly or indirectly. Today, CFC and CFC-FFL operate as separate organizations, and GK is independent from both, although supported by CFC through ANNCOP as part of its broader social ministry.[30] In the United States, the "status quo" was eventually forcibly broken by the Church, and Filipino Americans were left to decide which side they would take.

Most first-generation Filipino Americans in Houston, at least those interviewed, remained in CFC but have also changed their views on GK. Where they once supported the projects with open zeal, they now temper their enthusiasm, pointing to the fact that "Evangelization and family renewal are more important, and through ANNCOP, GK is just a part of the larger picture." Although many Filipino Americans in Houston declined my attempts to interview them after the split, those that did speak with me shared just how difficult it was on them emotionally. Explaining this, Joseph, a CFC member and former director for GK projects, told me, "We are all still friends and brothers and sisters in Christ, but many of us have not spoken to each other in a while. . . . I feel like we lost part of our family, but perhaps in the end it is for the best if it gets us all focused back on what is important."

When I asked Father José if members of either group had approached him to mediate or seek his council on the matter, he told me they had not. "It was truly sad you know, but they never came to me about that. . . . They followed what was happening in the Philippines and of course the ones there asked their bishops." When I asked him if the split affected his parish, he told me, "Not really, they used to use our facilities for their meetings, but when they split ones who were, I think from the north, stopped coming. . . . They weren't members of the parish so I think they just went back to their other parishes. . . . Most are still in the Couples for Christ not the other." Continuing, he explained that he supported CFC and its work, "I want to introduce the program [CLP] itself here." Although Father José did not endorse CFC during the split, he believes that CFC, as a wider part of a network of prayer groups and associations, is good for the parish. He also believes that the CLP program could be beneficial to his parishioners. Unlike the Bicol situation, Father José was not a major voice in mediating the CFC split over GK. Like his parishioners, he was forced to watch or offer condolences to his fellow Filipinos as the larger Church and its bishops in the Philippines issued official pronouncements on how to move forward.

CONCLUSION

The cases presented in this chapter highlight where political tensions, whether religious or secular in nature, can both unite and splinter first-generation Filipino Americans over a host of issues. While some of these matters remain local, others are well connected to larger national and transnational concerns. In some cases, the Catholic Church has been drawn into these situations by local parishioners. In other cases, the Church has willingly interceded based on what it deems best for the parish. Yet, in still other cases, such as the CFC split over GK, the Church has been forced to take action as the institutional authority in the dispute. The results, as we have seen, do not always bring about unity to the Filipino American community. In fact, in some cases it has brought about just the opposite. Filipinas such as Karla, for example, have left St. Catherine's and have largely stopped volunteering and giving money to its parish projects. Although Karla now attends a different parish, she is more cautious in her dealings with the Church after being pushed into positions of leadership by Bicolano priests. She has also turned somewhat more to secular institutions for her civic needs. For members of CFC, the larger Church's dealings with the GK split did not, for the most part, lead them to leave their parish churches in Houston, nor did it stop them from volunteering or giving to parish projects. It did, however, force them to rethink and reprioritize what was most important to them as a group— evangelization for the family or civic projects in the Philippines.

During the Couples for Christ dispute over Gawad Kalinga, the Church made it clear that while it valued GK and all that it has done for the Philippines, it was, or perhaps still is, concerned about it leaving its charismatic roots in CFC and taking on business partners whose products directly contradict Catholic teachings on the sanctity of the family. The Church essentially reasserted itself as the center of the CFC community and made it clear that it intends to remain an important voice in the Filipino Catholic diaspora. For the most part, first-generation Filipino Americans in Houston, whether they are members of CFC or not, agree with this assertion and welcome the Church's intercession.

Despite varying opinions over what the role of the Church should take in community politics, first-generation Filipino Americans still see the Church as very much at the center of their community. They also invite their priests, or in some cases bishops, to play a vital role in their lives and community affairs. This is both welcome and problematic. Although priests such as Father José are perhaps too close to the ethnic or regional nature of the community politics of their parishes, it is important to note that Filipinos' cultural understandings of community compel them to invite his council. Father José did not necessarily force himself into the Bicolano situation presented in this chapter because he is Bicolano or because he holds a tremendous amount of authority within his parish, but in large part because Bicolanos elected him as one of their spiritual advisors. While in hindsight perhaps some members of the Bicolano community regret this decision, the various Bicol groups today have all established similar ties with parish priests across Houston, including renewing or building new ties with Father José at St. Catherine's.

Complicating matters, although it may appear from the outside that patriarchy plays a role in these relations, first-generation Filipinas, while clearly respectful and reverent to the male hierarchy of the Church, do hold a measure of power both within and outside their parish churches. Filipinas such as Vera in CFC are vital to the faith of their families and the community in general. Drawing on the model of the Virgin Mary, they are also not afraid to clash with the clergy over what they believe is best for their community. This was clearly the case in the split in the Houston Bicolano community and the way in which the pioneering group challenged Church authority and negotiated the terms under which their parishes would conduct the celebrations and novenas associated with Our Lady of Peñafrancia.[31]

By means of communication networks established through numerous comadreships and associational memberships, Filipina leaders such as Maricar, who has 172 godchildren, in addition to being active in several Filipino associations, are intimately linked to the lives of women across Houston, if not beyond. As a result, they are also well connected to the broader civic workings of a host of communities, Filipino and other. This, as was noted, has clear implications beyond the Filipino American community itself. It speaks volumes about the future role of the laity, particularly women, in the reshaping of American Catholicism. It also sheds light on the potential role the Church, its priests, and lay groups in general may all play in shaping community relations in other new immigrant communities. Despite the clear contentiousness that can exist in the relationships between immigrant religiosity and the intimate workings of their communities, these relationships, at least as we have seen in the Filipino case, are central to their daily lives in diaspora.

Throughout the relatively short history of the Filipino American community in Houston, roughly fifty years, numerous umbrella organization have risen, but none has been able to completely unify the community, nor have they been successful at building a Filipino American center for community events and functions. Part of the difficulty Filipinos face in trying to unify the community lies within its immense diversity. Given its complexity and the sheer number of its regional and ethnic groups, it is hard to imagine a singular institution whose constructed boundaries can manage them all, let alone unite them. However, as we have seen throughout this chapter, many first-generation Filipino Americans long for unity and see it as the only way the community can reach its full potential or achieve its aims. To this point, at least in the Houston case, the only source for this unity has been the Church, despite its precarious involvement in community affairs. The one exception to this is the San Lorenzo Ruiz de Manila center (SLRM).

The SLRM center is the only first-generation Filipino Catholic community center with its own building that is fully independent of the Church and its parishes in Houston. While relatively small in terms of its official membership, it is an important site where Filipino immigrants, members or not, can gather as Catholics and as Filipinos. It is likewise an important site where Filipino immigrants can carve out a sense of independence from the Church and its authority. Exploring this further, the next chapter focuses on the struggle of first-generation Filipinos in Houston to build their own ethnic community centers both within the Church and independently of its authority. It chronicles the history of these attempts and then analyzes how Filipino Catholic cultural frameworks associated with the sanctity of the family can mobilize Filipinos in diaspora and bring about a sense of unity across its regional and ethnic diversity.

CHAPTER 5

BUILDING CENTERS
OF COMMUNITY

Every year first-generation Filipino Americans in Houston, like Filipinos in other cities across the United States, host a series of annual induction galas and celebrations for their various regional and community associations. The events are extravagant affairs with formal induction ceremonies, luscious buffets or multiple-course plate dinners, and often involve dancing into the early morning hours. They are an important place to be seen, and inevitably end up being covered in large photo spreads in local community newspapers. However, despite years of fundraising and countless pleas for unity, none of Houston's numerous Filipino American associations has built a community center to host these events. Like other Filipino community celebrations in Houston, these events are typically held at local hotels or the community halls of parish churches such as St. Catherine's. Although these venues provide adequate space and are more than capable of hosting formal catered affairs, many in the Filipino American community have grown increasingly frustrated that an independent community center has not been built.

"We are so tired of renting," Alice, a first-generation Filipina American in her late fifties, told me as the night's festivities came to a close at one gala I attended. Continuing, she explained, "You see, it is so expensive and we run through the money every time we put on these things. . . . I just don't understand why we can't get our act together." Alice was clearly upset, and her frustrations eventually spilled over from our conversation that night to an online community blog later in the week. "I have a few things to rant about and the first would be the development or lack thereof, of a Filipino Community Center!!! What happened to the funds FACOST [Filipino American Council of Southern Texas] set aside for a center?"

Raising a concern over possible misuse of funds and venting on the complete lack of unity and progress at building a center, Alice described her anxiety openly and unabashedly:

I remember people discussing this when I was a teenager—over twenty years ago . . . and still there has been no progress. Filipinos have been here [Houston] longer than many other ethnic groups, yet we are still behind them in terms of building an infrastructure for our own community. And the people that are suffering the most from this lack of infrastructure are the youth . . . can we open this dialogue among the elders of the community and get everyone to start working together on finally building a center? And can we make this a dialogue, one that does not require a membership fee, has transparent leadership and accountability, and makes records public so that everyone can see how the money will be used?

Like most first-generation Filipino Americans interviewed, Alice longs for a central venue where all groups can meet and share in the richness of being Filipino. Calling for an open dialogue in which the internal politics of Filipino associations can be managed with a measure of transparency and accountability, Alice fears what the impact may be on future generations. "These youth will either carry on a pride in their ethnic community or leave it in order to lead fulfilling civic lives elsewhere." Not unlike the fears expressed in other immigrant communities for the second generation or those born in their homelands but raised in United States, Alice is concerned that subsequent generations will leave the community if changes do not occur.[1]

Responding to this frustration, Regina, a Filipina member of PCCI (People Caring for the Community, Inc.), one of the countless umbrella organization attempting to unite the numerous Filipino associations in Houston, tried to moderate the situation as a number of people joined Alice on the blog to vent their frustrations. Explaining the present state of affairs among Filipino American associations, she posted, "Everyone, please be patient. Several Filipino and Filipino American leaders in the community are working on this project. Unfortunately, every one of us are ALL volunteers. We have families and jobs to attend to, and for the most part, the biggest drawback has been financial. Yes, we are asking for memberships of $100 . . . because it takes money to build a Filipino Community Center" (emphasis in original). Although not acquiescing to the demands to end membership fees or addressing concerns over leadership accountability, what Regina suggested in her defense, feeling the heat of increasing personal attacks, is very telling about where many first-generation Filipino Americans in Houston find their motivation and model for community life.

After intimately detailing how she has been hampered by illness, a failed marriage, and a host of other complications, Regina posted that she and others are still working diligently to build a community center. Responding to the personal attacks on the blog that questioned her motives and called into question her loyalty to the Filipino community, Regina stated, "Bottom line, I am continuing in my volunteer work and my community services in Houston, Texas as long as the Lord gives me strength and direction of what I can do as a citizen and human being for the good of ALL the Filipinos and Filipino-Americans. . . . IT IS ALL ABOUT MY TRUST IN MY LIFE IN GOD AND MOTHER MARY. . . . I have no personal agenda in getting out ONE Filipino Community Center BUILD ONCE AND FOR ALL" (emphasis in original).

Reflecting on her own personal faith, Regina went on to explain that the contentious politics that have plagued the Filipino American community can only be solved by looking to the Church for guidance. Explaining that problems such pioneer syndrome and crab mentalities are not unique to Filipinos, she posted, "All races have mentalities of, I am better than you are when it comes to volunteer work and community service, but this is NOT TRUE when it comes to the volunteering and community service rendered at St. Catherine's" (emphasis in original). As others chimed in on the blog, the personal attacks subsided a bit, and most agreed that there is something different about community life in their parishes. Tess, for example, posted that she is not always happy with her church's handling of community events and affairs, but stated, "At least we are all equal in the eyes of God and I think Father tries to live up to that vision."

Regina, agreeing with Tess and others, explained in subsequent posts how important the Church is to the Filipino American community. Describing the sense of unity and purpose she has found in her own parish, St. Catherine's, she called on those who had been debating intensely on the blog to look to their Catholic parishes as a model and example of success.

> At my church where I belong since October 1986, we volunteers are equal. Our talents, time, and treasures are not equal with each other and we accept it and we move on with projects like clockwork without jealousies with one another, who did more and who did what . . . that is why St. Catherine's Catholic Church is very successful. I PRAY TO GOD, THAT, WE FILIPINOS AND FILIPINO-AMERICANS WILL HAVE THE HEART AND MENTALITY LIKE THE PARISHONERS OF MY CATHOLIC CHURCH. (Emphasis in original.)

BREAKING GROUND OR BREAKING BREAD?

In the months and years that followed the blog exchanges above, debates raged on and grew increasingly heated. Fundraisers and galas continued to promote unity, and first-generation Filipino leaders continued to talk at great length about building a center, but no progress was made by any of Houston's Filipino American associations. Umbrella organizations like FACOAST and PCCI continued to plan and raise funds for a center, but controversy followed each step forward. Rumors of embezzled funds and one form of corruption or another began to circulate widely. However, what were once private debates or online exchanges became the subject of very public addresses and newspaper editorials.

In one such editorial in the *Manila-Headline*, a call was raised for a measure of accountability for the money that had been raised to build a community center. Clearly frustrated, Ben Ongoco wrote:

> Take the case of the construction of a community center. It is good that PCFI which stands for Philippine Cultural Foundation, Inc. is seemingly focusing on cultural revival like the "pabasa" and Santacruzan, rather than erecting a center, despite the canceled Mercedes Benz raffle. On the other hand, the People Caring for the Community, Inc. (PCCI) is still trying hard to build a center originally planned to spend $4 million based on the estimate that at least $1 million can be raised each year. Never happened. Still going through with the Mrs. Philippines-Texas/PCCI. During the old days of the Houston Fil-Ams Lions Club, Mrs. Philippines-Houston was racking money from the candidates, some of them even dropping the "bomb" of money, especially if they are married to an oilman or CEO of a corporation. With the economic meltdown, I doubt it now very much.[2]

Naming names and calling for a new paradigm in community relations in bold, well-circulated print, Ben expressed his sincere desire to see a Filipino community center built in his lifetime.

Continuing, Ben outlined his fears and concerns that barangay politics might prevent this from coming to fruition but also commended community leaders such as Regina for their efforts. Like other Filipino Americans interviewed, Ben believes that Filipino ethnic and regional associations hold a great deal of promise and have done a great deal for the community, especially back in the Philippines, but he, like others, is also very frustrated with the contentiousness of their politics:

> My congratulations to the new set of officers of PCCI.... I hope to see a center in my lifetime. But I suspect that some of her coterie of officers are trying to subvert the good intentions into being vindictive and pugilistic against critics or competitors.... Instead of having an inclusive organization, it is becoming an exclusive one. The "family" connotes the Italian Mafia from Sicily.... I was told by some that because the members of the PCCI are considered affluent that may have made it in America, they associated elitism with their conjecture. That is why the name transformed to present name PCCI to encompass membership because if it happens to ask for federal funds, the tax dollars should be for inclusivity. It used to be Philippine Community Center, Inc. I know, I was there from the start as an incorporator. I shelled out hard earned $1,000.... But lately, I am being alienated. Until to this very second while I am writing this column, I have not received any suiting words to alleviate my feeling of being taken for granted if not an apology.[3]

For Ben the sense of family that dominates PCCI is not inclusive and universal like the Catholic family but something more akin to the mafia. This is perhaps a bit harsh, but Ben, like others interviewed, question the future of a Filipino American center and their place in it, when or if it is ever built.

In May of 2011, PCCI broke ground on a two-acre lot it purchased in southwest Houston for a Filipino American community center. The announcement came as a shock for many first-generation Filipino Americans interviewed. Grace, for example, emailed me and asked, "Is this a joke or is something finally happening?" At the groundbreaking ceremony people were still in disbelief and expressed serious skepticism that the center would be built. Mary, as an example, told me after the ceremony, "I really don't care anymore. How much money has been raised and all we have to show for it after all these long years is an empty lot in the middle of nowhere. I doubt it will ever be built . . . the lot will just sit there and grow weeds." Others such as Sarah, another first-generation Filipina American, complained, "How many years have we been waiting for this and all we have to show is two acres for our growing community?" Dave, on the other hand was a bit more optimistic than others. He told me that although PCCI does not have the money needed to build a center yet, since the purchase of the lot, "People are gravitated to give and maybe in the next few years or so after more fundraising we will see it finally happen."

Breaking ground on a new lot marks true progress, but for a community with numerous socioeconomic resources it is very slow progress at best. Describing this dawdling pace, Ben likens any progress to the familiar analogy of the tortoise and the hare (rabbit). "Do you recall the anecdote about the race between the hare and the turtle? Slow moving turtle but persevering beat the hare who boasted about being faster and did many rests and even slept. The turtle beat the hare, because the latter overslept. The San Lorenzo Ruiz de Manila beat PCCI."[4] The San Lorenzo Ruiz de Manila center (SLRM), named after the first Filipino saint canonized by the Catholic Church, did indeed beat PCCI to building the first independent Filipino American center in Houston. However, the SLRM center is not directly affiliated with any Filipino American association or umbrella organization. The center was pioneered by a group of devout first-generation Filipino American Catholics who wanted an independent space where they could venerate San Lorenzo Ruiz de Manila, celebrate his life and martyrdom, and unite Filipinos in the process.[5]

While PCCI and other groups and associations have struggled for decades to break ground on a community center, Catholicism and the Catholic Church itself have continually been able to bring these disparate groups together—and successfully—year after year. This is no easy task. Given the complexity and diversity of the community, it is hard to imagine it could be contained within the constructed boundaries of any one organization or institution. However, given that 93 percent of the first-generation Filipino Americans surveyed consider the Church to be the center of their community, their common faith bonds are a powerful and legitimate source of unity.[6] For this reason, parish halls remain the top venues for first-generation Filipino American social gatherings and annual events such as the Philippine Independence Day celebration. Regional or national Filipino religious celebrations such as Simbang Gabi are likewise coordinated annually at parish churches with a surprising amount of ease.

This by no means suggests that conflict does not arise. As the last chapter highlighted, it can and does. Likewise, while the Church may be the legitimate source of unity in the community, it is not the only source. First-generation Filipino Americans, as was the case historically in the Philippines, want to carve out a sense of independence from Church authority through their own Filipino institutions. From its inception this was one of the original aims behind the SLRM center, and it remains the goal of PCCI and countless other groups and organizations in the community today.

Further charting these struggles, this chapter explores the mechanisms, namely, a cultural focus on the sanctity of the family, that facilitate the Church's ability to bring the community and its numerous associations together. It also demonstrates how similar mechanisms and their common Catholic faith more generally have paved successes for the San Lorenzo Ruiz de Manila center despite competing for members and space in the shadow of the Catholic Church itself. Beyond highlighting the clear importance of faith and family to the Filipino American community, the chapter suggests that Filipino Americans are not only introducing new religious practices into American Catholicism, hence reshaping its future, but are also civically engaging communities beyond their own through these practices.

Gathering for Simbang Gabi

"This is the most joyous time of the year," explained Kristi, a first-generation Filipina American teacher in her late twenties, as we entered the front door of St. Catherine's Catholic Church. It was the first night of Simbang Gabi, night mass in Tagalog, a nine-day Filipino Catholic tradition that celebrates the days and nights leading up to Christmas day. For Kristi and other Filipino American Catholic immigrants, it is one of the most enduring religious celebrations of the year. Simbang Gabi was first celebrated in the Philippines sometime after 1565, when Miguel López de Legazpi introduced the first Christmas novena masses to the Islands.[7] Originally the tradition was known as Misa de Gallo, morning mass in Tagalog, because it was held around four or five o'clock in the morning with the waking of the cock's crow. However, the tradition eventually changed names to Simbang Gabi over time, as longer work days and the complications of metropolitan life led many parishes in the Philippines to celebrate the masses at night.[8] Today the celebration thrives in the diasopra and has become one of the major cornerstones of community building for first-generation Filipino Americans.[9]

Although Kristi admitted that she misses the pageantry of Simbang Gabi in the Philippines, she suggested that the spirit of the celebration remains the same. "It feels like home, just a little smaller." Judy and Ramon, also first-generation Filipinos who were standing next to Kristi, agreed. After making the sign of the cross before entering the chapel for the mass, they told me how St. Catherine's literally transports them back home for the nine nights of Simbang Gabi. "On nights like this I can close my eyes and feel like we are home [in the Philippines] and the food after the mass just sweetens it. . . . This is our parish and our home away from home." Although the liturgy of the celebration is largely no different from that in the Philippines, the communal meals that follow are logistically more difficult to coordinate. In the Philippines, patrons and parish groups of a single or common regional heritage vie for the honor of sponsoring nights, but in the United States and other diaspora communities Filipinos from multiple regions and provinces must negotiate their places in the same few nights of service. This has resulted in the broader archdiocese, not just St. Catherine's, taking steps to insure everyone not only gets an opportunity to sponsor a night but share in the nine-day celebration.

Since the late 1990s, the Filipino council of the Galveston-Houston Archdiocese has used the celebration of Simbang Gabi as an opportunity to bring Filipino Americans together and build a sense of unity across its parishes and the wider Filipino American community. It has also used the occasion to introduce these Filipino Catholic traditions to its non-Filipino parishioners. The Church attempts to do this by widely advertising the events, actively managing the sponsorship schedule, and then highlighting themes within the liturgy of the novenas themselves that call on Filipinos and others to act as one Catholic family. Father José at St. Catherine's, explaining how it all works, told me that in previous years competition among groups and associations led to complications, but the logistics of coordinating the nights is what largely led to the Church to mediating the schedule, not necessarily conflict. Although Father José seemed reluctant to get into the full details about any prior incidents that had occurred between groups, he explained, "I am not even really sure how the council selects groups but it makes things easier for us. You still have groups that split and end up at other churches sponsoring different nights, but, for the most part, it's all fun and whoever has the best food has the best food. . . . It's not a competition, just loving faith and the Filipino tradition. It really is about the spirit of the season and everyone knows that they will get their turn to sponsor the festivities." Over the six years of this study, every group and association that wanted to participate did, at least to my knowledge.

In 2006, as an example, the nine nights of Simbang Gabi were sponsored by eighteen different groups. These groups included: the Black Nazarene fellowship, the Filipino Community of Notre Dame, Confredia Del Santo Niña, Visaya Mindanao association, Couples for Christ (CFC), Philippine American Masons of Texas

(PAMAT), Solidarity Lodge #1457, San Lorenzo Ruiz de Manila center, United States Senior Citizens Association of Texas, Philippine-American Senior Organization of Houston, Candelaria of Texas, the Aparece family, Bicol USA (the Houston chapter), Our Lady of Lourdes fellowship, Magnificat prayer group, Sandugo and Totus Tuus prayer groups, and the Bibingka prayer group. This long list of sponsors always changed from year to year and in some cases got even longer, but some groups such as PAMAT and CFC sponsored nights every year.

The food was always lavish, with buffet tables that seemed to go on for miles with everything from *chicken adobo* to *pancit* (noodles) and *Kare-kare* (Ta, vegetable and oxtail peanut stew). Despite the historical tensions that have existed both between and within some of these groups, the nights always appeared to run smoothly. Although Father José often remarked in private how difficult it was to coordinate things, the contentious nature of barangay politics never kept the nights from running as planned. Pointing to this, Charles, a first-generation Bicolano in his late forties, stated, "It's a lot of work and a great deal of coordination, but it's worth it. Just look at all the smiles." Among the smiles are those of Filipinos from every region and province that have immigrated to the United States since 1965. It is an immensely diverse gathering of the Filipino American community, but the masses are also attended by non-Filipinos, and increasingly so. Highlighting this, Father José suggested, "Every year more and more of our non-Filipino parishioners attend the mass—not just those who are married to Filipinas. Continuing he explained, "They [non-Filipinos] love the traditions and I encourage them to join in the celebration as way of deepening their faith and understanding of the season."

Beyond coordinating the logistics of the nights' events across this diversity, multiple members of the Filipino council of the Galveston-Houston Archdiocese typically attend the masses at St. Catherine's and use the opportunity to preach a message of unity to the Filipino American community. Although celebrations are held at other parish churches, the final novena mass is always held at St. Catherine's and draws a large crowd. In 2006, for example, the final night of Simbang Gabi drew in over four hundred Filipinos, mostly first-generation, fifty-nine non-Filipinos or over 10 percent of those gathered, and all from fifteen cities and fifty-four zip codes.[10] Understanding the opportunity that this presents, Monsignor Seth, a first-generation Filipino American priest and head of the Filipino American council, typically leads the last night's mass as the chief celebrant along with Father José. He uses the evening, much as Father José does during the celebration of Philippine Independence, as a call for unity and a reminder for the Filipino American community that their faith is what binds them. During the mass for the last night of Simbang Gabi observed in 2006, for example, Monsignor Seth stated, "Our Filipino tradition of Simbang Gabi is a timely preparation for Christmas. The nine-day novena of masses and Christmas carols together with Mary Our Mother can help us appreciate and benefit from the real meaning of Christians. . . . It is a time for us to become one family, brothers and sisters in Christ. Let us read from the wisdom of the message of the angels to the shepherds."

Turning to the pulpit, Monsignor Seth called on a young Filipina American, most likely first-generation, to read a passage from the novena. After completing the reading, Monsignor Seth repeated part of the passage, "We live in the struggle and conflict of life and death. How often do we not live as brothers, and even become enemies of each other. Christmas creates a new, at least for some moments, reconciliation and peace. Here before the crib [Nativity], we become brothers and sisters and friends again." Smiling broadly, Father José offered a resounding "Amen" before another hymn was sung. Although no mention was made of any specific conflict or group within the Filipino American community, the call for unity was clear. Dave, for example, a first-generation Filipino American sitting next to me whispered, "Well I guess we know what that's about, don't we." Continuing, he stated, "He's so right, just look around us. Just how many times a year do you see so many of us gathered together in one place? We would do well to embrace these words every day in everything we do all year long." Perhaps it was not clear to non-Filipino parishioners in attendance, but other Filipinos interviewed that night took it as message to put contentious politics aside and work toward unity. Highlighting this, Kristi, like Dave, later explained, "You know this is one of those rare times we all really seem to be united as one community—it's truly sad!"

After communion and before Father José gave the benediction, Monsignor Seth reminded the congregation that the preparations leading up to the last night of Simbang Gabi should remind good Catholics that Jesus' birth is about giving. Continuing the message he had written earlier in *Tambuli ng Panginoon*, a Catholic newsletter form the Archdiocese Filipino Council, Monsignor Seth called on the Filipino American community to answer Archbishop Emeritus Fioremza's request to raise money for the construction of the new co-cathedral. "For many years we have lived our Catholic faith and enjoyed the pastoral care in the archdiocese. . . . This gift will be a lasting dedication and gratitude from our Filipino community."[11] The following week I asked Father José if Filipinos ended up giving a lot of money for the co-cathedral. He told me that they made "a sizable dent" in the fifty thousand dollars that the Archbishop Emeritus had asked for and noted that "without them [Filipinos] it might never get built, really."

Outside of donating money, first-generation Filipino Americans also helped to replenish the parish food bank, stocked relief boxes for the homeless in Houston to be distributed during the nights of Simbang Gabi, and collected numerous toys and clothes to be distributed to families in need around the parish. At the same time, Father José was also able to raise thousands of dollars for the Bicol region of the Philippines, his home province that had recently been devastated by floods. When I called Kristi that week and asked her if she had contributed to any of these projects, she told me "No," but went on to say that she and her husband Mark had poured hours into building a traditional Filipino *parol* (Ta), a large decorative paper lantern symbolizing the Star of Bethlehem, for a charity auction sponsored by the Filipino American Council of South Texas (FACOST) at St. Catherine's. She then told me that after winning the competition and $500, she and Mark gave the money to Gawad Kalinga, the social ministry discussed in the last chapter that builds homes for the poor in the Philippines.

Although first-generation Filipino Americans like Kristi and Mark also contribute to a host of charitable projects throughout the year, these brief examples highlight the extent to which Simbang Gabi is not simply a Filipino religious tradition but also a celebration of Catholic cultural understanding of the sanctity and unity of the human family more generally. The tradition serves more than the spiritual needs of the Filipino American community. As Noemi Castillo, former director of Filipino affairs in the Archdiocese of San Francisco explains, "Filipino-Americans have found Simbang Gabi to be an effective way to build a community of faith, to express who they are as a people, to celebrate their religious traditions and culture, and to reach out to Filipinos in the parish." Continuing, she points out that the celebration is "a time to look at the example of Mary who was always ready for the stirring of God's grace, who promptly responded to God's call to be His witness of love and service to the community. . . . When Simbang Gabi is understood from the perspective of these challenges, it transcends cultural boundaries and is a unifying time in the parish. It is an opportunity for everyone in the parish to be one community of faith, to wait, with Mary, in silence and prayerful anticipation for the birth of her Son Jesus, our Lord and Messiah."[12]

Unshakable Foundations

Throughout the years of this study, contentious politics led to numerous first-generation Filipino American groups and associations splitting, but the Catholic Church remained intact through it all. Although some members of St. Catherine's left as a result of these conflicts and now attend other parishes, the Galveston-Houston archdiocese is still their home, and the universal Catholic Church remains the foundation of their community. Conflicts came and went, and regardless of the Church's level of involvement or the outcome of its mediations, first-generation Filipino Americans remained Catholic and very active in parish life. Beyond annual celebrations, such as Simbang Gabi and Philippine Independence, weekly masses consistently bring the Filipino American community together across ethnic and regional divides and engage them in a host of collaborative projects beyond their own communities. When I asked Father José why this is the case, he told me, "To be Filipino is to be Catholic; it's not a joke. We will always be together even if there is conflict. The Catholic Church is really organized so even if different groups split they will still come to mass . . . they cannot form their own church. It is because of the nature of the organization of the Catholic Church that these splits don't affect the priorities of our faith. We are one family working together and divorce is not permitted." Even though Father José was laughing as he talked about divorce literally not being sanctioned by the Church, his comments highlight how the rigid hierarchical structure of the Catholic Church does not deter parish and community life, as some social scientists might expect, but actually holds its diversity together as a single family.[13] Likewise, as subsequent chapters will illustrate, the centrality of the Church and the scope of its reach within the parish and beyond are equally powerful in mobilizing Filipinos to become involved in civic life. The same cannot be said for the organizational structure of first-generation Filipino American Protestant churches in Houston.[14]

The United Filipino Methodist Church, for example, the largest Filipino Protestant church in Houston, split into two churches during period of this study. The splinter churches also went on to split several times themselves. Although these splits typically occurred as a result of internal politics or questions over spiritual authority, they also fell along Filipino ethnic and regional lines. When I interviewed Reverend Bruce, the first-generation Filipino American pastor of the original Methodist splinter church, he told me, "This is just the way it is with us." Continuing, he explained, "I have actually started twenty-three new churches [not all in Houston] since I was ordained, and all of them were groups who just no longer felt the spirit with their current church. When you no longer feel the spirit you must move on and it is a blessing to build something new with all that passion. We need to build more churches where people feel God's love and are not lost in the coldness of a big cathedral." When I questioned Reverend Bruce about what he meant by "the coldness of a big cathedral," he told me, "The Catholics have got it all wrong, churches should be intimate and small . . . and when we Protestants build massive churches that mirror them it is no wonder people leave." Although the first-generation Filipino American Catholics interviewed in this study would overwhelmingly disagree about the coldness of their churches, Filipino Protestant churches clearly represent a different institutional model—one that is not only open to splitting but encouraged to split by some of its clergy.

Within any Catholic parish, the clergy hold clear positions of authority, and all below them are equal, regardless of the size of the church. When the Church actively mediates conflict between or within groups, it intercedes on its own behalf based on what it perceives to be good for the wider parish. Certainly not everyone agrees, as we have seen in previous chapters, but priests such as Father José believe this is the only way to insure that what needs to get accomplished for the larger parish, not just Filipino American interests, is done with as little conflict as possible. Explaining this further, Father José pointed out to me:

My role is to accommodate their needs. . . . For example, we Filipinos usually celebrate an anniversary of the nine days after death for forty days. Now American priests would not understand that, so they would not go to celebrate mass with them. So I try to accommodate them but at the same time in the context of the larger parish. We are not just Filipinos. We have different cultures and I try to lead across them. Take for example the building committee or the parish committee that contain different culture groups like the Hispanics, Anglo, Filipino, and Nigerians. No one group is in control. We are working on coming up and organizing a way so they can come together more. They contribute to the life of the church here in terms of their involvement and their ministries. They are important parts of our family and we want them to act as one family. It's my job to make them see what is best for the Church.

This is not to say that the Church is a malevolent authority in dealings with its parishioners. Father José does what he genuinely thinks is best for all Catholics in his parish. He also understands that his parishioners are free to switch parishes or even leave the Church. As such, he actively attempts to accommodate all their needs within the context of more universal Catholic values. He believes that this allows him to remain outside of divisive politics and campaigns of self-recognition. However, some members of the Bicolano American community or others may disagree with this assessment.

In either case, whether they are actively engaged in these conflicts personally or not, Father José and the Church more generally attempt to establish boundaries for how groups interact within the Church and all official parish affairs. Although the Church has little or no institutional authority over what goes on in people's prayer groups or ethnic and regional associations, it calls on them to act as "good Catholics" and attempts to direct their relationships with the wider community based on broad moral appeals centered on faith and family. These appeals can be very culturally pervasive, as we have seen. They can also instill a sense of moral obligation among first-generation Filipino Americans that extends well beyond the jurisdiction of any one parish. When this is the case, and when these values are made central to community efforts, they can have an equally powerful impact on Filipino American immigrants' attempts at unifying its immense diversity and building centers of community outside of the Church itself. Such is the case in the next example.

OF SAINTS AND CENTERS

In October 1987 Deacon Frank, a first-generation Filipino American member of the pastoral staff at St. Catherine's, flew to the Vatican in Rome with his wife, Sister Diana, also a first-generation Filipino American. The occasion was the canonization of San Lorenzo Ruiz de Manila, who is purportedly the first Filipino martyred for the Catholic faith and the first Filipino officially recognized by the

Church as a saint.[15] He is widely heralded by Filipinos as a true patriot, and his life story is considered a model of devout faith. After falsely being accused of killing a Spaniard in the Philippines, San Lorenzo joined some Dominican friars on a mission to Japan in 1636. While in exile, he was arrested along with the Dominican missionaries for preaching Christianity. Under Tokugawa rule Christianity was forbidden, and when San Lorenzo refused to renounce his Catholic faith he was tortured and killed in 1637.[16]

When I asked Deacon Frank about what it was like being in St. Peter's Square with Pope John Paul II for the canonization, he stated that he used the time to think more about San Lorenzo himself. "While I was in prayer I started to really think, who is this Filipino son San Lorenzo?" Continuing, Deacon Frank asked, "Did you know that San Lorenzo was half Chinese? His father was Chinese and his mother was Filipina. When I was listening to Pope John Paul II during the canonization, he mentioned this. I was inspired by the humility of the Pope because he said that this saint we have canonized represents immigrants because his father was an immigrant and he died an immigrant in another land. I was thinking then that I am also an immigrant and being an immigrant isn't always a very easy life here in Houston. This really moved me to do something." When I asked him why life had been difficult after immigrating to Houston, he told me he struggled back in the late 1980s to find a sense of community among his fellow Filipinos. "It's not America but Filipino politics that keeps us from building unity; it just confounds me and made me sad." When I asked what changed or inspired him at the canonization, he stated, "I was thinking the Church has always been a unifier, but maybe this was an opportunity to do something for Filipino immigrants in San Lorenzo Ruiz de Manila's name. That was my main point for starting the center, to unify the Filipinos as far as faith is concerned." With this vision and inspiration, Deacon Frank began the long journey toward building the first independent Filipino American community center in Houston when he returned from Rome in late October of 1987.

Throughout November, Deacon Frank brought together as many first-generation Filipino Americans as he could find to share his thoughts on San Lorenzo's canonization. Meeting in several homes, a group of about twenty families formed and began to meet regularly. Describing these early meetings, Deacon Frank noted, "Every Sunday after mass we would pray his [San Lorenzo's] novena and then work on making our vision come true." By December the group had written its constitution and outlined its mission for the center:

> Our mission is to follow the good example of our patron Saint San Lorenzo de Manila. To support Filipino Americans and other ethnic minority groups in their efforts to strengthen their family units, preserve their cultural heritage, [and] encourage spiritual and educational growth and development among the young and social support and activities for [the] aged and the infirm. San Lorenzo Ruiz de Manila aims to make a positive difference in the communities

in which they live and work by providing a place where people can meet, providing committed volunteers and healthy, varied sociocivic activities, foster
family unity and values, and enhance spiritual growth.

Placing faith and family at the center of its mission, the group started to work
on raising money to buy land. Throughout the nine nights of Simbang Gabi
the group went caroling door to door, singing Christmas hymns and asking for
donations. In little over a week it raised over $1,000.

Visiting with the board of the San Lorenzo Ruiz de Manila center (SLRM),
they told me how difficult it was to raise money when they first started. Jerome,
for example, explained, "People were very skeptical because we have a lot of organizations here, and there are all sorts of fundraising but even though they could
raise a lot of money they could not build anything. People wanted to know how
we were any different and I said, 'We trust in the Lord; you will see what He can
do through us.'" Adding her own thought, Emily admitted, "I didn't even believe
that things would really happen. But through the years and through faith, and I
know that it is really through God's grace that it happened because at the time,
at the start of every meeting, we had the prayer and then through the years it
became more deeper and deeper until we were finally able to reach other people
to join because they realized that there is really a genuine intent to make things
happen." By mid-year of 1988 the group elected its first board, began to hold a
weekly Bible study in members' homes, and had raised nearly $4,000. It is impor-
tant to note that nearly half of the officers at the SLRM center were and remain
women. Women such as Sister Diana, Deacon Frank's wife, play a prominent
role in the center both as leaders and in the planning and execution of its various activities. In 1989, for example, the center held its first youth program at St.
Catherine's community hall and filed for tax exemption status. In 1992, the group
raised $20,000 and held its first beauty pageant at St. Catherine's. These initial
events would not have been successful without the leadership and hard work of
the center's Filipinas.

By 1996 the center's donations rose from $20,000 to nearly $70,000, and the
group purchased 3.2 acres of land in southwest Houston for $41,000. Many ques-
tioned the location. As Joy described it, "It was in the middle of nowhere, but the
land was cheap, and well, as you see, it all worked out." During this time, feeling
that progress had been made, Deacon Frank and Sister Diana left Houston to
spend a year on a religious mission helping parishes around the United States.
They turned leadership over to Albert, who was elected as the first chairman of
SLRM. It was Albert who began the task of building the actual center.

Although the group still had nearly $30,000 left over after purchasing the
land, the cost of building materials was higher than expected, resulting in the
majority of the labor being done by volunteers and Albert himself. The frame
of the building went up rather quickly, but progress was slowed by weather and
the scarcity of hours volunteers had to contribute to the effort. During this

time the SLRM published its first quarterly newsletter and was granted bingo concessions from the state of Texas for the second Sunday of each month. Over the next several years, fundraising and membership increased as the center built momentum. By 2004, the building was nearly complete, but Albert tragically died while working at the center. In memorial, members of the SLRM board thanked Albert and commemorated him for "literally giving his life to make Deacon's vision a reality."

Three years after Albert's death, the county announced that the street that ran in front of SLRM was about to be widened, and offered to purchase the land on which the center sat for $169,000 in addition to providing an alternative plot at a low rate per acre. "This was divine providence," Deacon Frank suggested, so the group jumped at the opportunity and ended up gaining two acres in the process. With a new plot of land and new capital to build another center, the group moved forward quickly. In 2008, the center held its twentieth anniversary feast for San Lorenzo in the shell of a new home. Although far from complete, the building went up rather quickly and was finished well enough to hold celebrations. The old center sat on roughly three acres with a building that was about 3,200 square feet. The new center sits on five acres with a building that is nearly 13,000 square feet.

The twentieth anniversary feast celebration was presided over by Father José and accompanied by the Filipino choir from St. Catherine's. During the mass, Father José read from the Acts of Supplication in unison with those gathered, "O San Lorenzo Ruiz, you brought honor to our country, having been a level-headed and prudent father of family, a witness to Christ in your life until death. We present all our petitions to God through your help so that by our actions we may know more love and love more Jesus our Lord and Savior.... We humbly implore your intercession in this novena." While everyone was standing, he continued, "Dear San Lorenzo Ruiz, you showed yourself to be a responsible father of your family, you chose to live in the midst of suffering. Look with gracious eyes upon our family that is now beset with crisis." To which everyone responded, "San Lorenzo pray for us." Verse by verse Father José read from the novena and those in attendance responded. As I recorded the event, a member of the center standing next to me whispered, "This is what makes us different; listen to the words." As I listened even more intently to Father José, he continued, "You [San Lorenzo] had been a loyal servant of the church by fulfilling your duties to God.... San Lorenzo pray for us. You had been a hardworking member of parish organizations. Teach us to take an active part in parish activities and become worthy of Christ in works of charity.... San Lorenzo pray for us." At the end of the service I interviewed the first-generation Filipina who had been standing next to me. Before I could ask her a question she asked me, "Did you get it?" Not wanting to answer. I asked what was I supposed to get? She responded, "The novena and the mission of the center are the same. This is what makes us different."

Nearly a full year later, while attending the SLRM board meeting, I asked those present what they thought made the center unique. I asked them how they had succeeded when so many other Filipino American efforts at building a center had failed. Roger, a first generation Filipino American and the new chairman of the center, stated:

> People have left or died and all and we are still together . . . I think we have several reasons. To me, when you put God in the center of an organization or the family, anything, my opinion is that you will always be successful regardless; that is number one. Number two, I have heard people tell me personally that they like San Lorenzo because they can feel the sincerity of the members, that, no offense to other organizations, but they feel like that every member of this San Lorenzo have no personal gain that they want to have, that they are here for community service, that's all, which is true. I believe every single one here, especially the older ones. They really just feel like they want to have San Lorenzo because a sense of service to the community, a sense of being Filipino, they want to be proud but with no personal gain.

Agreeing with Roger, but expressing a certain amount of frustration with her past experiences in other groups and associations, Lea, also a first-generation Filipina American, explained,

> I will tell you exactly what it is because I have been there [in Filipino associations], that is why I left them. I don't mind saying it because that is the truth and the truth should come out because that is the only way you can improve things, right? If you go there, ok, here is my first impression of when I was there. They are always talking about parties, right, in hotels, Hyatt hotels, big name hotels. So where does all the money that is collected gonna go, how far can they go in building a community center? We just celebrated the twentieth anniversary of our center and with God's help we are still in existence and so far there are no splits.

As the conversation continued around the table, everyone, all of whom were first-generation Filipino Americans, expressed similar sentiments and experiences.

Lydia, for example, stated, "I think also one of the reasons why San Lorenzo is so unique which I have never found in any other organization, and thanks to Deacon Frank and Sister Diana, they have a Bible study here every week." Continuing, she explained, "I mean I feel a sense of fulfillment when I come over here on those weekends and I hope some more people will come but it's a matter of your personal. I mean of course I want anyone to come, but I think that's one of the best reasons why I'm here too. I don't think any other organizations, Filipino American organizations have that yet. Correct me if I'm wrong. . . . So, to me, that makes this organization unique. This center is built on God as the foundation and because of that he will reign king in this building" However, when I asked the board and the other members present if the SLRM center is just a Catholic religious center, they were not all in agreement. Some said "Yes." Others pointed to the fundraising dances and explained, "You have been here for our events. When do the most people show up? It is after we pray and after the blessing of the food. Some people come here to be with other Filipinos and dance, that's all." Somewhat agreeing, Roger explained to me, "We are a religious center, but it is multifaceted. We welcome non-Catholics and hold many events—it is partly religious, partly social, partly civic, and partly educational. We want to support health clinics and do more outreach to the community around us, not just for Filipinos. It is complicated and we always have to compete for members and their time at other events."

Parish or Perish?

During one of the numerous fundraising dances held at the San Lorenzo de Manila center on a Saturday night each month, questions arose about the competition the center faces with other groups and associations and the Church itself. Although the building was still not completely finished, the dance floor was polished and ready to go. On the stage above the dance floor, Rodger turned on a microphone that was attached to a stand-alone Karaoke machine and addressed the small crowed that had gathered. After reading the mission of SLRM and explaining a bit of the center's twenty-year history, he asked everyone to bow their heads for the blessing of the food. Then, with a resounding "Amen," people began to take their place in the buffet line.

The food, ranging from chicken adobo and pancit to Chinese fried rice from a local restaurant, was succulent and served in ample quantities. Sitting at one end of the buffet table was a tray of Lynn's famous hopia, which, as she pointed out in the interview quoted in Chapter 1, she makes every month for the fundraising dance. As people sat at the tables around the dance floor and began to eat their food, Emily, a member of the SLRM board, approached me and stated, "We normally have many more people—this is an off night for us." When I asked her why she thought attendance was so low, she told me several local Catholic parishes were celebrating Santacruzan.[17]

Later that evening, after people had finished their food, the music began and people started to dance, with little rest in between songs. As they danced for hours into the early morning, I asked Roger if he was happy with the attendance for the night. "We have about forty people here tonight and they all gave money so every little bit helps." Continuing, he explained, "Sometimes we compete with many other community events and this is what happens. Tonight our biggest competitor is the Church. It is Santacruzan, the last night of Flores de Mayo that honors Rena Elena. It's kinda big. All the Marian groups get together at the churches, not just Filipinos. It's also a beauty pageant. We can't compete with that, but it happened to fall on the same night we always hold the fundraiser each month. More will probably come after mass, but they also have their own parties to go to, sponsored by other associations too." Despite the competition with Santacruzan, the forty-two people in attendance that night came from sixteen different zip codes and thirteen Catholic parishes.[18] All but a few of the attendees were Catholic, and all were first-generation Filipino Americans. Clearly, the SLRM center is able to draw Filipino immigrants together as Deacon Frank had hoped, even if in small numbers at times. However, the Church remains the focus of their community. Of the first-generation Filipino Americans surveyed that night, 79 percent stated that they see the Church as the center of their community. This is significantly lower than the larger sample surveyed at St. Catherine's during Philippine Independence, 93 percent, but still the overwhelming majority.

At the next board meeting, I asked Roger and those in attendances how they see themselves in relation to the Church, given the competition the center faced during Santacruzan. Pointing to the larger mission of SLRM, Roger stated, "Look we support the Church and they support us. We are not wanting to take away from them; that is not our mission. We are our own group, mostly Catholics, who want our own center for us Filipinos. We honor San Lorenzo and we have done all this because of our faith and no one can take it away now." When I asked Roger about the rumors that several groups had tried to buy or take control of the center, he asked me where I had heard this. Somewhat upset by the question, Roger suggested that I talk to Deacon Frank.

A week later, I sat down with Deacon Frank. He told me that after purchasing the first plot of land for the old center, several groups inquired about sponsoring it or flat out buying it from SLRM. "During this time there were other Filipino groups that wanted to snatch our center since we were already established and ready to get the building. They wanted to take over and change the name to something else." When I asked who these groups were, Deacon would only say, "They were famous people. Everybody knows them because they are a big association. We will never be under them because once your main purpose is social or civic not religious, than you will not be successful. I thank God and San Lorenzo for still helping us." Although Deacon Frank was reluctant to name names, it appeared that either FACOST or PCCI, the only major Filipino umbrella associations in Houston, had attempted to buy or at least inquired into buying the SLRM center. Whether there was malicious intent or not, Deacon Frank was clearly upset by these events.

In the weeks that followed my conversations with members of the SLRM board, I sat down with Dora, a first-generation Filipina American who served at one point on the boards of both PCCI and FACOST. When I asked her what she thought about the San Lorenzo center, she stated, "I tell you, God is really good to that group . . . fortune smiled on them at every turn but it was their sweat equity, really sweat equity that made it happen." Continuing, she explained how frustrated she was that no one else had built a center yet. "You know we should have been first, we raised so much money. Looking back now we should have supported them [SLRM] instead of trying to take over. We saw an opportunity and they told us no. Perhaps we could have helped but they have done well without the associations. . . . The archdiocese actually approached them first but told them they must pay their dues like regular members and they didn't want to do that. Deacon Frank, I think, was afraid they cannot afford it but they were also afraid to be controlled." Seeing that I was shocked, Dora stated, "Yes, the Church tried to get there first but they [SLRM] didn't want anyone to control them."

A few days later I sat down with Father José and asked him about his thoughts on the SLRM center. He told me that the center is growing because of their new facility and they are starting to hold a lot of activities there. When I asked him if he thought the center was good for the Filipino American community, he told me, "Hopefully it can serve as a catalyst in terms of unity because it is the only Filipino center so far. I would like to see it, but also that's why there was a problem." Asking him what the problem was, he explained:

> The problem is that there are now two San Lorenzo celebrations and that was a conflict. It was some kind of personality thing that caused it before I even came to St. Catherine's. There was so much conflict for a while that you know they could not get a Filipino priest from the diocese because we did not want to do it until some kind of arrangement could be made on how and when we celebrate the annual feast of San Lorenzo. I would like to see just one celebration, but right now more people are attending their celebration and not the one organized here [St. Catherine's] by the Filipino Council [of the Archdiocese of Galveston-Houston]. . . . It should be the other way around.

As we continued to talk, I asked Father José if things had been worked out between the Church and the SLRM center, knowing he had been the celebrant at the twentieth anniversary feast held there. "There has been a reconciliation arrangement and now they don't celebrate on the same day—the Filipino ministry celebrates on the last Sunday of the month and the San Lorenzo group celebrates the week later." When I asked him if the Filipino Council in the archdiocese had ever tried to incorporate the center or had an interest in being more involved in its operation, he simply stated he had never heard anything about that or anything along those lines.

CONCLUSION

Today the SLRM center no longer fears that other groups are trying to take it over. In the last twenty years, through hardship and struggles, it has seen its membership more than double, it has built a beautiful new building that now sits on five acres of land, and it has negotiated a working relationship with the Church and St. Catherine's, specifically. Although the annual feast of San Lorenzo at the SLRM is actually better attended than the one at St. Catherine's, Father José is now the celebrant for both events. Deacon Frank, likewise, remains active on the pastoral staff at St. Catherine's and is still one of the key spiritual advisors for the SRLM center. Rather than completely circumventing the authority of the Church, the SLRM center has established a measure of independence in its shadows and with the blessings of the archdiocese's Filipino Council. While the SRLM center envisions serving the broader community, Filipino or otherwise, in much the same way as the Church, it remains the community's "best kept secret" as the *Manila-Headline* describes it.[19] The center is growing and has had numerous successes, but, to this point, it has yet to move very far beyond fundraising and hosting smaller Filipino American community events.

The SLRM center is not the center of the Filipino American community in Houston, but it is the only independent Filipino community center outside of the Church. Although first-generation Filipino Americans overwhelming believe that the Catholic Church is and should be at the center of their community, they clearly also want to carve out a sense of independence from its authority through their own Filipino institutions. The San Lorenzo de Manila center has achieved this where others have failed. Part of its success, at least according to the first-generation Filipino Americans interviewed, lies in the fact that religion, specifically a focus on the sanctity of the family, is central to the mission of the center. They venerate San Lorenzo as a Filipino martyr and father figure—a model of Catholic family that supports the wider values of their faith, and this engages them in building a sense of unity. Not unlike the unity found in Simbang Gabi, which calls on Filipinos to look to the example of mother Mary and respond to God's call for love and service to the community, the successes of the SLRM center have been paved by its emphasis on faith and family.

Despite the fact that PCCI broke ground for a new center in 2011, we can only speculate what the future will hold. While many interviewed wish them luck and remain rather optimistic, most question whether it can bring the community together as successfully as the Church or SLRM. Others question why it has taken so long and ask how a community with immense socioeconomic resources cannot move faster. Where other Asian American communities in Houston such as the Vietnamese or Chinese have built numerous cultural and community centers in less time, it has taken the Filipino American community roughly fifty years to break ground on a new lot for their first secular center. Outside of the large annual feast of San Lorenzo at the SLRM center that gathers first-generation Filipino American from around the city, the Church is the only other institution to consistently bring the community together. Whether it is at weekly mass, novenas for regional and provincial saints, or through annual events such as Simbang Gabi, Catholicism and the Church specifically remain the source of unity for Filipinos in the diaspora much as it has for hundreds of years in the Philippines.

More than mediating the community's numerous associations or simply managing its regional and ethnic diversity, the Church successfully engages first-generation Filipino Americans in a host of parish projects. It also links them to the wider community better than any other single institution. Although monthly Filipino masses at St. Catherine's are almost exclusively attended by Filipino immigrants, outside of non-Filipino spouses, all other masses are highly multiethnic/multiracial and introduce first-generation Filipino Americans to a host of community projects and concerns beyond their own. Annual events, such as Flores de Mayo, likewise draw the parish together across multiple groups of all ethnic/racial backgrounds and provide numerous opportunities to engage these boarder communities.

At the same time, celebrations such as Simbang Gabi introduce non-Filipinos to a Philippine brand of Catholicism that is different in many ways from what they are more accustomed to. As these traditions continue to be encouraged by Filipino priests such as Father José in parishes around the country, and as non-Filipinos increasingly attend them, it is yet another reminder of the potential impact Filipino immigrants may have in reshaping American Catholicism. In the end, their influence, coupled with that of other immigrants from the global South, may prove to be quite dramatic both within the Church itself and across the broader contours of American civil society. Celebrations such as Simbang Gabi, for example, are not simply religious events but also civic events. They can bring disparate groups together, regardless of race/ethnicity or nativity, and engage them in projects that not only benefit their parishes through raising funds to build a new cathedral or feeding and clothing those in need but touch the lives of people across Houston, the Philippines, and beyond.

Exploring this in greater detail, the next chapter moves from analyzing how first-generation Filipino Americans build community to how they engage it. The chapter highlights how Catholic cultural frameworks centered on the family motivate first-generation Filipino Americans to engage their community members as brothers and sisters through acts of informal helping and formal volunteering. It also analyzes how at a more cultural and linguistic level, the subtle nuances between the Tagalog words for help and volunteer, for example, can indicate radical differences not only in the meanings first-generation Filipino Americans attach to these endeavors but also the ways in which their cross-cutting memberships in a host of community and religious associations influence their understanding of them. This, as will become more apparent in the following pages, has tremendous implications on the ways in which we measure and understand where the civic engagement of new Catholic immigrants such as Filipinos fits into the broader context of the puzzle of American Catholic civic life.

CHAPTER 6

CARING FOR COMMUNITY

"It's really a crazy time of the year for us," Father José explained on the eve of the third annual Alief Health and Civic Resource Fair held at St. Catherine's Catholic Church.[1] As various groups and organizations, Filipino or otherwise, gathered at the parish hall for one last meeting of the parish council before the event, they checked over their lists of volunteers and supplies and debated various logistical issues. In the midst of these final preparations, I saw several familiar faces. Members of Bibingka, Couples for Christ, Pilipino American Masons of Texas (PAMAT), Philippine Nurse Association of Metropolitan Houston, and many other Filipino American groups, both religious and secular, were all present.

Some brought food to share, others were simply there to help in any way they could. Although most did not have time to talk for long outside of a quick *Como esta*, "How are you?," Bert, a first-generation Filipino American member of the Millennium Lions Club, stopped to speak a bit longer. When I asked him how the final preparations were going, he stated that all was well and even better than last year. "Each year it gets better because we pick up more sponsors and can do more for the community." Continuing, he explained,

> All the sponsors and groups make the event better and extend what we can do, but this is not the whole story. Having been a member of different organizations, I can tell you that they all have their strengths. For example, my Filipino Lion's Club have helped sponsor putting up community fairs like this for years. We have done medical fairs and stuff like that, but where are all of these events held? The Church, right? None of this would matter without the coordination and help of the Church. She [Church] makes it all come together year in and year out, and Father always makes sure it runs so smoothly. Wait and see, tomorrow will be a great day.

The next day, St. Catherine's was abuzz. Teams of people were building booths and setting up tables in the parish hall, while signs and posters were being thrown about like confetti. As people rushed to get everything in order, a crowd started to form outside. I was surprised by the number of people who were already gathering for the event. However, given the fact that St. Catherine's had hosted the Alief Health and Civic Resource Fair for several years and had been advertising the event year after year through churches, public schools, and local newspapers, the crowd should not have been surprising. The word was out and, unbeknownst to me at the time, the fair was and still is one the largest of its kind in the city. What had started in 1997 as a local outreach forum for community and parish problems entitled SAVE (Stand Against Violence Everyone), grew into a broad coalition of groups and individuals.[2] The first fair was held in 2002. It attracted a modest crowd of 1,000 attendees with nearly sixty providers and sponsors. Subsequent fairs grew to encompass several more sponsors and provide community resources on a scale unmatched in the area.[3]

In 2004, the first year I observed the event, the fair was sponsored by over one hundred providers and attendance swelled to over 2,000 attendees. That year over 135 children were immunized. Free health care screenings, such as mammograms or other tests for issues dealing with vision, blood pressure, cholesterol, glucose, and bone density were provided to over 1,000 attendees.[4] People also registered in large numbers for PSA tests, CHIP, and Gold Card insurance programs.[5] Booths and tables for the Scouts, YMCA, and other youth groups provided information and sign-up opportunities for area youth to get involved in a host of programs. School supplies and backpacks were also given away to over 300 area students. In total, 189 local underprivileged families also received 13,133 fresh produce items that had been collected by Southwest Houston Social Ministries and St. Catherine's own social ministry outreach.[6]

The following year (2005), 500 people got some form of health screening, 135 children received close to 450 immunizations, many getting three shots each, and 19 pints of blood were donated. At least 200 underprivileged families received nearly 14,000 fresh produce items, 600 children received backpacks and school supplies, and 80 people signed up for library cards.[7] The fair also served to educate the public on a host of issues and worked to get people involved in their community. Four hundred people visited the Houston Police Department's table for men against domestic abuse, as an example, and over 250 people picked up voter registration information or county service literature.[8] These successes, not to mention many other contributions, were matched and in many ways exceeded by subsequent fairs.[9] In fact, the fair grew to be such a success that SAVE decided that St. Catherine's parking lot and parish halls were not large enough to accommodate the number of people they anticipated for the next year and voted to move the fair to the larger school facilities in the Alief ISD school district.

Although St. Catherine's has not hosted the event on church grounds since 2005, it remains a major annual partner, as does the Filipino American community of Houston. Working side by side with groups and individuals from a host of backgrounds, the fair continues to engage members of St. Catherine's parish, Filipino or otherwise, in the broader civic concerns and needs of those living in the city. When I talked to Father José about the fair's venue change, he told me that he was sad to see it go but also stated that he was very pleased that it keeps growing each year. Two years later, walking around and talking to people at the annual fair held at Alief Middle School, just ten minutes away from St. Catherine's, I got the sense that this was indeed still the case. The fair was even larger than the prior two years and was undoubtedly still a major community event that continued to help meet the needs of families across Alief and Houston.

Talking to members of various Filipino groups, I also got the sense that nothing had really changed in terms of the first-generation Filipino American Catholic presence at the fair. Out of the hundred-plus sponsors and providers at the fair that year, first-generation Filipino American groups, such as Pilipino American Masons of Texas (PAMAT), Couples for Christ (CFC), Fil-Am Press, (Filipino American Council of South Texas (FACOST), Pilipinas Broadcasting USA, the various Lions groups, and Philippine Nurse Association of Metropolitan Houston, still provided hundreds of volunteers.[10] Likewise, beyond this formal list there were well over three hundred-plus walk-on volunteers, many of whom, according to Father José, were first-generation Filipino Americans from St. Catherine's parish.[11] Explaining this further, Father José noted:

> The Filipino presence, just in terms of their sheer numbers, is very vital in this parish and, of course, their involvement is key each year. They give life to the parish and its projects and the fair remains one our greatest projects. So nothing has changed, just the location. The church is still a part of those around us and we Filipinos are still helping. But I should point out that you can't just ask Filipinos to volunteer. You must extend a personal invitation to them because volunteering is just too formal. If you invite them to help, however, they show up. We all help each other for the betterment of the parish and the community. This is their church and family. When she calls they feel personally responsible, almost obligated to help and so they do. This is why we are so successful each year.

SILENTLY SERVING THE COMMUNITY

The annual Alief Health and Civic Resource Fair is by far the largest and most widely visible community project in which St. Catherine's Catholic Church and members of the Filipino American community are collaboratively involved, but it is certainly not the only one. From projects that address health care and the aging to feeding those in need or addressing immigration issues through the Catholic Charities and the St. Frances Cabrini Center, they are partners in a mind-boggling number of programs and annual projects that extend well beyond any one parish or their own ethnic communities. St. Catherine's has several partners outside of the Filipino American community helping with these efforts but, as Father José pointed out to me on numerous occasions, the church would not be nearly as successful without the aid of first-generation Filipino Americans. Certainly not all Filipinos in the parish volunteer, but among those that do there is little to no conflict. Although they do not always agree on what project should take precedence over another or how they should be carried out, by the time projects go beyond discussion and voting in the parish council, people, Filipino or not, tend to rally support and lend help where they feel they are best able to make a difference.

Although the general public, non-Filipinos, may not widely recognize Filipino Americans' contributions outside of their high visibility in health care, they are a vital part of the Houston community in many civic capacities. Through Operation Backpack, for example, many first-generation Filipino Americans at St. Catherine's annually collect and distribute school supplies and shoes for young children, in addition to the numerous resources they already donate to the Alief Health and Civic Resource Fair. For the annual Christmas drive for tots and woolens at St. Catherine's that coincides with the celebration of Simbang Gabi, many first-generation Filipino Americans also raise money and/or donate space heaters, clothes, and blankets to distribute to those in need during harsh winter freezes and storms.[12] And these are but a few examples.

Within the Houston Filipino American community itself, St. Catherine's and its Filipino parishioners also collaborated on a host of projects from aiding local families who recently immigrated from the Philippines to raising money for people devastated by natural disasters in their hometowns or those who fled Hurricane Katrina.[13] They have also worked together in helping to process legal documents for immigrants in the community. In 2009, for example, St. Catherine's, in partnership with FACOST, hosted a Consular Outreach program for the Filipino American community with representatives from the Philippine Consulate General in Los Angeles, to facilitate the renewal of passports, the retention and reacquisition of Philippine citizenship (Dual Republic Act 9225), and to register people for overseas absentee voting. Over 1,600 applications for these consular services were received and processed over the two-day event.[14]

When I asked Father José about the frequent involvement of Filipino Americans in these kinds of projects and why I had rarely seen a news story or editorial about their community volunteerism in Houston in non-Filipino media, he told me:

> Perhaps it has something to do with the Filipino temperament, especially here people are very outgoing and it is the American way. Filipinos just watch if there's something they can do, then they do it. Filipinos are silent workers. They participate in projects and activities, but they do not want to be in the limelight. Most of the time they're just in the background but they are there. They are involved in practically every ministry and organizations like Knights

of Columbus, but they also have their own groups that do work for the community too. We all help each other for the betterment of the parish and the community. That's one of the good things about Filipinos; it is very easy to get them involved.

When I asked Father José why Filipinos do not seek greater recognition for their community efforts, he joked, "This is what their associations are for." After laughing a bit, Father José went on to suggest that there is a difference between seeking recognition among your fellow Filipinos and the broader public. "We generally do not want to draw too much attention to ourselves outside the [Filipino] community . . . we want to blend in with the average American and help out where we can."

Asking any first-generation Filipino American in Houston to define volunteerism or to explain what it is they are doing civically, even while they are doing it, is not an easy task. Throughout the six years of studying community and parish events, asking Filipino Americans questions such as, "Are you a volunteer?" or "Are you volunteering?" were either met with confusion or denial despite clear observations that they were obviously helping out in some capacity. Filipino Americans do volunteer, and at high rates compared to other Asian Americans, as other scholars have demonstrated.[15] However, they are also engaged in a host of more informal forms of sharing and giving that many Filipinos may not perceive as formal volunteering.[16]

At a more cultural and linguistic level, the subtle nuances between the Tagalog words for help (*tulong*), volunteer (*magboluntaryo*), and participate (*sumali* or *lumahok*) may also indicate radical differences not only in the meanings first-generation Filipino Americans attach to these endeavors but also the ways in which their cross-cutting memberships in a host of community and religious associations influence their understanding of them. Each word, the context, and the meanings associated with them matter.[17] Highlighting this, when I asked a first-generation Filipina American nurse at the Alief Health and Civic Resource Fair to describe or classify what it was she was doing to help out at the blood donation booth, she stated, "It is what you Americans would call volunteering, but that is not the words I would use—I would say that I am simply helping out."

When I asked the same question of a first-generation Filipino Americans member of CFC who was also at the fair, helping to pass out school supplies to children, he answered the question in a similar way and emphatically stated he was not a volunteer. "No, I am not a volunteer. I am a Christian in the real sense. I am not a social activist. I am more into just helping and being more kind to other people, you know, just doing what you can to get people through tough times. It's just compassion, thinking less and less about myself and more about others." Continuing, he explained, "God works in mysterious ways. The more you do things for him, the more he entrust work for you to do. However, he provides the tools and resources to accomplish them. It is not volunteering, but his will."

Throughout the study, whether it was the word "volunteerism" itself that did not translate well with what many first-generation Filipino Americans perceived they were doing or whether it was a conscious religious decision to describe it in other terms, volunteerism meant something different to everyone depending on the situation or context.

Many first-generation Filipino Americans made a clear distinction between formal volunteering and the civic things they were doing. Diana, a parishioner at St. Catherine's, for example, stated, "Unfortunately I am not really doing any social service directly. I give money, so through our church I support social ministries or I have donated whatever is needed. Like during the start of the school year there is a shoe drive and I gave fifty pair of shoes. Oh, and I helped pack school bags for the kids too, with supplies we bought for them, and then we went to the schools and gave them out. We even held a little immunization workshop and talked about health and gave out pamphlets and tooth brushes and other stuff, but this is not what I consider volunteering."

Even at the group level, members of religious fellowship such as Bibingka perceive their civic life through a more informal lens. Explaining this, Cheryl stated, "Our group does a lot, but it is not really volunteering so much as it is family helping each other. When we joined [the group] we felt that this was a family to help us grow. Take a path that we thought we should. We don't have big projects like some groups, but all of us have things going that we pull each other into. We also take care of each other and sometime that requires a lot of work and coordination. Like the time Jimmy was laid off and we helped to cook meals and raise money until he got back on his feet." Clarifying this further, Adler, who was sitting next to Cheryl during our conversation, explained, "Volunteering means signing up, putting your name on the line—I can't do that, no time, I just show up and help when I can, when they need me the most . . . it's just a matter of helping, being there for those in need, and giving care—*gawad kalinga!*" As I continued the conversation with other members of Bibingka and extended it to other groups and individuals throughout the study, Adler's definition of volunteerism was shared by most, if not all, of the first-generation Filipino Americans interviewed.

This, perhaps, explains some of the reasons why Filipino Americans are not recognized more often by the general public for their community involvement. They are not actively seeking to be recognized by the wider public, for the most part, and many do not even consider what they are doing as volunteerism or civic engagement. As a result, first-generation Filipino Americans may underreport their civic activities on formal surveys or not even consider what they are doing to be all that civic.[18] This is important, because it provides a measure of insight into where immigrants inform the supposed enigma of American Catholic civic life. Scholars have long been puzzled by the fact that American Catholicism is devoted to messages of community and provides numerous opportunities for involvement but does not necessarily lead its members to volunteering or

participate in other forms of civic engagement at rates higher or even comparable to that of American Protestants.

First-generation Filipinos American Catholics do volunteer in the academic
or traditional sense, despite what they may call it or how it is viewed from their
own Catholic and Filipino lenses. However, the frequency of their involvement
and what they actually do may have as much to do with their faith and opportunity as it does with any cultural characteristics that are uniquely Filipino. This
chapter further explores this by highlighting where the Church provides opportunities for engaging in civic life that extend well beyond their parishes. Given
that participating in the Church beyond worship services may in fact actually
mean working on a community project, the chapter demonstrates how these
community engagements, carried out through the Church, can easily get lost
or overlooked in the wider analysis of Filipino American Catholics' civic lives.
Beyond analyzing these community engagements and bringing them to the
forefront of discussions about Catholic immigrant civic life, the chapter assesses
where Filipino religious groups and fellowships fit into this puzzle and weighs
in on the debate as to whether these types of groups detract or facilitate engagement with American civil society.

Serving Community through the Church

In 2009, the Archdiocese of Galveston-Houston raised $11.2 million dollars for
its Diocesan Service Fund.[19] That same year St. Catherine's parish alone spent
nearly $25,000 for youth, family life, and social ministries for its own parish, in
addition to raising money to support broader service fund ministries. The ministries supported by these funds include:

Apostleship of the Sea	One Daily Bread
Catholic Schools Office	San José Clinic
Chapels	St. Dominic Center for the Deaf
Communications	Clergy Pastoral Outreach
Continuing Christian Education	Department of Seminarians
Diocesan High School Grants	Diaconate Formation Program
Ecumenism Commission	Good Leaders, Good Shepherds
Office of Worship	Ministry to Priests
Angela House	Office of Permanent Deacons
Camp Kappe	Office of Vocations for Priests
Ethnic Ministries	and Religious Life
Family Life Ministries	Pope John XXIII Residence for
Hispanic Ministries	Retired Priests
Respect Life Office	Aging Ministry
Rural Life Bureau	Pastoral and Educational
Special Youth Services	Ministry

Catholic Chaplin Corpse
Catholic Charities
Correctional Ministries
Foreign Missions
Office of Peace and Justice
Catholic Campaign for Human
    Development
St. Dominic Village
Circle Lake Family Retreat
    Center
Vicar for Judicial Affairs
Young Adult and Campus
    Ministries
Youth Ministries

This long list of programs spans every social service need or social justice issue imaginable, and provides both a diversity of projects and ample opportunity for Filipino Americans to get involved in their parish and Houston more generally.

Other institutions and groups, religious or otherwise, do not have the same number of resources or the vast networks of programs that the Archdiocese of Galveston-Houston can bring to those who want to be involved in their parish or community. Each of these opportunities is well advertised in a host of venues, from St. Catherine's newsletter and the *Texas Catholic Herald* newspaper to posters and boards around the church and its halls. Father José also frequently invites the parish to participate in these efforts during his weekly community update during mass or through his own homilies on giving back to the community. This by no means suggests there are not other numerous groups and projects working for the community outside of the archdiocese. There are. However, volunteerism has traditionally been found to increase when opportunities are ample, readily available, and people are asked to get involved.[20] For the first-generation Filipino Americans in this study, St. Catherine's is considered the center of their community and thus the projects and resources in the archdiocese often offer them the greatest opportunity to get involved in the wider community. Likewise, these opportunities are often presented within the parish and do not require people to travel too far from home or what is familiar to them to make a broad impact.

Filipino American groups and associations, on the other hand, are not as independently involved in the wider community, that is, outside of partnering with the Church, as they are in working for their own ethnic communities. This is by choice in some cases, but is also a matter of resources. Throughout the six years of this study, groups like PAMAT or Solidarity Lodge, for example, hosted blood drive campaigns at St. Catherine's independent of the Alief Health and Civic Resource Fair. Flyers for these events often highlighted messages such as, "Let us spread our love and care for the community" and were well staffed by first-generation Filipino nurses. While attending one of these events, I asked Ramon, a first-generation Filipino American Mason, about his work in the Solidarity Lodge and any differences he saw between service to the Masons and service in the parish.

> We do a lot of good things in Masonry. We sponsor patients from the Philippines and we recommend them to the Shriners for medical attention. We help put on these blood drives, too, but somehow with the parish it's different.

Personally, it's more satisfying [working in the parish]. It's because it's more than for myself and my own satisfaction. With the church it's giving and doing God's work, it's not just a social program or doing something just to make me feel good. It's more than that, more than that. It's God's work, not that the other isn't. I guess it can be both and events like this [blood drive] highlight that. Plus it is easier to work with the church because it is so central to the community.

Groups like the Masons or even Bicol USA that volunteer for programs like Project CURE clearly do a great deal of work for Filipinos in Houston and in the Philippines,[21] but when the focus is the wider Houston community and non-Filipinos, it is easier, as Ramon points out, to utilize the centrality and resources at St. Catherine's or other churches in the archdiocese to accomplish their projects.

In other cases, members of budding independent Filipino American community centers like the San Lorenzo Ruiz de Manila Center (SLRM), want to be involved in the community in a greater capacity but simply do not have the resources at this point. Explaining this to me, Sara, a first-generation member of the San Lorenzo board, stated, "We want to be a real community center not limited to our own selves or Filipino or Fil-Ams [Filipino Americans], but everyone around us, the surrounding community. We really want to reach out and help the seniors. I have seen nursing homes and it breaks up the family. No offense, but the American way is wrong. We have bingo now but we want to do more. We want to do so much, but we need to get the center finished first." The SLRM center did have a community garage sale during the time of my observations, but as Sara pointed out, the participants bought most of what each other had brought to the event. Despite this, the desire to serve the broader community through the center was clearly present with all those interviewed at the SLRM center. Yet, most of the first-generation Filipino Americans interviewed also stated that working to build the center is an important part of what they consider to be their civic and religious life as well. Simply put, working at SLRM is both religious and civic engagement for Filipinos at the center. Roger, the chairman of the SLRM board, highlighting this, explained, "We are all active in our parishes too, but we are working here to honor San Lorenzo and put God and family at the heart of this community. . . . What we do for the center helps build the community and it is important to us civically and spiritually. For many of us the center consumes all our hard work and devotion but it's fulfilling and rewarding." From Lyn, who bakes hopia for the SLRM fundraisers every month, to Albert. who died constructing the original center building, this certainly appears to be the case.[22] At the same time, being active in their parishes does not necessarily limit what they do in their groups and communities but actually facilitates greater involvement.

Drawing on survey findings, Figure 3 further illustrates that first-generation Filipino American Catholics surveyed in Houston who are active in their parish are more likely to be involved in the community through volunteering,

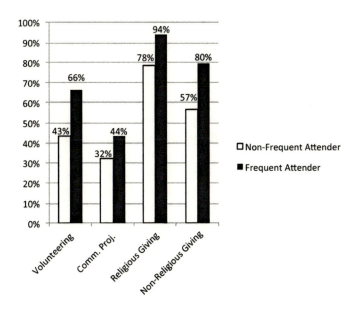

Church Participation Beyond Attendance

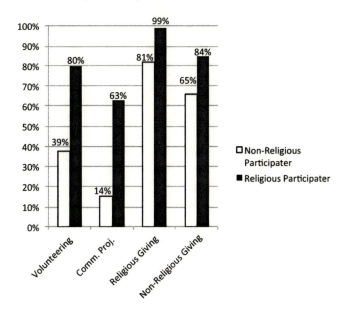

Figure 3 Percentage of First-Generation Filipino Americans in Houston Engaged in the Community by Religiosity. *Source:* The Houston Filipino American Survey 2010; see Methodological Appendix for further details.

community projects, and both religious and non-religious giving than those who are not religiously active.[23] Although rates may actually be higher, given the use of the word "volunteer" versus "participate" or "help," 66 percent of first-generation Filipino American Catholics who attend mass frequently—weekly or more and almost weekly—stated they had volunteered in the past twelve months, compared to only 43 percent of those who only attend a few times a year or less. This is a 23 percent difference. The difference between the percentage of frequent attenders and nonfrequent attenders who had worked on a community project in the last twelve months was considerably less, 12 percent, but still significant, as was the relative gap between the percentage of those who gave money to both religious and nonreligious causes and institutions.

Looking at the same set of community engagements (see Figure 3), those who stated that they had participated in church activities in addition to or outside of attending mass were likewise more involved in their community than those who stated they were not. Of first-generation Filipino American Catholics who participate in extra-church activities, 80 percent stated that they had volunteered in the past twelve months compared, to only 39 percent who did not, a 41 percent difference. Additionally, 63 percent of first-generation Filipino American Catholics who participate in extra-church activities stated they had worked on a community project in the last twelve months compared to only 14 percent who did not, a 49 percent difference. Participation in the church is civic participation and, as we have seen, can easily extend beyond the parish.

Although the difference between those who gave money to both religious and nonreligious causes and institutions was not as large, it was still significant. Across all domains, the percentage of those who volunteered, worked on a community project, or gave money was greater among those who participate in extra-church activities. This suggests, at least for the first-generation Filipino Americans surveyed, that getting involved in the church is good for civic life despite the findings of other studies which suggest that messages of community service may not be getting conveyed well to Asian Americans by the Catholic Church.[24] These messages are being conveyed very well, and people, not just Filipinos, are collaboratively acting on them.

The Church clearly plays a major role in bringing numerous groups, institutions, and causes together for events such as the Alief Health and Civic Resource Fair. Much like the events of Simbang Gabi discussed in Chapter 5, divisive politics within the Filipino American community or other communities is mediated by an institutional mechanism that allows the Church to serve the community better through a host of partners and volunteers from diverse backgrounds. The fact that religion facilitates first-generation Filipino American civic involvement specifically should not be surprising. As many scholars have pointed out, religion can provide opportunities to cross social boundaries, forge ties with people from other groups, and bridge individuals to the wider society.[25] Half of all American volunteerism occurs in a religious context, if not through a place of worship, and this certainly appears to be the case for first-generation Filipino Americans in Houston.[26] Beyond the extensive networks and numerous resources the Catholic Church can present to Filipino Americans that may increase the likelihood that they volunteer or get involved in the community, it can also mobilize more intrinsic motivations that instill a sense of duty to serve others, as Father José pointed out at the beginning of the chapter.[27] This is not just a one-time mobilization, but something more heartfelt and lasting that is seen as a part of what it means to be devoutly Catholic.

In April, for example, people around the United States participated in National Volunteer Week. In Houston, many of the first-generation Filipino Americans interviewed took part in several projects at St. Catherine's that coincided with this week. When I asked them about National Volunteer Week, most did not know about it. Shirley, for example, told me she was just helping out and did not know about the national events. "The fact that it is part of something bigger is just a bonus I suppose." Covering these events, but not mentioning Filipinos specifically, an editorial in the *Texas Catholic Herald* suggested, "For Catholics, rolling up sleeves to do volunteer work is about more than helping others . . . It's about fulfilling a commitment made at Baptism."[28] First-generation Filipino Americans appear to exemplify this commitment, particularly those who are religiously active. They are morally bound to serve the Church and demonstrate this through their involvement in parish programs and projects. However, St. Catherine's depends as much on their organized groups within the parish as it does on them individually.

Pointing this out, Father José explained that the various religious groups within the parish are an important part of St. Catherine's ability to organize programs and events. "I am just the ringmaster sometimes." Continuing, he also explained,

> Their religious groups [Filipino Americans] are a big help to the parish spiritually beyond being a source I can call on for contact and projects. That is why we have the groups in the parish. It helps the members to grow, to grow in their knowledge and their faith and their appreciation of their faith. It's a good thing. When we have Stewardship Sunday or host the stewardship ministries, they are all there and are part of our social ministries. Sometimes they have tables and booths of their own. So many depend on us and what we do through the Church but we cannot do it alone. We need partners.

Turning to these partners in the following pages, the remainder of the chapter explores the role of Catholicism in first-generation Filipino American community life through religious groups and fellowships. It highlights two cases, Bibingka and Couples for Christ. In some situations, participation in these groups facilitates community or parish involvement, as Father José pointed out. In other situations, these groups can become the focus of their community life, and thus deter first-generation Filipino Americans from parish or wider community projects. Beyond describing how Filipino Americans get involved in the community through these groups, the following sections also explore what getting involved in the community means to first-generation Filipino Americans within them and the ways in which a uniquely Catholic and Filipino expression of care can engage Filipinos in projects that transcend communities and national borders.

MANY GROUPS, MANY CAUSES

On any given Friday night, the fellowship in religious groups such as Bibingka demonstrate how first-generation Filipino Americans' Catholic faith and devotional practices can engender a sense of civic responsibility. They also further demonstrate where the opportunity to become involved in civic life can often originate. After praying the Rosary and singing several hymns, the members of Bibingka typically read a selection of scripture from the Bible and then reflect on it based on their own personal experiences and perspectives. Although the scripture readings change from week to week, the subject often centers on themes such as "living your faith" or "putting faith into action." Doctrinally, these themes are not unique among Catholics, but they are interpreted through purely Filipino lenses and what they mean to the group as Filipino Catholics living in the United States.

"I really don't understand this country sometimes," stated Adler. "My coworker complains about taking care of his parents and is thinking about putting them in a nursing home." Continuing, Adler questioned this from both a Filipino and Catholic perspective. "They raise us and care for us. How can anyone put them into a home? Children should take care of their parents; they should be in our homes and lives. That is the Filipino way, but I also think it is what God would ask of us, am I right?" Responding, Jun agreed, but then joked, "Perhaps it's the fault of Filipino nurses—we love their parents more than they do." Rose, a Filipina nurse herself, disagreed with Jun and explained, "We don't love them more, many of them [adult children of parents] just can't do it or they don't understand how giving care, no matter how difficult it may be, is doing God's work." Trying to motivate the group to open up even more to discussing the theme of living one's faith, Rose stated that her care for those in the hospital is not just a job, but a way to live the values they discuss every Friday night.

Applauding Rose's words with a resounding "Amen," Stan agreed and added, "We must be able to see where our faith matters, put it in context or question if it is irrelevant." Continuing, Stan said that this was of central importance to the group. "We come here to pray for Lola Louise and direct our faith towards her healing. This is what brought us together, but we also need to ask ourselves if our faith is growing . . . are we putting it into action, are we living the faith and seeing where all of this matters in our lives." As each member shared what the scripture reading meant to them and how they see their week and lives more generally, they began to talk about their projects in the community and what God would want them to do in each case. Adler, looking to lighten the mood a bit after an hour of serious contemplation, pointed out, "You know I was lucky this week, and although I did not see it then, my actions are important—God is watching, and I am thankful he caught me in a good moment!" Everyone laughed, but as the laughter came to calm, Cheryl offered one last message through prayer before the group broke for its midnight snack. "Lord, help us do your will, help us put our faith in action and bless our efforts as we attempt to build a community and lives worthy of your Son's love. Mother Mary protect us, lead us to your Son and guide us in as we do what is right for our communities in his name." With another resounding "Amen," the group adjourned to the kitchen.

After eating and enjoying each other's company over discussions that ranged from jokes to light-hearted debates over politics in the Philippines, the group slowly split into smaller groups throughout the house. Although this did not seem to be planned, various members of the group spontaneously gathered people around themselves to discuss projects and business. Working my way through the house, I found that the conversations centered on everything from collecting money for buying a birthday present for a member of Bibingka to recruiting help for other groups and causes.[29] At one end of the house, for example, Fred announced, "Okay guys, so you are going to be at the church [St. Catherine's] Saturday right? We [PAMAT] need your help!" While a few offered reasons why they could not be there, most said they would help. No sign-up sheets were passed around, but a contract of sorts was made. In the kitchen, Angie announced that the Legion of Mary and Our Lady of Lourdes prayer groups will be collecting food and clothes for her parish ministries. Responding, Jun, in whose house the fellowship was being held, immediately went to the pantry and pulled out a bag of canned goods to donate.

In the living room, Lyn reminded everyone that the San Lorenzo Ruiz de Manila center was going to have a fundraiser the next Saturday night. Overhearing this, Jake, who had been talking to Fred about helping PAMAT at St. Catherine's, asked Lyn, "How are we supposed to do both?" Replying, Lyn stated that the PAMAT event was during the day and the fundraiser was at night. "You don't have to come but I will be baking hopia." Jake, laughing a bit, then stated, "Well I guess I have to be there, now, don't I." Although lighthearted, this exchange is yet another example of how food does not just fill bellies at these gatherings. Food can act as a social lubricant. It is the *grasa* (Ta) or grease that often facilitates conversation and creates a comfortable atmosphere that can seal a deal or insure that people will help in any given cause.[30]

Most of the members of Bibingka are members of multiple groups and causes outside of their Friday fellowship. They are also members of several local parish churches. Jun, as an example, is an avid volunteer at St. Michael's Catholic Church and a member of Texas Association of Mapua Alumni. Before Jun's wife Louise became ill, the two of them were very active in the Houston Bicolano association as well as active tennis enthusiasts in a local club. After Louise became ill, this changed. Jun and Louise still maintain their contacts and even get out to an occasional community function, but not as frequently. Fred, on the other hand, is a Mason and an active member of St. Catherine's Catholic Church. He and his wife Alice are very involved in both the parish and the wider Filipino American community. Alice, like Lyn, as an example, frequently bakes for community fundraisers. Likewise, other members such as Jake and his wife Dina are members of St. Michael's and frequently help out in the parish in addition to singing at church events and fundraisers. And these are but a few examples.

Like Bibingka's fellowship, Friday night gatherings in Couples for Christ households equally inspire their members to live their faith and actively engage their community. Although their fellowship is a bit more structured within the broader international scope of CFC's programs, the messages are often centered on the same themes—"living one's faith" or "putting one's faith into action." Explaining this, John stated that after eight years in the CFC community he could not think of a single reason why anyone would not be "inspired or challenged" to get more involved helping others. "For us, community life either parish-wise or CFC-wise has always been in one of our top priorities." Continuing, he suggested that through CFC, "We experience firsthand the shift, gradual and drastic, of our values and way of life. . . . In the [CFC] community we learned that the more we give ourselves, the more life becomes vibrant and fulfilling. It is through this premise that my wife and I along with the many members who experience the liberation from life's mundane existence, make ourselves available for God's work." This sentiment was shared by most of the first-generation Filipino American members of CFC interviewed.

Lita, for example, stated she was not nearly as active in her parish or community before she joined CFC. "I helped out in my kid's PTA and helped the parish food drives, but that all has a different meaning now—I see things differently now and do more." Agreeing with Lita, Dan, her husband who was sitting next to her during our conversation, stated, "I believe that there are several stages in the realization of community. . . . When I first joined the CFC community, I started not littering, I learned to volunteer, as you put it, and got more involved in the school. I started to lead people in prayer and support others emotionally whether they were a part of the community or not. I started giving and helping more to the poor, including the homeless, through Gawad Kalinga." Unlike Bibingka,

CFC is involved in rather large civic projects such as Gawad Kalinga (GK) that not only transcend national boarders but engage first-generation Filipino Americans extensively across them.

Many of the members of CFC interviewed, at least prior to the international group officially splitting over GK, not only helped to raise money for GK projects but frequently built homes in GK villages while vacationing in the Philippines. Highlighting this, Mark, explained, "Home is where the heart is. We now live in the U.S. but still consider the Philippines our homeland. The miracle which brought my wife and I together in the U.S. came from the same God who tells us to support Gawad Kalinga all out." In some cases these projects are the sole reason that first-generation Filipino Americans remained in CFC. Tim, for example, stated, "Gawad Kalinga put a meaning to the CFC community. I believe my wife and I would not have stayed in the CFC community if we did not see that it is meant for the good of the less fortunate." This explains, at least in part, how GK has been so successful in mobilizing the Filipino diaspora.[31] It is also yet another example of how CFC instills a belief in its members that "Faith is empty without works," as Kristi, Mark's husband, describes it.

Beyond inspiring its members to get involved in their local community and transnational projects in the Philippines such as Gawad Kalinga, many of the members of CFC suggested they were not well educated in their Catholic faith before joining CFC and stated that this was at one point a major barrier to their civic life. Vera, a first-generation nurse and long-time member of CFC, for example, explained she was born in a Catholic nation, the Philippines, raised in a Catholic household, and even attended a Catholic university, but was not really knowledgeable about her faith until she went through the CFC's Christian Life Program with her husband.

> With CFC, yeah it changed; it has more of a fond meaning now. I study the various parts of the mass and am more appreciative of it than before; so I would say it's a change spiritually, intellectually, and that is what the changes are all about. . . . I have a different attitude than before because with CFC it's faith through service. You can't just pray and pray—it's faith plus work. Your faith must be demonstrated by actions and services; so I have a better attitude towards service now. I am more willing to serve than before because now I know the reason behind it and why we do it and why we should help other people.

Unlike the lay-led Bible study in Bibingka, CFC's Christian Life Program is part of a larger international effort to educate Catholics and engage them in their communities. This by no means suggests it is more effective at doing either, but highlights the fact that while both are lay led, there are considerable difference in the size and scope of these groups.

Does Group Size Matter?

Church leaders such as Father José at St. Catherine's believe that these groups, regardless of their size, allow first-generation Filipino Americans to deepen their Catholic faith through their own cultural understandings and practices. He believes that these groups are a vital part of St. Catherine's mission to reach its diverse parish, and he depends on them to help run the parish's numerous programs and projects. He also depends on these groups to help facilitate events surrounding religious celebrations such as Simbang Gabi that emphasize Filipino Catholic traditions and broader events such as Flores de Mayo that link multiple ethnic groups within the parish. However, considerable debate still exists among the clergy about the cumulative impact of these groups on the religious and civic life of their parishioners. This is particularly true of their opinions of CFC.

Father Roberto at St. Stephen's, for example, questions the loyalty of first-generation Filipino Americans to groups such as Couples for Christ and believes that they have established independent identities that deter them from getting involved in their parishes. "Couples for Christ is like its own church . . . they have their own leaders and their own projects that are not necessarily in keeping with the Church. They say they are Catholic but if faced with a choice, they would choose CFC versus answering the call of the Church." Continuing, Father Roberto explained that groups such as CFC that are large and have developed international organization can present certain challenges to the Church and its authority. "This CFC is an international Catholic movement that wants the blessing of the Church but GK [Gawad Kalinga] shows you that they can choose to ignore her [the Church's] teachings. We can offer advice, but they will eventually do what they want and that is not a good role model for Catholics."[32] When I asked Father Roberto if these issues were unique to CFC, he told me "No," but also stated that CFC was the "most extreme case."

When I spoke with Father José, he did not agree with Father Roberto's assessment of CFC and repeatedly stated that he considers them and other large groups to be important partners in his parish's service to the community. While it is true the Church has very little authority or control over these groups beyond their moral commitments as Catholics, this does not mean they are not engaged in the parish or the broader community.[33] Just as each of these groups can have its own special ethnic or regional devotions, each of them also varies both in size and the scope of its involvement in their parishes and communities.

In general, first-generation Filipino Americans who are members of these religious groups are more likely to be engaged in other groups and take part in community projects—and this not unique to Filipinos, as many scholars of American civic life have repeatedly pointed out.[34] Drawing again on survey data, Figure 4 illustrates that 70 percent of first-generation Filipino American Catholics who are members of religious groups stated that they had volunteered in the previous twelve months, compared to only 54 percent who were not members

Member of Religious Group

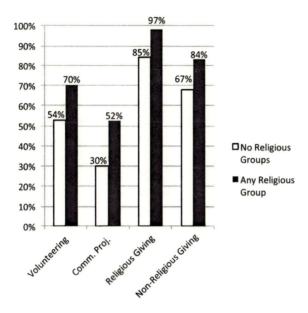

Figure 4 Percentage of First-Generation Filipino Americans in Houston Engaged in the Community by Religious Group. *Source:* The Houston Filipino American Survey 2010; see Methodological Appendix for further details.

of a religious group, a 16 percent difference. Once again, while these percentages may be lower than the actual rates, given the use of the word "volunteer," there is still a sizable difference.

Looking at other forms of engagement, 52 percent of first-generation Filipino American Catholics who are members of religious groups stated that they had worked on a community project in the last twelve months, compared to only 30 percent of those who were not a member. This represents a 22 percent difference. Like the other indicators of religiosity (see Figure 3), the difference between those who gave money to both religious and nonreligious causes and institutions was not large, but still significant.

Ultimately the size of groups such as Bibingka and CFC does matter, as Father Roberto alluded to, but not necessarily in the way he suggested. Both Bibingka and CFC have a membership of over ten people, but do not exceed twenty to thirty members for any given Friday night fellowship. This suggests the groups are small enough to make decisions and encourage interaction but also large enough to convince members they can make a difference in the wider community. Bibingka and CFC both clearly make a difference in their communities and parishes, whether it is through raising money for causes, volunteering their time for projects, or cooking for community events. However, among the six religious groups surveyed in this study, members of Bibingka, the smallest group in terms of membership, were the least likely to volunteer. Of Bibingka's members, 50 percent stated that they had volunteered in the previous twelve months, compared to an average of 75 percent among the other five groups.[35] Members of Bibingka were also the least likely to work on a community project. Of the members, 30 percent stated they worked on a project, compared to an average of 62 percent among the other groups. Members of CFC were neither at the top nor the bottom of either domain. Although this complicates the picture of what scholars of American civic life might expect to find, it highlights the dynamic forces that make each of these groups unique. In both case, it is important to point out that members of these religious groups are engaged in their community more than those who are not members these types of groups. Any differences between them may be attributed to the availability of resources and opportunities that each group brings to the civic sphere. They may also depend on the ways in which first-generation Filipino Americans view what they do in the community and the words they use to describe it, as we have seen.

Conclusion

Whether it is nurses volunteering at medical booths or members of local prayer groups such as Lyn cooking pastries for fundraisers at the San Lorenzo Ruiz de Manila Center, Filipino Americans are an active and important part of community and parish life in the city of Houston. Without them, large-scale events such as the Alief Health and Civic resource fair would not be nearly as successful, nor would smaller parish food drives and various community projects and programs. Churches such as St. Catherine's stand at the center of Filipino American civic life. Although first-generation Filipino Americans have built their own independent centers and have established numerous voluntary civic associations, these efforts cannot match the resources and opportunities that the archdiocese can and does present for Filipino American civic life. Calling on first-generation Filipino Americans to work collaboratively across their own diversity and that of the wider parish, institutional mechanisms, such as representative parish councils, allow the Church to draw parishioners together for projects and programs that extend well beyond any one parish or ethnic community. As a result, the Church is more than the center of the Filipino American community. It is in many respects the civic link or series of networks that engage Filipino immigrants and others in the wider city of Houston through concerns and needs that are not necessarily their own.

This is not to say that other groups and associations do not animate Filipino American civic life; they do. Groups such as CFC, for example, contribute a great deal to the civic aims of their local churches. They also further engage Filipino

Americans in projects such as Gawad Kalinga that transcend parish and national boundaries. However, the point is that many Filipino Americans are most active in their Catholic churches or groups associated with them, and hence, the Church is perhaps the easiest or most established way for them to get involved in the community. Both survey results and observations in the community confirm this. First-generation Filipino Americans who frequently attend mass and participate in the parish beyond service are the most involved in community projects. They are also the most likely to state they have volunteered in the last twelve months. Where previous studies have suggested that Asian American Catholics may face certain internal concerns or barriers that limit their community life, this is not the case for Filipino immigrants in this study. Internal concerns are mediated by the Church, as we have seen in previous chapters, and any barriers are largely overcome by insuring that each project or program is supported by multiple partners, groups, and communities.

Messages of community service are indeed being conveyed well to Filipinos in these parishes, and they are acting on them. Far from being secluded to ethnic enclaves or their own community concerns, Filipino immigrants are engaged because the Church calls on them as a part of the Catholic family to do so. They are morally bound not just as Filipino Catholics but also as American Catholics. Similar to what other scholars have found among other American Catholic immigrant populations, the American Catholic Church supports Filipinos' diverse and unique cultural traditions but at the same time calls on them to act collectively as American Catholics.[36] By doing so, the Church hopes to unite all people in the parish as an extended family by building cultural frameworks that instill in them a deep communitarian ethic. Regardless of sex, race, ethnicity, or even nativity, the Church, at least in Houston, has been quite successful at doing this.

This said, what Filipino Americans actually do in these projects and programs is not always seen by them as volunteering or being civically active. It is often seen as simply "helping out" or "giving care" to others. At the center of this view of caring for the community is an understanding that family extends beyond the biological to encompass a more universal understanding of family. Helping your fellow brothers and sisters is thus not always considered volunteerism. Given Filipino Americans' rather formal definition of volunteerism and civic involvement, it is not inconceivable that national rates of Filipino American volunteerism may be underreported.[37] This may partially explain why some scholars have found a discrepancy between the volunteerism of Asian American Catholics and Protestants.[38] At the same time, these discrepancies may also be a matter of place, where social scientists often think of volunteerism occurring. Members of CFC who participate in GK projects, for example, may not register their efforts in the Philippines as volunteerism but rather something they simply did to help out their hometown while on vacation in the Philippines. In fact, many of the members of CFC interviewed during this study often scheduled working on GK projects during their vacations back home and never describe these trips or their labors in building GK villages as a form of civic engagement.

The rich civic lives presented in this chapter and the devout faith that drives them provide some of several possible answers to where immigrants fit into American civic life. Immigration policy remains one of the greatest debates of our time. Although largely driven by fears that the continued growth of foreign-born populations will cause lower wages or worsened conditions for American-born workers,[39] issues have also been raised over the assimilability of new immigrants.[40] Both scholars and social pundits question how, if at all, new immigrants will contribute to or give back to their new American communities. The answer, at least in the Filipino case, is quite clear. Filipinos are giving back and at rates that exceed those of native-born Americans. If you consider that roughly 27 percent of Americans volunteer, the Filipinos surveyed in this study are volunteering at rates nearly double this percentage.[41]

This is important. However, more than demonstrating that new immigrants are civically engaged beyond their own ethnic communities, the civic lives presented in this chapter also provide a measure of insight into what some scholars have defined as the puzzle of American Catholic civic life. If Filipino Catholic immigrants are not actively seeking to be recognized by the wider public for their civic efforts and do not consider what they are doing as volunteerism or civic engagement, then it is not surprising our view of their civic lives up to this point has been somewhat skewed. This is particularly true in cases where the analysis of larger national data collections do not account for their unique understandings of "giving care" to their communities. First-generation Filipino American Catholics, as evidenced in this chapter, are very civically active. They are also poised to be an important part of the future of American civil life as they continue to engage their cultural understandings of faith and family.

Exploring this importance further, the next chapter demonstrates how the centrality of Catholic cultural frameworks not only shapes first-generation Filipino Americans' views on family values, gay marriage, and abortion but also compels them to take action on these issues. Providing an immigrant perspective on American civil society, the chapter analyzes how first-generation Filipino Americans view the role of Catholicism in American politics. It also explores how they view their own impact on American politics as they engage issues such as immigration reform and the right to life.

CHAPTER 7

PROTECTING
FAMILY AND LIFE

When President Bush announced that one of the top priorities of his second term was to reform the nation's immigration policy by granting millions of undocumented workers the opportunity to attain legal status, the Catholic Church applauded the move but also knew that Republicans in the House, members of Bush's own party, were staunchly against the idea or any other reforms that would establish a guest-worker program.[1] With the realization that House Resolution 4437 was also gaining momentum and could threaten the way the Church served its parish and the community by prosecuting those who aid or help undocumented immigrants, the Church began a national campaign to educate its parishioners about these issues and engage them further in the immigration debate.[2] In Houston, a battleground in the nation's ongoing immigration debate, the Galveston-Houston archdiocese called on its priests to speak out on the issue, conduct workshops for its parishioners, and challenge their congregations to do more. The local *Texas Catholic Herald* also ran a series of articles that not only carved out where the Church stood on immigration but highlighted the threat new legislation, specifically House Resolution 4437, could pose to good Catholics engaged in acts of charity across the nation.

At St. Catherine's Catholic Church, a church with one of the largest and most diverse immigrant populations in the archdiocese, Father José made immigration the focus of several of his homilies throughout the year. On one Sunday, Father José dedicated the entire mass to addressing the immigration debate and HR 4437 specifically. Toward the beginning of the mass, Father José invited Bryan, a representative from the Justice for Immigrants organization, to the pulpit. While introducing Bryan, Father José told the congregation that it must be sensitive and think compassionately about the nation's ongoing immigration debate. "I know this can be a sensitive topic, but we must address it with an open mind and then fill that mind with the understanding of what we as Catholics are charged to do. We are bound by God to uphold and protect his family. God's family and kingdom has no borders and does not require a visa or a passport." Agreeing, as Father José stepped aside, Bryan began to talk to the congregation about what they could do to inform themselves better about what was going on and where the Church stood.

Directing parishioners to the website for Justice for Immigrants for further information, Bryan then stated there were four simple steps everyone could take to help improve the lives of immigrants and stabilize the nation's borders.[3] First, he suggested that everyone should purchase "fair trade goods" that were produced with transparency and respect to the people who labored to make them. Second, he suggested that people should get to know their congregation and parish better by developing relationships with its diverse population. "Some of us here today are undocumented or live with the threat that our visas may run out soon—these people are our neighbors and our fellow parishioners. We must learn about their struggles or how these issues affect their families." Third, following the same theme, Bryan suggested that anyone who knew an immigrant who was either struggling or in a desperate situation, should refer them to legal clinics such as those held at the St. Frances Cabrini Immigrant Legal Assistance Center.[4] Fourth, and finally, he suggested that people should look in their own backyards. "Ask yourself, do you know or hire workers that are illegal?"[5]

The point of much of Bryan's talk was not to cease giving charity to those in the parish or community who were undocumented immigrants, but to actually increase it despite the threat of HR 4437. He suggested that immigration affects us all economically, politically, and spiritually. "Under this new legislation Father José could get prosecuted for simply serving Holy Communion to his parishioners, but I know that is not going to stop him from doing what is right—we are one family under God." Quoting Cardinals McCarrick and Mahoney, Bryan went on to remark, "Our diverse faith traditions teach us to welcome our brothers and sisters with love and compassion—this is our duty and responsibility as Catholics."[6] Bryan then concluded by singing a hymn in Spanish, accompanied by guitar, and passing out prepaid and preaddressed postcards to Senators John Cornyn and Kay Bailey Hutchinson with a form letter on the immigration issue. Bryan then stated, "Read the card, sign it if you agree, and then mail it to your senator—make your voice heard." The cards, which were the same as those mailed out in the *Texas Catholic Herald* in prior months, stated:

Dear Senator,
Our immigration system is broken. Comprehensive immigration reform is needed now! I ask you to oppose HR 4437. I ask you to support comprehensive immigration reform as described in bill SB 1033, proposed by McCain and Kennedy. I urge you to conduct the immigration reform

debate in a civil and respectful manner, mindful not to blame immigrants for social or economic ills or for the atrocities committed by those who have carried out acts of terrorism.

Respectfully Yours,

_____ sign here[7]

After an attendant collected cards from members of the congregation who had already signed them, the remainder of the mass followed in usual fashion until Father José's homily.

Calling on the congregation to recall the words of Mathew 25:35, "I was a stranger and you welcomed me," Father José then asked, "What would Christ have us do?" Continuing, he rhetorically asked, "Are we not to give compassion to our fellow brothers and sisters in need? Think of the love he has shown the world. These immigrants are members of the parish and children of God! We are charged as Catholics to love our neighbors without condition. It does not matter where they came from or what their situation may be." Echoing a sense of moral obligation and an edict of divine love, Father José's message was clear. Like Bryan, he implored the congregation to think about what they could do to make a difference.

After the mass, some parishioners, including some Filipino Americans, stated that they saw the issue as a so-called "Mexican problem" and not one pressing their own communities in Houston. The majority, however, praised Father José's earnestness and suggested they wanted to help. One Filipina with whom I spoke, for example, pointed out, "Being an immigrant myself, I could sympathize with the immigrants' plight. Most of them are honest, hard-working people and contribute to the country's economy." Continuing, she stated that she wanted to get more involved in helping her fellow immigrants in the parish because "that is what a good Catholic should do," but she also pointed out, "I came through the legal system, which diminishes my sympathy for them. This is a big issue in the Filipino community, especially in California, where there is an enormous number of illegals. They are family and deserve our care, but it is complicated and I have mixed feelings about it." These thoughts reflected the sentiments of many Filipino Americans interviewed after the mass. Most agreed with Father José and what was printed on the cards Bryan passed out. Helen, for example, simply stated that "We must do something and we must change the system, it is not fair no matter how you look at it!"

Many were also quick to point out that in California there are a number of legal-permit Filipinos who have stayed beyond their time and are now TNT— *tago ng tago* (Ta)—that is, "playing hide and seek" with immigration authorities. Others, while somewhat reserved in what they would say, suggested that the situation in Houston is not very different. Dora, for example, who is well connected to the Philippine Consulate in California, openly stated that there may be as many as 10,000 undocumented Filipinos in Houston, according to her sources. "They are mostly domestic workers but in home health care. If their tourist visa is approved they just don't go home [to the Philippines], so they are undocumented health workers and then they use their relatives' social security numbers. They also work in Houston hotels, bakeries, and restaurants. My friend employs six undocumented workers. They are good workers and good Catholics." Continuing, she explained, "Some of them stay at my house sometimes. We play cards until three A.M. and talk about life and home [Philippines]. . . . On Tuesdays I usually pick them up after their mid-day duties and take them to Blessed Sacrament. Other times in the week we get together and pray the Rosary to the Blessed Mother. On Sundays I also take them to mass. This is what Father asks of us. They are Filipinos, they are Catholics, and they are our family too."

A POLITICAL FOCUS ON FAITH AND FAMILY

Although most of the Filipino Americans interviewed were not quite as candid as Dora about their knowledge of and or support of undocumented Filipinos in Houston, many had their own stories to tell. Some admitted they had at one point overstayed their own visas en route to gaining citizenship. Others talked about friends or family they knew who were TNT. Most preferred to talk about the current situation in California and their fears for family and friends who either want to come to the United States or those who are already here and trying to gain citizenship. Pia, for example, asked me if I had been reading the news about the Cuevas family, who were recently deported in California. "It could happen to any of our families—it is a real concern and most Americans don't even know." Continuing, Pia explained, "It is not just a Mexican issue like some might tell you; this country is getting unwelcoming to immigrants including those of us who are legal and keeping the hospitals running—it is just wrong what is happening." What Pia was referring to was the fact that over a multiple-year period, from 2001 to 2003, the number of Filipino immigrants deported rose by 65 percent. In cases of deportation considered noncriminal, not a result of a crime or national security risk, the increase was 134 percent over the same period, and this trend continued for several years.[8]

Among the more publicized deportation cases was that of the Cuevas family in 2004. The Cuevas family had been in the United States since the early 1980s on visitor visas, and during this time they were able to secure jobs and overstayed their visas some ten years. Despite the fact that the Cuevases had hired an attorney to act on their behalf with the INS (Immigration and Naturalization Services) to officially apply for citizenship well prior to their troubles in 2004, the attempt to legalize their status was never heard, and the stiffening of laws during a time of national crisis after September 11 made the case rather difficult to adjudicate. For many Filipino Americans the timing of the deportation, including eighty-nine other Filipinos a week later, was more than coincidental. Pointing to this, the Gabriela Network (General Assembly Binding [Women] for Reform, Integrity, Equality, and Action), a Filipina organization for social justice noted:

> Just hours after the Philippine government's decision to save the life of a Fili-
> pino overseas worker by withdrawing its troops from Iraq, the Bush govern-
> ment abruptly deported Filipinos from the U.S. . . . Despite official claims that
> the deportations were "routine," the action was obviously both retaliation and
> threat. Just as his Iraqi captors used Angelo de la Cruz to pressure Philippine
> government policy, it would seem that the U.S. government is also using Fili-
> pinos residing and working in the United States as pressure points to bring
> the Philippine government to its knees. . . . The effect has been to terrorize
> Filipinos in the United States. Rumors, reports and tales of woe concerning the
> deportations panicked the community. With more than half of the community
> comprised of immigrants, documented and undocumented.[9]

Beyond just editorializing, the rising number of Filipinos deported was indeed a legitimate and growing concern for many Filipino Americans interviewed in Houston.[10] However, it was not the only concern they expressed to me after Father José and Bryan spoke at mass.

Many of the Filipino Americans interviewed later in the parish hall stated that they felt the world had changed for the worse after the terrorists attacks of September 11.[11] They suggested that there were a host of issues both here in the United States and in the Philippines that concerned them beyond just immigra-tion. Maricel and Tony Reyes, for example, stated, "The key issues that concern us the most are about life and things that affect the family—these are not things that just affect people here in the States." Agreeing with them, Julius, who was sitting at the table next to us, stated, "Immigration is just one of many problems." As we continued to talk, he explained, "Father José is right to draw attention to the issue, but there are several things that concern me about the world right now." Broadening the scope of our conversation, Julius suggested, "We have lost our focus on the family. Immigration is a family issue, just as abortion, and the rights of those who lack the care they need. All of these are part of a larger life issue and our rights as humans. We have to keep this in mind. My family is not just here but in the Philippines. Our nation is poor, that is why we come here. As Catholics, we need to see humanity as a global family and take on political matu-rity to do what is right here and there [Philippines] or wherever people need help." Julius and the Reyes family's concerns were not unique among Filipino Americans interviewed. Most were concerned about immigration but were also quick to point out that immigration is tied to a host of global issues on which they believe Catholics are compelled to take action.[12] Drawing attention to this, Dan, a member of Couples for Christ and St. Catherine's, explained, "Although the Church does not make me do anything, it teaches that every issue has a moral dimension. . . . In the end it is up to the member who decides what to do!"

Through homilies, special programs, newsletters, and papal encyclicals, among other sources, the Church directs its parishioners to engage in politics on its behalf and for the betterment of the Catholic family. Highlighting this, an editorial in the *Texas Catholic Herald* during this time made it clear not only why the Church was engaging American politics on issues such as abortion and immigration but how parishioners should also get involved:

> The Church wishes to help form conscience in political life and to stimulate greater insight into the authentic requirements of justice as well as greater readiness to act accordingly, even when this might involve conflict with situations of personal interests. . . . Yet at the same time, she [the Church] cannot and must not remain in the sidelines in the fight for justice. She has to play her part through rational argument, and she has to reawaken the spiritual energy without which justice, which always demands sacrifice, cannot prevail and prosper. A just society must be the achievement of politics, not of the Church. Yet the promotion of justice through efforts to bring about openness of mind and will to demands of the common good is something which concerns the Church deeply. . . . Believers are called to become informed, active, and responsible participants in the political process. As the Catechism states—know the facts, consult church documents and theologians, and pray for guidance.[13]

While the Church clearly does not force Filipino Americans or anyone else to act on these issues, as Dan noted, messages like the one above are being conveyed to them through a host of sources, including respected clergy members such as Father José. There is no true separation of church and state as far as the Church sees it. As a result, Filipinos feel obligated to take action on these issues because this is what good Catholics should do.

Elaborating on this point, Angie, a member of the religious group Bibingka, stated that the issues that are most important to her and the group's discussions are "pro-life issues like abortion, euthanasia, human cloning, and stem-cell research." When I asked her if her Catholic faith or the Church shapes her opinions on these issues, she emphatically stated, "Definitely! Our religion plays an important role in the decisions we make and the choices we make in our politics. It is up to us to protect life through our actions and those we elect. It is really our duty as Catholics to protect the family." Like Angie, Mel, who is also a member of Bibingka, stated, "Life issues that affect the sanctity of the family unit are very important to us Filipinos." Continuing, he went on to explain, "We might not make the news but in the crowds that are protesting HR 4437, we are there and we were at the capitol marching for life too—we are part of a larger Catholic voice and we make a difference."

It is true that Filipino Americans did not receive much press outside their own ethnic newspapers during these events, but they were there, as Mel noted. Perhaps their comparatively small numbers were overshadowed by other groups, namely Latinos. Perhaps they were even misidentified as Latinos, given their Spanish surnames. Whatever the case may have been, they were there, and as one Filipino told a reporter for the *Filipino-Express* while protesting HR 4437 at City Hall in New York, "Latinos are not the only ones affected by these immigration reform proposals. . . . Asians, especially Filipinos, have a stake in these bills as well."[14] Beyond simply being an issue that impacts the Filipino American community, immigration is a Catholic issue and one in which Filipino Americans feel morally obligated to lend their voice. Some voices, such as that of Bishop Solis of Los Angles, the first Filipino bishop in the United States and head of the national steering committee for Justice for Immigrants, may be heard louder and farther than those of other Filipinos, but this does not mean they are not collectively making a difference outside of the efforts of the Church itself.

Belle, a new resident of Houston and parishioner at St. Catherine's, for example, noted that she believes Filipino American Catholics are having a "big impact" on American politics both inside and outside the Church. "We have Bishop Solis, but it's not the same as clergy rising up the way Cardinal Sin did on Radio Veritas during the People Power movement."[15] "His leadership matters," she explained, but also noted,

> here [in Houston] and in Chicago, my old home, at least, one does not have to be clergy to convince and mobilize people to their cause. . . . We were Catholic before we came here and we were Catholic before the U.S. was even a nation. We know right from wrong. . . . There is also the argument however that you fight using the tools that the government uses; so, for one, you can call or write your legislator as often as you want and get everyone else to do it too. You can also vote and protest to make your voice heard. We are fortunate that we live in a nation where the tools God gave us can be put to use.

Turning to these tools, as Belle describes them, the remainder of the chapter explores the various ways in which Filipino Americans engage American politics and make their voices heard on issues beyond immigration. Whether it is through voting in presidential elections, writing letters and signing petitions, or even protesting against abortion, as Mel briefly alluded to, this chapter analyzes how Filipino Americans, although only part of a much larger voice, are attempting to shape policies they believe are threatening the sanctity of the family or go against the teaching of the Catholic Church. It demonstrates how Filipino American Catholics' conservative cultural and institutional understandings of family have the potential to push broader local and even national communities, Filipino or not, to enact more conservative policies or take political action to voice their views.

PRESIDENT FOR LIFE

Historically, Filipino Americans have voted for Democrats in national and local elections or at least leaned toward the Democratic Party.[16] They overwhelmingly supported Bill Clinton throughout both his terms, for example, and Clinton's appointment of several Filipino Americans to positions within his administrations further solidified the community's support for the Democratic Party for over a decade.[17] In the 2000 presidential election, Filipino Americans also overwhelmingly voted for Gore, a Democrat and Clinton's former vice president.[18] However, the community's support for Democrats waned in 2004, when John Kerry became the Democratic nominee. While Gore benefited from his ties to the Clinton administration in the 2000 election, Kerry could not rally the same interest among Filipino Americans. It is hard to imagine that things changed so dramatically in just four years, especially with the Democratic nominee being Catholic, but it did.

In the months leading up to the 2004 U.S. presidential election, there was considerable debate in the national Filipino American community over whom to vote for.[19] Unlike previous elections, many Filipino Americans did not support the Democratic candidate forthrightly and were split over a host of issues.[20] As the election drew nearer, they also had serious doubts about the impact the Filipino American community would have on the outcome of the election. Of the five states with the largest Filipino American population—California, Hawaii, New York, New Jersey, and Illinois—Kerry had a running lead, but among Filipinos, making up over 800,000 eligible voters, there was no clear consensus on a candidate outside of a growing distrust of Kerry. Those who staunchly opposed Kerry were also deeply concerned that their vote would not matter in the Electoral College.[21]

In Houston, a key city in Texas's largely Republican electoral base, many Filipino Americans interviewed were confident that their vote for Bush would simply validate the voice of the state. However, with the previous presidential election in 2000 coming down to the wire, decided by fewer than 600 votes, the "one vote matters" campaign seemed to echo loudly among those interviewed. Connie, for example, a member of St. Catherine's and the Our Lady of Lourdes fellowship, pointed out, "We can't let things go the way they did last time, we need to vote—it felt like the elections back home [Philippines]." When I asked her to clarify what she meant by this, she stated, "We can matter here, but back home I'm not sure that is always the case—they always stuff the ballot box and that's how you end up with someone like Marcos."

Connie was not unique in her concern. Even in the national Filipino American community, the election seemed to take on a sense of urgency. Highlighting this, the Filipino social pundit and newspaper columnist Perry Diaz editorialized, "With 1.2 million Filipino-American qualified voters in the entire United States, less than 100,000 Filipino Americans could influence the outcome of the presidential election on November 2, 2004. That's power. Let's use it!"[22] When I asked Filipino Americans in Houston, like Connie, what was fueling this concern or sense of urgency, many told me it was a "matter of life or death." Luis, for example, a member of St. Catherine's and a former member of the parish advisory council stated, "The president is not voted in for life but while he is there, he should protect life not kill it." Continuing, he explained, "You ask any Filipino or good Catholic for that matter and they will tell you they cannot stand by and watch someone who supports abortion get elected."

Many Filipino Americans interviewed stated that Kerry was "taking the Catholic vote for granted." They suggested that while Kerry was Catholic, he did "very little to show it." Key to these perceptions was what many described as "life issues." There was a great deal of concern that if Kerry was elected to office, he would not address issues such as the right-to-life from a purely Catholic doctrinal point of view. Being Catholic did not matter. What mattered was being a good Catholic. Compounding the perceptions that Kerry was not a good Catholic were the actions of Cardinal Ratzinger, who ordered a ban on serving communion to Catholic candidates, such as Kerry, who supported pro-choice positions. Although Ratzinger pointed out this was not done as an act of judgment on any particular candidate, he also stated, "Not all moral issues have the same moral weight as abortion and euthanasia. . . . There may be a legitimate diversity of opinion among Catholics about waging war and applying the death penalty, but not, however, with regards to abortion and euthanasia."[23] By making this distinction clear, Ratzinger, and the Church more generally, did inadvertently endorse Bush and sent a clear message to many Filipino Americans that Kerry was not their candidate of choice—at least that is how those interviewed saw it.

Ratzinger's actions were often the focus of discussions among Filipino Americans after masses at St. Catherine's and in prayer groups such as Bibingka and CFC. Some questioned how the Church could refuse communion to a fellow Catholic. Others feared that a line had been crossed, presenting a real problem for the democratic process. Explaining this, Aaron, a member of St. Catherine's, stated, "I believe in the separation of church and state and I believe that faith should not be a factor in choosing a candidate. Some politicians showcase faith to get elected in America but oppose religion from becoming a major factor in forming other governments such as Iraq and Iran." Aaron went on to suggest that the Church had no place in politics and should "stick to issues of morality."

For most Filipino Americans interviewed, Ratzinger's actions were seen as a clear condemnation of Kerry's faith as a Catholic, even if they disapproved of his not being offered communion. Emphasizing this, Dan, a member of CFC stated, "I have always voted since I became a citizen and faith is a factor . . . anything anti-God, I vote against. . . . I am anti-abortion. I will not vote for that Democrat for this reason!" For many Filipino-Americans interviewed, moral or religious issues appeared to drive them to the polls. Anything "anti-God," at least in terms of how the Church defines it, was cause for getting out the vote and this was different from prior elections. Pointing this out and discussing her own views on Ratzinger's actions, Gale, for example, stated, "I must say that I did not use to vote based on religious beliefs, even back in 2000, but because the candidates and some factions have made moral issues become central, issues like the right-to-life has become the litmus test!" Agreeing, Melvin, Gale's husband, suggested, "I'm not sure how you can be Catholic and pro-choice? Where would we be if Mother Mary got an abortion? Think about it." This moral emphasis appeared to stimulate a religious awakening of sorts in the Houston Filipino American community. Of the 167 first-generation Filipino Americans interviewed who were eligible to vote, 78 percent voted for Bush. Like much of the national Filipino American community, this marked a rather dramatic shift for many from the Democratic Party to the Republican Party.

After the election, this switch was made even clearer. Ray, for example, a staunch Democrat and active member of the local party, lamented, "Let me point you to a simple fact, Asian Americans mostly voted for Kerry in the last election. There is one group that deviated from that, the Filipino Americans. . . . When asked why Filipino Americans instead voted for Bush, a common reply was that Filipino Americans can relate to the Republican definition of moral values—I don't think I have to direct you to my favorite liberal, Bill Maher's interpretation of the Republican definition of moral values, do I?[24] I voted for Kerry but not many of us did." Ray's frustration was not unique to Kerry supporters. Several Filipino Americans interviewed suggested that Kerry simply left them with little choice. Pointing to this, Suzette, asked, "Where is our generation's Kennedy . . . now that was a man you could feel good about voting for." In the end whether it was push, a case of Filipino Americans being repelled by the pro-choice stance of a fellow Catholic, Kerry, or pull, a case of Filipino Americans being attracted to the more conservative positions of Bush, a switch did occur.

Four years later, the Filipino American community's support for Bush began to wane. Frustrated with the economy and the ongoing war in Iraq, Filipino Americans, at least those interviewed in Houston, stated that they were leaning toward voting for a Democrat in the next presidential election. Some suggested that Bush and Cheney did not "walk the talk." Vera, for example, a member of CFC, pointed out that Cheney's daughter was in an open lesbian relationship and this did not sit well with her understanding of the moral values the Bush administration was supposed to support. "He [Bush] should have told Cheney to say something to the effect that he does not condone his daughter's immorality."

Others interviewed, particularly Filipinas, were excited about Hillary Clinton's entrance into the race. Highlighting this, Mercedes, a Filipina nurse, stated, "It's about time we got a woman in office." Continuing, she explained, "If Mother Mary can lead us to Heaven, then maybe Hillary can lead us out of this earthly mess we are in. The Clintons have always supported our community and I don't think that would change this time around. It's like we get a two for one deal—Bill and Hillary." Many Filipinas agreed with or shared similar sentiments. However, while many Filipino Americans, both men and women, were somewhat excited about Hillary's possible nomination, they also expressed concerns about the rumors that Obama was a Muslim.[25] Pointing to this, Ramon, stated, "It's not that I am all that opposed to a Muslim being president, I mean Kerry was supposedly a Catholic, but I'm just ignorant about what Muslims think about right-to-life issues."

When Obama won the nomination and did not select Hillary as his running mate, many Filipino Americans interviewed suggested that they would vote for McCain simply because they knew where he stood on key life issues. As Alice pointed out, "In the end it is about family values and making your voice heard on these issues." Continuing, she stated, "I am anti-abortion. I think killing an unborn child is wrong. Yes, it is my body, but that is being selfish if I am only thinking of my body. A human embryo is life." Heading into the final months of the 2008 election, the Filipino American vote was split somewhat equally between Obama and McCain, but most were undecided.[26] The cause of this indecision, at least among those interviewed, came down to how they felt they could best express the values of their Catholic faith. Raul, for example, a member of St. Catherine's, explained, "It is our duty to make our voice heard—some say the Church should stay out of politics, but who else will speak for those who can't or those who lack the values to say what is true."

VOICES AND VALUES

Throughout the presidential campaigns discussed in the previous pages, Filipino Americans in Houston were seen actively debating the issues at hand in their parishes, homes, associational meetings, and Friday night religious fellowships. Far from being politically disinterested, they demonstrated that they not only had a stake in these elections but were willing to aggressively push others to the polls to vote on matters of faith. Explaining this, Keith, a member of CFC, stated, "I did everything I could to get Filipinos and even my white colleagues at work to the polls during the last election." However, as we continued to talk, Keith pointed out that this was not the only action he took on the issues that were important to him. "It is true that voting really matters and is a powerful tool of democracy, but it's not the only weapon you can fight with and it's not the only thing I've done"

Agreeing with Keith, Jimmy, also member of CFC who joined our discussion at their Friday night fellowship, stated that there were several things members of CFC had done beyond voting to engage issues that are important to them. "Our elders encourage us to contact or be active in evangelization or when you talk to people to ask for support for on the issue of pro-life." Continuing, Jimmy added, "I have written my Congressman several times and I have on a few occasions signed petitions . . . I'm not really sure how effective these are, but I think they serve the good purpose of letting the adversary and society in general know that we're not sleeping, that we stand behind good moral principles . . . and will not be led by default towards the wrong path that the prevailing culture wants us to go." Keith and Jimmy were not unique among the Filipino Americans interviewed. For many Filipino Americans, their faith engenders a moral commitment to issues such as immigration and pro-life that starts within the Church and extends not only to their home devotional and prayer groups but also to their active involvement with like-minded political organizations such as Grassfire Alliance and Justice for Immigrants. These groups serve as an important resource for Filipino Americans who are looking to mobilize on these issues beyond voting. Explaining this, members of both Bibingka and CFC stated that they had signed petitions on pro-life issues from time to time and had forwarded emails and articles from various groups such as Grassfire Alliance to friends and family.[27]

Although members of Bibingka were quick to point out that they tried to keep heated political issues out of their Friday night conversations and only brought up these issues as they pertain to their own members' situations, they also stated that they were more active on these issues throughout the week online. Many pointed out that online blogs and groups had facilitated their involvement on the pro-life issues. Jake, for example, told me that he regularly forwards emails and petitions to the group as well as friends and family about a host of issues that "good Catholics should be concerned about." Others, such as Angie, stated that she had forwarded emails and articles from various groups and added, "I even electronically signed an email petition for the Cuevas family during that horrible ordeal." Like Jimmy in CFC, both Angie and Jake admitted that they were not sure how effective these petitions were. Others such as Janis added, "It at least makes me feel like I am making my voice heard on these issues." Continuing, she explained, "Sometimes I don't want to raise these issues on Friday, but online I can just forward something and say you all might want to read this—it's more of a suggestion."

While members of Bibingka, such as Jake and Angie, seemed to be a bit more reserved in discussing political issues within the group face to face or in the petitions they forward via email, this was not the case with CFC. Highlighting this, Kristi, a member of CFC and St. Catherine's, stated, "The Fire Society has helped me get the word out on abortion and keeps me up to date on what others are doing around the country." Continuing, she noted, "Sometimes the things I send the group [CFC] set the tone for our fellowship—we always discuss the news and what we can do next to make a difference." When I asked if abortion or pro-life issues were the only issues they discussed, she stated:

> We also talk about other issues as well. We talk about the gay community saying that it was Adam and Eve, not Adam and Steve—I think we got that from a movie or something. We express our thoughts about gays but we aren't trying

to force people not to be gay; there is nothing you can do about that. It's a topic that frankly we really don't talk about but we are against it. If it pops up we discuss it, but I myself don't want to discuss it because I think it could be critical toward people who are gay and they are good people. Perhaps others don't share my thoughts but I have co-workers and friends who are gay and I don't tell them what to do or what is wrong. I'm not going to chastise them because they are gay. I think we should love all of God's children. It doesn't mean we have to agree on everything.

Throughout my conversations with members of CFC, there was a wide range of thought on what counted or could be considered a life issue by the group. Many were split on the issue of gay marriage. Some, like Kristi, considered gay marriage a life issue inasmuch as homosexuals cannot have children as "God intended," but also stated that she did not want to talk personally about the issue. Others, such as Mayee, stated that homosexuality was "anti-family" and added, "Most American Catholics are too liberal when it comes to social issues like gay marriage—that is why we are Couples [emphasizing couples] for Christ; we are a model of what is right."

The one issue that all members of CFC interviewed agreed on and highlighted as the most pressing life issue for the group was abortion. Explaining this, Dave stated, "We can talk about condoms and gay marriage as they relate to what God wants for the model of his family, but what is most disturbing to us as Catholics is the killing of life—we must make it end." Echoing this same sentiment, Evelyn, like Mayee, suggested that CFC was a model of what she believes to be right for life and the family, "As a nurse I can understand why people use them [condoms], but we should be thankful for the children God gives us. . . . My point is that at the least we all don't get abortions. We would support our children if they got pregnant before marriage, but I would hope that we have taught them better." Agreeing, Mark, Kristi's husband, who was sitting next to Evelyn, added, "It is more than just being a model for others, CFC sees itself as a political action movement that can make a difference."

When I asked Mark to explain how CFC was making a difference, he stated, "It starts with being an example like Evelyn said, but we also have a pro-life ministry to make sure we are on the right path to being that model." Continuing, he explained, "Our pro-life ministry [meaning a CFC ministry for pro-life issues] is barely starting here in Houston. Those directly involved with the ministry are currently preparing the groundwork. As far as I know, the committee wants to look at the local CFC community first, as far as its position, understanding, awareness, etcetera on pro-life issues is concerned before making a move outside of the community . . . it's kind of self-house cleaning, if you understand what I mean?" CFC aims to make its community a model of Catholic family and virtue. Although mobilization on pro-life issues outside of the community is being planned, much of their collective action has been either "self-house cleaning," as Mark puts it, or facilitated by other organizations through petitions and letter writing campaigns. However, individual members such as Ernie have been very active in protesting against abortion nationally and have, at least on several occasion, rallied fellow members to join him protesting "in support of life" at the state capital. This was not unique to members of CFC but something shared with other Filipino Americans in other groups and members in various Catholic parishes such as St. Catherine's, all of which made trips to the Texas capital to make their voices heard.[28]

Capitol Crusade

On the first weekend after the thirty-fourth anniversary of Roe v. Wade, Ernie and his wife Sue, both first-generation Filipino Americans and members of Couples for Christ, packed up their car with their four young children, ages twenty-three months through thirteen years old, and headed to Austin to demonstrate their support for life issues and protest abortion. The Mercados had been up since six in the morning and were tired. Getting together snacks, packing extra clothes, and preparing signs for the rally, Ernie later stated he was not sure that his children completely understood the day's events but suggested that involving his children was important to him nonetheless. As Ernie continued to explain what transpired that morning, he stated, "When my wife and I surrendered our lives to God eight and half years ago, we already made a decision that even our kids will be in the battlefield with us." Continuing, he noted, "The younger ones [his children] might not get it, but they know we were doing something together as a family that is important."

Earlier in the week, Ernie and Sue were in Washington, DC at a national pro-life rally. Inspired by what they saw, the Mercados felt compelled to get others to join them in Austin by sending out mass emails to their fellow members in CFC and other Filipino Americans they knew in St. Catherine's parish. Clearly invigorated by their experience, Ernie crafted an email together with Sue that highlighted the power of the event as they saw it. "You know, we saw yesterday that there is a chance! Yes, there is! During the mass at Verizon Center yesterday, [a] throng of people in different age, occupation, vocation, young and old, laity and religious gathered together to worship and bow down to the source of all LIFE! Then in the field [during the march] one could easily sense the hand of God moving the crowd—everyone is at peace and hopeful that one day victory will come! (emphasis in original)" As the email continued, the Mercados not only shared their experience but called on fellow members of CFC specifically to sacrifice their time and join them in Austin, the capital of Texas. "There is a chance! Only if people just like you and me would give our time. Just like what you have done already in the different pillars of CFC, now is the time to show another facet of God's power thru this pillar . . . and so I'm encouraging you to do the same sacrifice that our CFC brothers and sisters did in other states." The email was an open invitation and an emotional plea, but beyond the Cruz and Gonzales families who immediately replied that they would join them, the Mercados later told me that they were not sure at the time how effective their message was going to be.

Impassioned and driven, the Mercados tried to coordinate their plans with other families, but later stated they were not really concerned who joined them. "If it is just the three of us [three families], so be it—at least we are doing all that we can for what is right." Agreeing, Sue added, "Wherever God brings us, either further into this ministry or on the other field of service, we know only one thing, as we echo the words of Peter, Lord to whom shall we go? You have the words of eternal life!"[29] The Mercados did not see the anniversary of Roe v. Wade or any other pro-life rallies as political events per se, but as opportunities and a spiritual obligation to engage their faith on issues that are important to them as Catholics. This sentiment was shared by many first-generation Filipino Americans interviewed.

Across town, while the Mercados prepared to head to Austin, Dave and Agnes Gonzalez were also getting their two children, ages fourteen and nine, ready to make the same drive. Somewhat skeptical about the day's events and the impact he could make, Dave later stated that he had questioned whether he should make the drive or not. Explaining this, he noted, "I must admit that I was thinking; why should I travel two and half hours just to walk a mile or so? Will I, one person, really count? I know others must wonder about that too." Continuing, Dave suggested if it were not for the faith of his fellow CFC members he might not have made the drive. "I was really doubting things today but then Dan and Lita called me and asked me if we were bringing the kids and you know that just hit me because that is what this is all really about." Although the Cruz family did not realize their phone call had made such an impact on Dave, they told me they had called him earlier in the day to inspire their own kids, who were tired. "We called Dave because we wanted to tell our own three [children] that they would have someone to play with." Like the Mercados, Dan and Lita believe that it is important to get their children, ages seven through eleven, involved in their religious and civic life. Whether it is through their volunteering at Loaves and Fishes soup kitchen or protests against abortion, Lita explained, "This is our first rally and I'm not sure the children will completely understand, but hopefully they get some of God's message like we hope in everything we take them to."

Once they all arrived in Austin, the three families found each other in the crowd. Much to their surprise, they were not alone. Over fifty-two members of CFC in Houston, both couples and extended families, made the journey, as did other Filipino American members of St. Catherine's parish who are not a part of CFC. Louie, for example, came over and greeted everyone in the CFC gathering and stated, "I'm so proud we are all here doing what is needed—there are so many of you, God bless CFC."[30] Others, such as Janice, shouted across the crowd, "I thought I would see you all here!" As they stood side by side next to each other, most wearing CFC t-shirts, they formed a vibrant presence among the 1,500 protestors that gathered in Republic Square, roughly a mile and a half away from the capitol. Heralded as the "Texas Rally for Life," over thirty-two local and national pro-life groups as well as individuals and families from around the state gathered to protest against abortion and pray for what they see as a tragic loss of life.[31] As CFC members marched toward the capitol they began to recite the Rosary. Inspired by those around them, Agnes and Dave stated how thankful they were that their children were with them. "By bringing our daughter and son, we are teaching them by showing them they have a voice in this cause, or for any cause they believe in. We are already planting a seed in their hearts. Beyond the material and earthly possessions, these are life-lessons and values we wish to leave them, our legacy, priceless!" Echoing these sentiments, Ernie later told me, "Those children that were at the rally knew why we were having the rally . . . they might not understand everything but the seed is planted."

Making their way to the capitol steps, some pushing their children in strollers or carrying them on their shoulders, one group of protestors released 212 white balloons representing the number of babies they claimed are aborted in Texas every day, while another group released 212 red balloons representing the women they say are having the abortions. Throughout the crowd, people expressed themselves in various other ways. Some held posters with pictures of aborted fetuses on them or carried posters with pictures of what seemed to be their own living children with phrases like "How could you kill God's creations?" or "Murder kills." Others, including members of CFC, sang hymns like "Amazing Grace" or recited prayers.[32] It was hard to gauge the response of onlookers to these acts, but it was also clear that the rally was not just about abortion for the people in attendance. Explaining this, Agnes later stated, "We have to uphold the culture of life at every opportunity that beckons us. Amidst the confusion, violence, unrest, apathy, cynicism, and disregard for life in the world today, it is important to show that there is hope for goodness to triumph. We have won, in fact, 2,000 years ago when Christ conquered all. . . . The [rally] is not just anti-abortion, it is for everything that Christ stands for, his incarnation tells us how much dignity God bestows on human life!" Continuing, she suggested that her faith compels her to take actions on life issues beyond abortion. "We march because it is our duty. . . . this filters down to our everyday activities and all. It is pro-life to drive the speed limit. It is pro-life to exercise. It is pro-life to avoid smoking and drugs. It is pro-life to eat healthy food. It is pro-life to uphold the sacredness of sex and see its meaning within the framework of God's plan. To be Catholic is to be pro-life! To be a member of CFC is to be pro-life! To love Jesus is to be pro-life!" Sharing this view, Ernie, suggested, "Being pro-life is more than not having an abortion—it is a lifestyle built on faith and real family values."

After the rally, I sat down with members of CFC back in Houston and asked them what they thought about the day. Agnes stated, "It is very encouraging to see tens of thousands of people waging war against [the] culture of death." Continuing, she explained that in seeing people from different political, religious, social, and ethnic backgrounds all sharing the same conviction about the "integrity of life," it made her realize three things, "One, that there is hope. Two, regardless of how divided this world may seem, God can bring about unity in a very unexpected way. And three, we can only expect God to help us change our circumstances if we decide to make ourselves available for God's purpose—when we start living not only for ourselves but for others as well!" All of those at the rally with whom I later spoke agreed with Agnes or expressed similar thoughts. Most were not sure how their actions impacted others, but stated they felt like they were doing the right things. Bob, for example, emphatically pointed out, "Look we are doing more than most and that makes me feel like I am walking a righteous path." As we continued to talk, he explained, "Every little bit we do helps break down the evil that plagues this country—we don't need separation of church and state but the unity of faith and politics in action."

CHURCH AND STATE

Although the rally for the thirty-fourth anniversary of Roe v. Wade at the Texas capitol was covered widely by local and national media, Filipino Americans did not gain any recognition or coverage for their presence and efforts. This did not bother any of the first-generation Filipino Americans interviewed. In fact, most, like Rita, a member of CFC and St. Catherine's, stated, "I don't care if people see me as a Filipino in action or not—all I can do is go to church, hear God's word and act on it as a good Catholic." Whether it is through voting in national election, signing petitions, forwarding emails and articles, or marching in pro-life rallies at the Texas Capital, first-generation Filipino Americans are acting on their faith. Likewise, those who are most active in the practice of their faith are the ones who are also most active politically, as we have seen. Drawing on survey findings, Figure 5 further illustrates this point.

First-generation Filipino American Catholics surveyed in Houston who are religiously active are more likely to be involved in politics through voting, signing petitions or writing letters to their representatives, and participating in rallies, marches, and protests.[33] Of Filipino Americans who attend mass frequently—weekly or more and almost weekly—60 percent stated that they had voted in the last presidential election (2008), compared to only 38 percent of those who only attend a few times a year or less, a 22 percent difference. Although the difference between the percentage of frequent attenders and nonfrequent attenders who had signed a petition or contacted their representative on an issue in the last twelve months was not significant, a difference of only 3 percent, the difference

Church Attendance

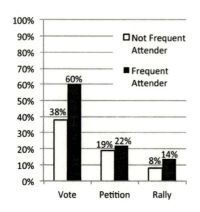

Church Participation Beyond Attendance

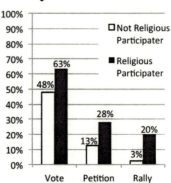

Member of Religious Group

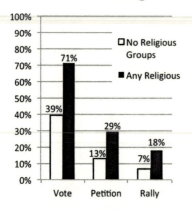

85.2% of first-generation Filipino Americans surveyed in Houston stated that their religious beliefs shaped their opinions on the issue of abortion (HFAS 2010)

Figure 5   Percentage of First-Generation Filipino Americans in Houston Engaged in Politics by Religiosity. *Source:* The Houston Filipino American Survey 2010; see Methodological Appendix for further details.

between frequent attenders and nonfrequent attenders who had participated in a rally, march, or protest was somewhat larger—a difference of 6 percent.

Looking at the same set of political engagements in Figure 5, those who stated they had participated in church activities in addition to or outside of attending mass were likewise more politically involved than those who stated they were not. Of first-generation Filipino American Catholics who participate in extra-church activities, 63 percent stated they had voted in the past presidential election, compared to only 48 percent who did not, a 15 percent difference. Likewise, 28 percent of first-generation Filipino American Catholics who participate in extra-church activities stated they had signed a petition or contacted a representative on an issue, compared to only 13 percent who did not, a 15 percent difference. The difference between those who participated in a rally, march, or protest was also significant. Of those who participated in church activities in addition to or outside of attending mass, 20 percent stated they had been involved in these activities in the last twelve months, compared to only 3 percent, a 17 percent difference.

Not surprisingly, given the events discussed in previous pages, first-generation Filipino American Catholics who are members of religious groups were significantly more involved in political activities than those who are not members of these groups. Of those who are members of groups such CFC or Bibingka, 71 percent voted in the 2008 presidential election, compared to 39 percent of those who are not members of a religious group, a 32 percent difference (see Figure 5). Likewise, 29 percent of those who are members of these groups stated they had signed a petition or contacted their representative about an issue in the last twelve months, compared to only 13 percent of those who were not a member, a 16 percent difference. Eighteen percent of those who are members of these groups also stated they had participated in a rally, march, or protest in the last twelve months, compared to only 7 percent of those who are not members of a religious group—an 11 percent difference.

CONCLUSION

In the decade since political scientist Robert Putnam first questioned what killed civic engagement in the last third of the American twentieth century, the civic engagement of first-generation Filipino Americans described in this chapter reminds us that immigrants are a vital and active part of American civil society.[34] In an age when the majority of Americans undertake no other political activity outside of voting in national elections, and that is rather low as well, the involvement of Filipino Americans in getting out the vote or signing petitions and rallying on issues such as immigration and abortion points to a sense of civic concern that is vibrant and well connected to the traditional social structures, such as voluntary associations, the Church, and political parties that some scholars once feared were in atrophy. If civic participation stands at the heart of American democracy, as some scholars have suggested, its heart and its future, at least in the case of first-generation Filipino Americans in Houston, may very well be imported.

Filipino Americans are not politically disinterested, but actively debate and take action on a host of issues that concern them. Most of these issues are matters of faith and are shaped by cultural frameworks that place the sanctity of the family at the center of their lives. Looking at the activists that marched to the Texas capitol after driving three hours with their families in tow, they demonstrated a sense of passion and a clear commitment to civic life. They are immigrants and Americans who not only express their love for the democratic process by exhausting all means to make their voices heard but also demonstrate an earnest desire, from their own perspectives, to make the country a better place. Above it all, they are also Catholics who are active in their parish churches both in attendance and through social service and are active in religious fellowship such as CFC or Bibingka. What drives them or compels them to act is their devout faith.

Filipino Americans, at least those interviewed, believe it is their duty to protect the sanctity of the family and uphold life. They are not civically inhibited by their Catholic faith or the hierarchical structure of Church itself, as some scholars might anticipate, but rather mobilized by them. Through access to a wealth of religious resources and opportunities, Catholicism facilitates their mobilization on civic concerns. Seeking greater connections between church and state, the Filipino Americans in this study, by and large, not only believe that the Church should be involved in politics but see it as one of the only voices that are speaking out on issues that are important to them. Pointing to this fact, the Filipino American social commentator Perry Diaz, suggests:

> Filipino-Americans as a Catholic group is not as big as the Irish-Americans, the Italian-Americans or the Hispanic-Americans. However, Filipino-Americans' presence in Sunday masses seems to indicate that they are more committed to their Catholic faith than other Catholic groups. Yes, in these days of sound-bytes and cyberspace surfing, Americans of Filipino descent have a higher propensity for fulfilling their religious obligations. . . . Our religious upbringing, our strong family ties, our deep-rooted tradition of self-reliance, and our time-honored spirit of "*bayanihan*" [Ta, caring for your fellow neighbor or countryman] have ingrained in us a core of values that directs how our brains think and how our hearts beat. Intellectually and emotionally, Filipinos are social and fiscal conservatives. Our core values have to be in harmony with environment including governance.[35]

Both in heart and mind, Filipinos are devoted Catholics who feel a sense of duty to act on their faith. They also believe that in acting they are making a difference on issues that shape the culture and civic life of the nation, whether it occurs through their actions as individuals or through their groups and associations.

At the national level, first-generation Filipino Americans such as Bishop Solis, who heads the Catholic Church's national steering committee for Justice for Immigrants, are making an impact well beyond the Filipino American community itself. As a prominent national voice, his words and strategic planning are at the forefront of national debates over immigration policy. While most likely influencing fellow Catholics more than the general public, the Church is a major force in these debates nevertheless, and non-Catholics are well aware of their presence in these debates. This said, smaller groups such as the Gabriela Network, now renamed the Association of Filipinas, Feminists Fighting Imperialism, Re-feudalization, and Marginalization (AF3IRM), highlight where other groups, particularly Filipina women, are also mobilizing on immigration issues and making their presence felt. Locally in Houston, female members of groups such as CFC and Bibingka are likewise powerful voices in shaping the political discussions and actions of their groups. This is particularly true when it comes to broader right-to-life or family issues.

Drawing on their faith, the model of Mother Mary, and their central roles in their own families, Filipinas see themselves as important voices in their groups and communities. Filipino men, for the most part, respect the legitimacy of their voices for these very same reasons and see them as leaders and equals in the community. Regardless of sex, Filipinos often work side by side with non-Filipinos in voicing or taking action on their civic concerns. Many times, as we have seen, this is carried out through the mobilization of families who share similar cultural views on faith and family. This is not unique, but at the group level, the mobilizations of fellowship groups such as CFC are also not what most scholars of American civic life would expect. Scholars have often noted that with the exception of a few lobbying groups, small groups such as CFC or Bibingka do not typically stage protests or try to initiate public policy.[36] Although in both of these cases this is somewhat true, the march on the Texas capitol, for example, was largely driven by individuals and families, and it is through their group affiliations and network resources that they were able to mobilize and to take action. In some cases, such as the CFC group that gathered at the capitol, these individuals can take action as representatives of their groups, marching in unison, despite the fact these mobilizations are not officially sanctioned as CFC events. This is important and highlights yet another way in which Filipino immigrants, both collectively and individually, can and do make a civic impact beyond their own ethnic communities. Likewise, as strong voices within these groups and their own Catholic parishes, it also highlights where Filipinos and their more conservative views have the potential to reshape American Catholicism as well.

Turning to the broader question of this impact not only on the American Catholic Church but on American civic life, the next chapter explores the implications of this study in the context of scholarly and popular concerns over the future of American civic life and the place of new immigrants in American society. The chapter summarizes the major arguments and evidence presented in previous chapters and weighs in on what a study of first-generation Filipino Americans tells about the future of American Catholicism and the puzzle of American Catholic civic life. It argues, given the fact the Filipino American community is one of the largest immigrant populations in the nation and is expected to grow over the next several decades, that first-generation Filipino Americans not only have the potential to reshape American Catholicism by their sheer numbers, but are already doing so through their active involvement in the Church both in local parishes and within the structure of the larger national hierarchy. Additionally, the chapter concludes that Filipino immigrants are building communities that engage and impact American civic life as they take action on their Catholic faith and the sanctity of the family.

CHAPTER 8

GROWING PRESENCE AND POTENTIAL IMPACTS

In 1992, Tessie Manuel, with a coalition of other first-generation Filipino Americans that included a small group from Texas, wrote Monsignor Bransfield, the rector of the Basilica of the National Shrine of the Immaculate Conception in Washington, DC, to inquire what it would take to build a chapel for Our Lady of Antipolo—an apparition of the Virgin Mary of Peace and Good Voyage in the Philippines known as Birhenng Antipolo.[1] For decades, Filipinos visiting the national shrine had questioned Birhenng Antipolo's absence and longed for their own faith journey to take a final resting place in the basilica. Diana, for example, a first-generation Filipino American now living in Houston, explained, "It's hard to believe that for all the years Filipinos have lived in this country and filled its parishes, that our Mother Mary was not welcome on these shores." Two years after initial conversations began, in January of 1994, the Antipolo Shrine Project Committee started to raise money for the chapel with the assistance of Father Fidel de Ramos, a Filipino American and the associate pastor of a heavily Filipino-populated parish in Oxon Hill, Maryland. A few months later, a draft for the design of the chapel was completed and the project was made the focus of the Fourth National Convention of Filipino Apostolates (SANDIWA IV) in Virginia.

The SANDIWA conferences, meaning "of one consciousness or spirit" in Tagalog, helped to raise national awareness for the project in the Filipino American community and dramatically increased its ability to fundraise over the next several years. By 1996, the project met and exceeded its goal of raising $400,000, with the aid of over 8,000 individual Filipinos, twenty-two archdioceses across the country, over forty Filipino American organizations, and thirty Filipino American Catholic prayer groups. That same year the National Basilica officially announced that construction of the chapel to Antipolo would begin. One year later, in June of 1997, a 125-year-old image of Birhenng Antipolo, an exact replica of the original in the Basilica of Antipolo in the Philippines, was enshrined and dedicated by Cardinal Hickey of the Archdiocese of Washington, DC, and

Father Gungon, the bishop of Antipolo in the Philippines. Since the enshrine-ment, the oratory chapel has been the site of pilgrimage for thousands of Filipino Americans, many of whom have been first-generation immigrants. The chapel also hosts an annual pilgrimage and Feast of Antipolo that draw hundreds of Filipinos from around the country and the Philippines each year.

On the eleventh annual pilgrimage to the Oratory of Our Lady of Peace and Good Voyage Antipolo in June of 2008, hundreds of Filipino Americans, mostly first-generation immigrants, gathered to celebrate their Catholic faith and their journey with Mary to America. Although the celebration was perhaps no dif-ferent in liturgy and attendance from that in any of the previous ten years, the celebrant and host for this particular year was not a Philippine bishop or a non-Filipino representative of the Church but Oscar Azarcon Solis, the auxil-iary bishop of Los Angeles and the first Filipino American bishop in the United States. Marking a doubly special occasion, the Hymn to Antipolo seemed to resonate with even greater meaning for the Filipino American immigrants in attendance. Shirley, for example, a first-generation Filipina American nurse and member of St. Catherine's recalled, "I remember singing the words and thinking about my own journey to this country, how true it is."

> O Virgin of Antipolo, to you we lift our every woe
> May your love and guiding presence remain with us where every we go
> Ave Ave Ave, Ave Maria light our path and make clear
> O Mary Mother Dear,
> You are our guide on our journey, you calm our fears and you light our way. . . .
> —from the hymn O Birhen Ng Antipolo[2]

After a long and turbulent history in the United States, through hardships and successes, the growing presence of Filipino American Catholics today has an offi-cial voice within the hierarchy of the Church and a national shrine to the Virgin of Antipolo that not only stands as a testament to Filipinos' faith and devotion but announces that they are an important part of the new American story.

Changing the Face of America

By 2050, the United States is expected to become a majority minority population, with no one racial or ethnic group being the clear majority of the nation. Much of this expected demographic change is a direct result of continued and increased immigration since 1965. These new immigrants, post-1965, are distinctly different from earlier historical waves of immigration to the nation. They come from a greater variety of countries and, as a result, have significantly increased the num-ber of nonwhite racial and ethnic minorities in the nation. In the 2010 census, one of the largest demographic gains of any census category was Asian Ameri-cans.[3] In fact, Asian Americans, for the first time, surpassed Hispanics/Latinos as the fastest growing population.[4] Among the groups responsible for this gain was Filipino Americans, both foreign-born and native-born, who not only diversify the Asian American subcategory but represent an immense diversity within themselves. The Filipino American community is not one community or a singular population, as Chapter 3 illustrated, but a community of communities that stretches across representatives of over 7,000 islands and a wealth of cultural and ethnic diversity. Filipinos are Bicolano, Biholano, Cebuano, Ilocano, and Tagalog, to name a few groups, and collectively they represent one of the largest immigrant populations in the nation.

At a purely demographic level, the growth and diversity of the Filipino American community matters. From 1990 to 2000, the Filipino American community grew by 32 percent. In the years leading up to the 2010 census, this trend, coupled with mounting complaints from the Filipino American community itself, led the United States census to create a separate category for Filipinos, who had been forced in prior years to check Pacific Islander or something else. From 2000 to 2010, the Filipino American population grew an estimated 38 percent in the "Filipino alone" category and by 44 percent overall.[5] As a result, based on these emerging estimates, the Filipino American community is now at least 3.4 million people, including both foreign-born and native-born. Filipino Americans represent roughly 5 percent of the nation's foreign-born population, and this does not include an estimated 280,000 undocumented Filipinos living in the country. To put this in perspective, the Filipino American community is larger than the total number of Japanese and Korean Americans combined, and if present trends continue, Filipino Americans could become the largest Asian American community, surpassing Chinese Americans, in the near future.

In places such as California and Hawaii that have been major historical destinations for Filipino immigration, Filipino Americans now represents anywhere from roughly 3 to 15 percent of these states' total populations.[6] Although this is not surprising, this growth has also significantly diversified the racial and ethnic landscapes of other states across the nation that are not typically considered historical Filipino immigrant destinations. The Filipino American population in Nevada, for example, dramatically grew by 236 percent from 1990 to 2000 and by 142 percent from 2000 to 2010. Likewise, in other states, such as Texas, Alabama, North Carolina, Wyoming, Idaho, and Arizona, the Filipino American population has grown anywhere from 77 percent to 116 percent in the last ten years.[7] It is a startling pattern of growth, fueled in part by American nursing and engineer shortages, and one that stretches geographically far beyond the traditional metropolitan centers, such as New York, Chicago, and Los Angeles that have long been the gateways for Filipino immigration. Where Filipino Americans at one point in time may not have had a large visible presence across the nation outside of California or New York, this is increasingly not the case. However, this does not necessarily mean that the average American recognizes the importance of their presence.

Sergio Arau's 2004 critically acclaimed film *A Day without Mexicans* asks the question of what would happen if the seemingly invisible or taken-for-granted contributions of a single group of people were to be rendered completely invisible by making them disappear. Satirically looking at the long-range effects on California if all of the state's Mexican population, both citizens and undocumented immigrants, were to suddenly disappear, the film easily could be extended to question on a larger scale what would happen to the nation in general should the country's Mexican populations disappear. The results would be devastating to the national economy and life as we know it. However, we might rightly say this about any of the nation's immigrant populations, should they disappear. Looking hypothetically at the case of Filipino Americans, just what would a day without Filipinos be like? The answers are equally troubling as Sergio Arau's film.

As of 2008, Filipina Americans were more likely to participate in the civilian labor force than all other foreign-born women in the United States.[8] Much of this can be attributed to the continued growth of Filipino Americans in American health care. According to a study conducted by the American Medical Association in 2007, Philippine-trained physicians represent the second largest group of foreign-trained physicians practicing in the United States.[9] Likewise, from 2004 to 2007, Filipino American nurses accounted for slightly less than half of all foreign-trained nurses and over half of all foreign-born people taking the American nursing licensure exam.[10] Although these numbers have declined somewhat in the last few years with a troubled economy, given the "graying of America" and its continued shortages of health care professionals, these numbers are likely to rise again in the near future. Beyond this, in 2007, dentists from the Philippines represented the second largest group of foreign-trained dentists in the country, and Filipino medical professionals in other related health care fields, such as physical therapy, radiologic technology, and medical technology, continue to be well represented.[11] What does this mean? If Filipinos were to disappear for a day, the health care industry in the United States alone would be drastically impacted, and this is but one area of the American economy to which Filipinos, like Mexicans, silently and without recognition make major contributions.[12]

Despite their continued growth and their geographic spread across the nation, Filipinos remain the forgotten Asian American community. They are largely an "invisible and silent minority."[13] The question is, why? According to researchers from the Center for Civic Innovation at the Manhattan Institute, first-generation Filipino Americans are the second most "assimilated" population of the top ten American immigrant populations coming to the nation, second only to Canadians.[14] Economically, Filipino immigrants were found to be no different from the wider native-born population in terms of their income, labor force participation, education, and home ownership, among other factors. Culturally, according to the report, Filipino immigrants were found to be 72 percent similar to the wider native-born population, second again to Canadians, in terms of English proficiency, intermarriage with native-born people, marital status, and the number of children they have.[15] Civically, the report suggests that Filipino immigrants were 65 percent similar to the wider native-born population, second only to Vietnamese, in terms of naturalization rates and military service. Although the theoretical underpinnings of the report hearken back to classical assimilation theories from the early 1960s that have long been challenged, particularly in how we understand processes of immigrant acculturation, structural adaptation, and incorporation, the findings do raise the question of whether Filipinos are "too American" for anyone to notice their civic or economic contributions and the cultural impact of their increased presence.

The one exception to this possibility is that fellow American Catholics, from Oregon to New York, have slowly begun to write about Filipino immigrants' increased and unique presence in their parishes. In 1999, Ed Langlois of the *Catholic Sentinel*, for example, wrote an article about the rich spiritual tradition Filipino American Catholics bring to the United States and Northwest, in particular.[16] Highlighting this, Langlois also noted that while Filipinos' vibrant and enthusiastic practices are "not the norm in Oregon," their presence may be somewhat overlooked. Continuing, Langlois stated, based on the observations of Norma Lacorte, a Filipina who serves as the director of religious education at St. Mary Our Lady of the Dunes parish in Florence, Oregon, that Filipinos' lack of visibility in the Church may have something to do with their high levels of integration into their parishes and communities.

In other words, people may simply forget about them because they do not draw attention to themselves. Explaining this further, Lacorte, citing Father Culaba, the Filipino Redemptorist head of Holy Redeemer parish in Portland, notes, "Historically, we have been taught to assimilate but that may be a good thing, because it leads us to stick to the security of the faith and the value systems and family orientation . . . things all Catholics can learn."[17] Father Culaba's words explain something important that many scholars of immigration have missed by ignoring the Filipino American case. New immigrants, such as Filipino Americans, are indeed changing the face of the American racial and religious landscape, but they are in many ways doing so silently. By sticking to their Catholic faith and making family central to their lives, Filipino Americans are like many other Americans. They work, they play, they go to church, and they buy homes in the suburbs where they raise their families. However, while their increasing but somewhat silent presence has gone largely unnoticed by many, through their vibrant religious practices and cultural frameworks that sanctify the centrality of family, Filipino Americans are poised to play a vital role in shaping the future of the new American story.

Although it is difficult to speculate what lasting impacts Filipino Americans will have on the future of the United States, several trends are becoming increasing clear and merit further discussion. First, Filipino Americans are already reshaping American Catholicism, and in doing so, are challenging the traditional norms of Catholics across the nation. Second, as part of this wider challenge, Filipino Americans have called on fellow Catholics, immigrant or not, to engage civil society on family and life issues that are important to them and the Catholic Church. Third, by taking social action on these issues themselves, Filipino Americans have already begun to unravel many of the long-standing questions surrounding the puzzle of American Catholic civic life.

FUTURE OF AMERICAN CATHOLICISM

In the next forty years, not only will the United States become a majority minority nation but the Philippines will surpass it as the third largest Catholic nation and the largest English-speaking Catholic nation in the world.[18] This emerging trend has several implications for the future of global Catholicism and the American Catholic Church itself. First, at a purely institutional level, the United States, like many nations around the world, is increasingly unable to replace its aging priesthood with native-born priests and has grown dependent on foreign-born priests to keep their parishes staffed.[19] Given Filipinos' high English proficiency and the fact the Philippines is one of the few nations in the world that has young men still actively entering the priesthood, Filipino priests are in high demand across the globe. This increased demand, however, is not without its complications and serves as a stark reminder that the ongoing "brain drain" that is fueling the current cultural and economic crises in the Philippines is not just a result of nurses and engineers leaving the country. While filling the needs of a global faithful, the exodus of Filipino priests from the Philippines has resulted in a ratio in which one Filipino priest in the Philippines now serves an estimated 15,000 Filipino parishioners.[20] What is saving American parishes continues to threaten them in the Philippines.

Historically, this trend is nothing new for the Philippines. From their very emergence as a Catholic nation under Spanish colonial rule, they struggled to find priests to serve their growing numbers. Today, as was the case then, Filipinos have turned to lay leadership to fill this void. In the United States, and even globally, this trend continues, particularly in the growth of prayer groups and fellowships that facilitate Filipino traditions and practices both within and outside of the Church.[21] These groups and their leaders, such as Deacon Frank and Sister Dianna discussed in Chapter 5, serve as bridges between Filipino parishioners at St. Catherine's and its clergy. They are also active leaders in and of themselves who are not only largely responsible for the establishment of community centers, such as the San Lorenzo Ruiz de Manila Center in Houston, but facilitate a space between the larger Filipino American community and its growing presence in the American Church.

In 1995 it was estimated that there were roughly three hundred priests serving in the United States. Some thirteen years later, this number has tripled.[22] As of 2008, there were an estimated nine hundred Filipino priests and over two hundred nuns serving in various official capacities in the American Catholic Church from California to Virginia, and this does not include several hundred additional Filipino priests and nuns who are visiting the country and giving pastoral care while they are here.[23] Although their numbers are larger in places like California, where an estimated forty priests now help to serve the increasing presence of Filipinos in their dioceses, Filipino priests, by in large, are not solely serving the needs of Filipino parishioners, but the wider American Church as well. More than simply serving these parishes, Filipino American priests are challenging the wider Church to recognize them as they introduce beliefs and practices that have the potential to reshape American Catholicism. Celebrations such as Simbang Gabi, for example, introduce non-Filipinos to a Philippine brand of Catholicism that is different in many ways from what they are more accustomed to. Whereas American Catholics typically celebrate the Advent season in their homes and in mass on the Sundays leading up to Christmas day or the twelve days of Christmas from Christmas day through Epiphany on January 6th, Filipinos draw additional attention to the importance of Mary's personal journey in nine days leading up to Jesus' birth both through novenas in their homes and in nightly masses and celebrations at their parish churches. As Filipino priests such as Father José in parishes around the country continue to encourage non-Filipinos to join them and they increasingly do so, it is yet another reminder of the potential impact Filipino priests may have on the future of American Catholic practices and beliefs. While the average native-born American Catholic may not be very cognizant of this potential, Filipinos are and have increasingly demanded that the Church recognize their growing importance.[24]

Starting in the early 1990s, the increasing presence of Filipino priests and the growth of Filipinos in the American Church in general led Filipino Catholic leaders such as Naomi Castillo to establish SANDIWA and hold a series of national conferences to proclaim their identity and establish their place in the Church. The culmination of these conferences was the enshrinement of the Virgin of Antipolo at the National Basilica in Washington in 1997, the elevation of Father Solis to be the auxiliary bishop of Los Angeles in 2004, and the establishment of the Chapel of San Lorenzo Ruiz de Manila in New York in 2005 as the first national church dedicated the Filipino Apostolate—the second of its kind globally, with the other chapel being in Rome, Italy.[25] In 2008, under the leadership of Bishop Solis as head of the United States Conference of Catholic Bishops' subcommittee for Asian and Pacific Islanders, Filipino Americans also established a national organization for Filipino priests serving in the United States and called for a national assembly to be held in 2011—this, too, was a first of its kind.[26]

Beyond the priests' numeric importance to the Church and their growing momentum in gaining increased recognition within it, few scholars have
explored what the presence of Filipino priests may mean to the reshaping of
American Catholicism. Today's Filipino priests are not theologically the same as
their retiring Italian and Irish American counterparts. They come from a nation
whose importance to global Catholicism is not only on the rise and quickly
surpassing its European counterparts but staunchly conservative compared to
the more liberal views of Catholics in nations such as Ireland, Germany, Spain,
Poland, Italy, and the United States. Filipino priests also come from a nation in
which the Church played a major role in the toppling of the Marcos regime, the
EDSA 1 People Power movement, and subsequent seminarians, such as Father
José, have been educated in a form of "liberation theology" that may be unfa-
miliar to the average native-born American Catholic. Throughout this book,
for example, Filipino priests, such as Father José or lay leaders such as Deacon
Frank and Sister Diana in Houston, have demonstrated how they often walk a
fine line between the separation of church and state, and are not afraid of directly
engaging national or local political issues both inside and outside their parishes.
Articulating messages that emphasize cultural frameworks that assert the sanctity of family through church newsletters and homilies, many of these priests and
lay leaders see the Church as the fourth branch of government. Although they
do not tell their parishioners who to vote for, they have a significant influence in
shaping how their parishioners take action and on what issues. As we have seen,
they compel Filipinos and others to engage civil society because it is the right
thing to do as good Catholics.

Beyond the potential institutional influence Filipino priests or lay leaders may
have within their parishes and the American Church itself, the increasing presence of devout Filipino parishioners in the United States is just as likely to not
only reinforce these patterns of influence but bring about their own independent
impact on American Catholicism as well. From the late nineteenth through the
early twentieth centuries, successive waves of immigration to the United States
elevated the American Catholic Church to the largest single religious denomination in the country. Today, new waves of Catholic immigrants are once again
propelling Catholicism to the same status, and Filipino Americans are an important part of this emerging story. While 65 percent of American Catholics today
are white, they are also older and being replaced by youth from Latin America
and the Philippines.[27] While the Latin case has garnered more attention, and perhaps rightfully so based on its numeric size, the Philippines is the second largest
source of Catholic immigration to the United States, second only to Mexico, and
this population is just as important to the future of American Catholicism.

Like Filipino American priests and lay leaders, first-generation Filipino
Americans, who make up roughly 56 percent of the national Filipino American community, typically attend mass at higher rates and are more socially

conservative than native-born Americans. Roughly 86 percent of first-generation Filipino Americans surveyed in Houston, for example, said they attended weekly mass, compared to only 41 percent of the general American Catholic population.[28] In an age when American Catholics are leaving the Church at increasing rates or are no longer attending regularly, Filipino American are filling their vacant pews.[29] Theologically, Filipinos believe that the Pope should be less open to change in the Church, they oppose priests getting married, and they believe that priests should be more focused on religious issues rather than what life is like for the ordinary person—all in sharp contrast to the more liberal or moderate views of native-born American Catholics.[30] On key issues such as abortion, Filipino Americans, as evident from the discussions and survey findings in Chapter 7, are likewise more conservative in believing that abortion should be illegal in all cases, compared to 51 percent of American Catholics in general, who believe that abortion should be legal in all or most cases.[31]

Like other Christians from around the global South, Filipinos, in general, are not only largely charismatic in their religious practices but are increasingly led by women lay leaders. Throughout this book, women such as Cheryl, Karla, Maricar, Regina, and Sister Diana, to name a few, have demonstrated that women are often the key movers within the Filipino American community and the Church itself. Part of this may be attributed to the fact that Filipinas are immigrating to the United States at disproportionally higher rates than men, but their historical role both in the home and the community may also suggest otherwise. Filipinas have always been the center of Filipino faith and family. When their number began to increase, especially after 1965, Filipino religiosity grew exponentially. This is not a coincidence, given that studies repeatedly suggest that women are more religious than men, and thus it is not surprising that the demands of recognition for Filipinos within the Church and its hierarchy were led by women such as Tess Manuel and Naomi Castillo. Drawing on their faith, the model of Mother Mary, and their roles as comadres that intimately link them to vast networks of communication as godmothers, Filipinas not only see themselves as important voices both within the Church and their ethnic communities but are also respected as such.

Although Catholic patriarchy has greatly influenced Filipinas' understandings of family and home, the previous chapters clearly demonstrate that women such as Dora do have a certain amount of power or say in shaping Church decisions, particularly when it comes to organizing and carrying out projects through parish councils. They are also keenly involved in shaping community opinion outside of the Church and do not shy away from questioning the Church or its priests when they feel the Church has overstepped its authority.[32] Drawing on models of faith and family both within and outside the Church, Filipinas have negotiated spaces within their parishes that allow them to voice their concerns and gain a measure of agency in shaping decisions on the issues that are most important to them.[33] Acknowledging this, it is important to point out that the presence of lay women in the Church and their increased voice in parish affairs is not unique to Filipinas, but part of a larger trend within the wider American Church, where 80 percent of all lay ecclesiastical ministers in 2005 were women.[34] However, what is special about Filipinas, is that they are equally conservative in their social and religious views as their male counterparts or other immigrants from the global South, and in some cases, more so. Hence, Filipinas bring a different perspective and voice to the Church. As the vocal centers of their families, and hence their home devotional groups and fellowships that are linked to a host of parish projects and celebrations, they also introduce other non-Filipino parishioners to beliefs and practices that may be less familiar.

In general, Filipino Americans, both men and women, like other immigrants from the global South, have the potential to reshape American Catholicism through their beliefs in spiritual healing, the existence of supernatural forces, and the power of exorcism.[35] These beliefs are not widely held by the average American Catholic, but are clearly present in prayer groups such as Bibingka, which are discussed throughout this book. While their Friday night fellowships are largely no different liturgically from normative American Catholicism outside of their ethnic or regional specific novenas, Bibingka was initially formed to pray for and bring about the healing of Louise, one of its key members. Today, members of Bibingka still ardently believe that their faith and devotion will heal her. Although scholars have largely ignored this trend, Philippine Catholicism, as evident in other groups such as Lord's Flock Charismatic Community in Houston, is also increasing evangelical and/or charismatic and stands as one of the only reasons why Protestant Pentecostalism has not spread as rapidly in the Philippines as it has in rest of the global South.[36]

Whether it is through their increased presence in the American clergy, their growth in lay leadership, or their growing presence as parishioners, Filipino immigrants are a mounting force within American Catholicism. Although they were at one time seen as a silent minority, their increasing demands for recognition, coupled with their numeric growth, is changing this. Although in some respects they are like the average American Catholic, their unique and historic relationship to Catholicism in the Philippines makes them more akin to other Catholics from the global South. As such, Filipino Americans are not only challenging the more liberal and moderate beliefs of their fellow American Catholics but are changing the Church itself. Likewise, with a cultural and religious obligation to protect the sanctity of the family, Filipino immigrants are also making their presence felt as they continue to engage American civil society.

Unraveling the Catholic Puzzle

Despite the fact that Catholic institutions and teachings continue to foster a communitarian ethic, many scholars have declared that the civic life of American Catholics is a puzzle.[37] Pointing to mounting empirical evidence that suggests that American Catholics either participate in civic life less or no differently from people of other religious traditions, these studies suggest the average size of most American Catholic parishes is rather large, which results in less social capital being generated for civic life per individual parishioner compared to those in Protestant denominations. Echoing classical arguments that the Catholic Church inhibits American Catholics' ability to acquire civic skills, these studies also suggest that despite changes in Catholic culture since Vatican II, the locus of moral authority within the Church remains highly centralized and does not allow for parishioners to get democratically involved in their parishes or take part in the decision-making processes within the operation of the Church itself.

Looking specifically at the case of Asian American Catholics, scholars have also suggested that Asian American Catholics not only participate less in their communities compared to Asian American Protestants but are faced with other internal concerns or barriers that limit their community life. If this is indeed the case, where does this leave first-generation Filipino Americans and the future of American civic life? As one of the largest immigrant communities in the nation, the question is important. Are Filipino American immigrants twice as likely not to get involved in American civic life because they are the second largest Asian American community and represent the second largest source of Catholic immigration to the nation?

The answer, as the previous chapters have clearly demonstrated, is no. First-generation Filipino Americans are very active in American civic life. In fact, according to findings from the 2008 National Asian American Survey, Filipinos are considered the most "activist group" of all Asian Americans in the nation; they acquire citizenship at high rates, register to vote and vote at high rates, and are very active in civic organizations and community projects, including writing letters to elected officials about problems facing their communities.[38] It is true, as Chapter 4 highlights, that contentious politics can be a major barrier to Filipino American civic life and can create certain internal problems along ethnic or regional lines that stifle their participation in mainstream American civic life. However, acknowledging this, the Church tends to mediate these issues, although not always to everyone's liking, and more often than not, broader civic aims do get accomplished. The only true unity that Filipinos have found across their diversity is through the Catholic Church. The Church is their community. Thus, what often motivates and compels them to live active civic lives are their Catholic faith and the cultural importance they place on the sanctity of the family. Likewise, what holds them together and binds them to this community is the Church itself—the very thing many scholars contend should be impeding their civic life.

This is an important point. Where scholars have long heralded the democratic nature of the structure of American Protestantism, they have often overlooked the fact that in the case of new immigrants, the Catholic Church has been comparatively successful in drawing together its diversity. Yes, Catholic parishes are large, but despite their size they do not split along ethnic or racial lines to form new churches, as is the case with many immigrant Protestant churches. Protestant immigrant churches also tend to be more mono-racial or establish smaller churches within specific ethnic enclaves.[39] As we saw in Chapter 5, for example, Filipino American Protestant ministers such as Reverend Bruce acknowledge that they have encouraged congregations to split and have started numerous churches themselves. The Catholic Church is a vastly different institutional model. While Catholics may ultimately disagree with the Church's involvement in community affairs or the results of its mediations, Filipino Catholics do not form new churches, but more often than not still attend the same mass every Sunday or frequent another parish additionally.

This is not to say the Church cannot or does not present certain barriers to Filipinos civic lives. As Chapter 4 highlighted in the case of the splits over disputed elections in the Bicolano association, the Church's involvement, whatever it may have been, may have actually contributed to the problem and subsequently made relations between the Bicolano community and the Church rather tense. Although these tensions eventually subsided, some Bicolonaos left St. Catherine's parish for another parish. Others such as Karla stopped giving money to the Church and participating in parish projects. On a larger scale, the Church's international involvement in the Couples for Christ split over Gawad Kalinga was largely a matter of Catholic principles and called on Filipinos to question what was more important to them as Catholics, faith or certain civic projects. The Church made it clear that although it valued GK and all that it had or has done for the Philippines, it was concerned about CFC leaving its charismatic roots and working with business partners whose products directly contradict Catholic teachings on the sanctity of the family. The Church asserted itself as the center of the CFC community and made it clear it intended to remain the voice of authority in the Filipino Catholic diaspora. While GK remains alive and well today and has actually grown larger in the scope of its projects in the last several years, many Filipino Americans, especially those in CFC, no longer see it as their top priority. They have returned to evangelization and a focus on the family as their main concern, which in some ways has limited at least one of their potential civic outlets.

In other cases, independent civic centers such as the San Lorenzo Ruiz de Manila center, which originally stood as a competitor for the Church's own annual San Lorenzo celebrations, has negotiated an arrangement with the Filipino American Council of the Galveston-Houston archdiocese that has allowed both groups to flourish. One supports the other and, for the most part, everyone is happy with the arrangement. Although the SLRM remains limited in the scope of its civic outreach, this has little to do with its relationship to the Church and is more a function of resources and opportunity. Both Deacon Frank and Father José remain active at St. Catherine's and in facilitating celebrations at the SLRM center, but the larger Church remains the literal and figurative center of the Filipino American community. As a result, the Church remains Filipino immigrants' greatest civic outlet. Part of these successes, as we have seen, can be attributed to the fact the Church and its priests have been able to bring the community together and forge a host of lasting partnerships.

Filipino American priests such as Father José see it as their duty to bring their parishioners, Filipino or otherwise, together. Parish councils reflect the diversity within the parish itself, and every effort is made to encourage parishioners to be "American Catholics" while still maintaining their ethnic specific practices. Celebrations such as Simbang Gabi at St. Catherine's are a testament of how both can be achieved. It is one of the rare occasions when the entire Filipino American community in Houston is gathered together to celebrate collectively as Filipinos. However, St. Catherine's is equally accommodating to the needs of its other parishioners despite the fact that its main priest is Filipino. Father José works to bring all parishioners together beyond ethnic and general masses through events such as Flores de Mayo, which celebrates the various regional apparitions of Mary that are venerated around the world and throughout the parish. This is not the case in Filipino Protestant churches and this is not unique to Houston.

Several scholars have found that despite structural concerns over the American Catholic Church and its ability to mobilize people beyond collectivist conceptions of moral authority, Catholic churches in Chicago, where Filipino Americans are the largest and most visible ethnic group, deviate from these patterns and place considerable value on individual freedom.[40] In other words, the Catholic Church is not a barrier to their community life but stands at its center. Similar differences have also been found between Salvadoran Protestant and Catholic churches in other studies.[41] Although in this case both churches equally supported new Salvadorian immigrants and connected them to their community, they did so in different ways. The Protestants were more homogeneous, smaller in congregational size, focused on a specific ethnic or regional group, and were more inclined to split, just as is the case with Filipino Protestants in Houston. Catholics, on the other hand, were more diverse ethnically and concerned with uniting all people in the parish through an extended communitarian ethic. Although few scholars have explored these differences, they are important to understanding how religion shapes immigrants' sense of community and the ways in which they engage it.

Today, despite the fact that scholars and social pundits alike question the contributions and place of Catholic immigrants in America, they should be encouraged by the case of Filipino Americans presented in this book. Although some scholars suggest that the Catholic Church benefits more from immigration than the immigrants themselves, particularly Mexican Catholics, this is not necessarily the case for Filipino Americans. Even outside of the Church, Catholicism is vital not only to first-generation Filipino American community unity but also to their ability to physically build its infrastructure. The only Filipino American community center built outside the Church in Houston is the San Lorenzo Ruiz de Manila Center and, as we have seen in Chapter 5, Catholicism and the Church itself had a great deal to do with its successes. Although SLRM has not been as successful at engaging the larger community as the larger Church, the same spirit and emphasis on faith and family drives them in their attempts to expand their programs and projects beyond fundraising.

Churches such as St. Catherine's, on the other hand, have been very successful at engaging the community beyond its own parish. Events such as the Alief Health and Civic Resource Fair, discussed in Chapter 6, serve as a key reminder that the Church and its first-generation Filipino American parishioners are highly engaged in American civic life. The Church provides numerous opportunities and resources for Filipino Americans to get involved with a host of people and partners in their community, and they do. They get involved because that is what good Catholics should do. From giving money to support the Diocesan Fund to working for any of the forty programs the fund sponsors, first-generation Filipino Americans feel obligated to serve because of the cultural frameworks that widen their understanding of family and morally bind them to the Church. It should not be a surprise, as the survey findings discussed in Chapter 6 demonstrate, that those who attend Church frequently and participate in the Church beyond or in addition to weekly attendance are more likely to volunteer, work on a community project, and give more to both secular and religious causes. This is not to say that first-generation Filipino Americans are not engaging their community except through the Church—they are, particularly through their prayer and devotional groups. The problem, however, is that the average Americans and scholars alike may not recognize their more silent contributions.

Throughout Chapter 6, the Filipino American immigrants interviewed suggested that they preferred not to be recognized for their volunteerism and often disputed traditional labels for their civic endeavors. From the Cruz family who volunteer at the soup kitchen Fishes and Loaves to Lyn who bakes hopia for the SRLM Center fundraisers, or Diana who donated shoes and school supplies for parish drives, these efforts were seen as giving care. As a result of this perception, I would argue that part of the discrepancy between Asian American Catholic and Protestant volunteerism found in previous studies may be largely methodological.[42] Simply put, Filipino American immigrants do not always perceive what they are doing as volunteering. At a more qualitative level, however, it is clear that many community events in Houston would either not be as successful, or in the case of health-related projects, would not occur at all without their participation. In fact, looking at the broader picture of American civic life, Filipinos are giving back to their communities through these acts of volunteerism at rates that far exceed that of native-born Americans. Although the same cannot be said, perhaps, for protests against immigration legislation such as HR 4437 or pro-life rallies at the Texas capitol, first-generation Filipino Americans' ardent focus on faith and protecting the sanctity of family makes them a vital part of a larger voice that is shaping the future of American civic life.

In an age in which scholars have questioned the death of American civil society, first-generation Filipino Americans remind us that immigrants are crucial to the future of American civic life. As Chapter 7 demonstrated, Filipino Americans are not politically disinterested but driven by their faith to the polls and into the streets. During the 2004 election, for example, the Filipino American community was an important part of a larger swing vote that Kerry lost. The reason that Kerry lost this support, at least among Filipino Americans in Houston, hinged on the fact that he was not Catholic enough and did not support life issues, as many felt a good Catholic should. Filipino Americans know what a good Catholic is because the messages and teachings that shape their views are clearly and collectively articulated through a host of Catholic sources and venues. Not surprisingly, as survey results in Chapter 7 demonstrated, first-generation Filipino Americans who attended mass frequently, participated in the Church outside of or in addition to attendance, and are members of religious groups such as Couples for Christ, not only voted more than those who were not religiously involved but were more likely to contact their elected officials about issues that concern them and or rally or protest over these same issues. Whether it is in the Church, through the Church, or in prayer and devotional groups, Filipino American faith matters and is key to their involvement in American politics.

As public debates over issues such as abortion, gay marriage, and stem cell research are likely to continue and possibly grow even more heated in decades to come, Filipino immigrants, whether through their prayer groups or simply on the basis of their faith and devotion to the teachings of the Catholic Church, are an important and growing voice in these national debates. Although they are not likely to decide the outcome of any single issue by themselves, they are a potentially powerful swing vote and, as Raul pointed out in Chapter 7, they feel it is their moral duty to make their voice heard. Some may not hear it now or even recognize its source, but as their presence in the United States continues to increase and as they continue to take social action on their faith, Filipinos will compel people to listen or extend a hand to others to join them. From the pulpits and pews of Catholic churches across the nation to protests at state capitols or unsung acts of volunteerism in major metropolitan cities throughout America, their voice matters and is a vibrant part of the future of American civil society.

METHODOLOGICAL
APPENDIX

This methodological appendix details the varied ways in which I studied the first-generation Filipino American community in Houston, Texas. In addition to describing the rationale behind the various methodological choices I made throughout the study, it addresses the key concerns that often arise when selecting cases for study and outlines more broadly the advantages these data present for studying the intersection of civic and religious life for first-generation immigrants.

WHY STUDY FIRST-GENERATION FILIPINO AMERICANS IN HOUSTON?

As was highlighted in the introduction, Filipino American immigrants are not simply one of several groups we should be studying today, but a group we must study if we are going to fully understand how the nation's growing foreign-born populations are changing and challenging the religious and civic landscape of the United States. Reiterating some of these key points: Filipino Americans are one of the largest immigrant populations in the nation, and the Philippines is the second largest source of Catholic immigration to the United States. Filipinos are surpassed only by Mexican immigrants in size and scope. While the Mexican case has received a great deal of academic attention, and perhaps rightfully so, the Filipino case has been sorely understudied despite their long historical relationship to the nation and their continued numeric growth. The Filipino American community today is still largely first generation, 53 percent, and thus while studying the second generation is important and will be increasingly so in years to come, given the paucity of academic work on the first generation, I felt it was important to tell their story first. In terms of location, Houston has a fairly new but steadily growing Filipino American community. As an emerging community, Houston serves an excellent location for studying how recent Filipino American immigrants, post-1965, are not only reshaping American Catholicism but engaging American civil society through communities built on faith and family. The selection of Houston also allows for a comparative case outside of the typical studies of Filipinos' large presence on the West Coast.

Beyond the clear academic reasons for studying first-generation Filipino American immigrants, the selection of this particular group and the Houston locale was also personal. During the time of my graduate studies at the University of Texas (2004), I was fortunate to attend a guest brown-bag lecture given by Stephen Warner on the impact of new immigrants on the nation. To my surprise, in the midst of discussing the potential various populations hold for reshaping the American racial and religious landscape, he stated that we know very little about Filipino immigrants specifically and the impact of Catholicism on their lives and communities. Somewhat overzealously, I raised my hand during the question and answer period and announced that I knew a great deal about the Filipino American community. Dr. Warner suggested if that was truly the case we needed to talk more after the session.

During the conversation that followed, I explained to Dr. Warner that I had lived in the Filipino American community in Houston during high school, had learned some of the basics of Tagalog—the national language of the Philippines—from friends and adopted families, was currently married to a first-generation Filipina from this same area—as I still am—and was raising our two children with at least one foot in the Filipino American community, metaphorically speaking. Continuing, I explained I was exploring the 1903 United States census of the Philippines for a possible dissertation topic; but given my twenty plus years of experience and unique connections to the Filipino American community, Dr. Warner suggested that I should look at the present context and read a bit more before making my final decision. After a few weeks of researching, I discovered that there was not a single study that had been written about the intersection of religious and civic life in the Filipino American community.[1] The next step was obvious to me.

When I told my wife about my plans, she cautioned that my particular interest in religion and politics/civic life might not be something people in the community would want to talk about or necessarily would be willing to talk about. She feared I would become frustrated. However, given the seeming importance of the work, I decided to contact people and at least gauge the community's initial interests. I first contacted and then met with Father José (pseudonym) at St. Catherine's Catholic Church (pseudonym) in Houston. To my surprise, he was very open to discussing the project and suggested that I discuss it with other members of the Filipino American Council of the Archdiocese of Houston-Galveston. After putting me in contact with other members of the council, Father José introduced me to his parishioners during a monthly Filipino mass and urged people to speak with me about the project. Immediately after the service, several people approached me, and from there I began to build my snowball sample in the parish. One particular first-generation Filipino American, Frank (pseudonym), pulled me aside and told me, "I am glad that Father [José] brought you before us, but understand that religion and politics is tricky for us and not everyone here or in the community has always been happy with the Church or Father José's involvement." From that point forward I better understood my wife's concern, but I had also gained a valuable contact in Frank, who helped me build a second snowball sample outside of those who were embedded in the parish as regular church attenders or those who had left it for another parish. In the end, the two samples overlapped considerably. Outside of these samples, I also continued to contact community leaders—including founding members of the San Lorenzo Ruiz de Manila Center, various Filipino associations, and Filipino prayer groups—until I had built a strong enough foundation that I felt I could not only map the general contours of the community but draw on a diversity of voices that represented their differing views on religion and civic life.

As both an insider and outsider, I found myself conducting research over a six-year period in a community with which I was very familiar through friends and family, but one that was not my own by birth or upbringing. As Sandra Acker points out, in questioning when we even know we are inside or outside or somewhere in between, I found myself working creatively within the tensions of what scholars have long cited as the advantages and disadvantages across all sides of this methodological debate.[2] As an insider, I had the advantage that the first-generation Filipino Americans I studied did not question why as a white man I was studying the community. Many knew me or of me and my family. Those who did not eventually read about my ongoing research in editorials written about my work in the *Manila-Headlines*, the largest Filipino American newspaper in circulation in Houston, or heard my name from Catholic clergy members or other various members of the Filipino American Council of the Archdiocese of Houston-Galveston that actively encouraged people to work with me on the project. In sum, most saw me as an insider. As a result, I felt very accepted in the settings I studied. The only challenging question I typically got asked was, "Why are we so important?" to which I had to explain the very details I outlined in the introduction of this book.

As an insider, I wanted to make sure my research vividly captured the community I knew. However, as an outsider I was free to ask questions and explore topics that Filipino researchers might not have been able to undertake. Because I was not a vested part of any Filipino American organization or parish nor actively involved in the community's politics, people, including the clergy at various churches, expressed that they felt a certain amount of ease in telling me "How it really is." They might not have felt as free to do so otherwise. What they told me was in some cases controversial or could be seen as such by some in the community. I often heard competing stories, allegations, or pleas to "Get the truth out there," but felt no pressure to take sides or a desire to engage these debates outside of analyzing what they tell us academically about religion and civic life in the community. Because of my unique relationship to the community, in the end, people did act more authentically during my observations—often forgetting I was there, but they were also perhaps even more honest in sharing their feelings about their faith and families during interviews than they may have been if I was truly one of them.

Studying St. Catherine's and Other Sites

As was discussed briefly in the introduction, my research is based primarily on ethnographic data collected in the Houston Filipino American community with extensive analysis of St. Catherine's Catholic Church (pseudonym), the San Lorenzo Ruiz de Manila Center, and a host of religious and secular associations over a six-year period. For the sake of anonymity and confidentiality, and given the very personal and political nature of some our discussions, the names of all respondents, with the exception of those whose published work is cited, were all given pseudonyms in the book. Likewise, given the contentious nature of politics in the community and the relationship of the Church to these issues, the central church in this study was also given a pseudonym. This was not done for the San Lorenzo Ruiz de Manila Center or the religious group Couples for Christ, given that both are the only organizations of their type and could be easily identified regardless of these types of measures.[3]

St. Catherine's Catholic Church was selected as the central site of this study because, first, it is one of the largest, if not the largest Filipino American Catholic congregation in Houston and, second, I had/have unique entrée to the parish through community leaders, friends, and family. St. Catherine's is located in a lower- to middle-class socioeconomic area of southwest Houston. The area is highly diverse and predominately nonwhite. However, members of St. Catherine's, particularly Filipinos, do not necessarily live within the geographic jurisdiction of the parish but come from across Houston to attend and serve this specific parish.

In the late 1960s, around the time Filipino immigrants started to come to Houston in large numbers, St. Catherine's founding parishioners were roughly 90 percent white, with the remaining percentages being black and Hispanic. From 1980 to 1990, the ethnic and racial make-up of the church dramatically changed as immigrants from Africa, Asia, and Latin American moved into the area. The percentage of white parishioners dropped from the clear majority to only 15 percent. Asians, largely Filipino and Vietnamese immigrants, become the majority (64 percent), with Hispanics being the next largest group (20 percent). Today, St. Catherine's remains a very diverse congregation. Fifty-four percent of the congregation is Asian, the majority of whom are Filipino, 40 percent is Hispanic, 12 percent is African American—largely African immigrants—and only 4 percent is white. Mass is held every Sunday in Spanish and English, and once a month in Tagalog. The clergy, which in the 1960s was exclusively white, primarily of Italian and Irish decent, is now headed by a Filipino, Monsignor Father José (pseudonym), an Indian parochial vicar who speaks Tagalog, a Hispanic permanent deacon, a white permanent deacon, and a Filipino permanent deacon.

The San Lorenzo Ruiz de Manila Center, like St. Catherine's, is also located in southwest Houston but outside St. Catherine's parish in a remote part of the adjacent county. The center is the only independent Filipino American center in Houston outside of community center spaces located on Church properties in various parishes. The idea for the center started after Deacon Frank and his wife Sister Diana (pseudonyms) attended the canonization of the first Filipino saint San Lorenzo in Rome in 1987. When they returned to Houston, and over the next six years, Deacon Frank and his wife Sister Diana were able to mobilize the Filipino community and raise funds for a center in San Lorenzo's honor. The center broke ground in 1996 and today rests on five acres of land, and with a 13,000-square-foot building that serves as a meeting space for novenas to San Lorenzo, community events, and other annual celebrations. Although no official records are kept, the center largely serves first-generation Filipino Americans from various ethnic and provincial backgrounds, despite a vision to serve the larger community around them, Filipino or not.

Among a host of religious and secular groups that comprise this study, I spent extensive time with two specific religious fellowships—Bibingka (pseudonym) and Couples for Christ (CFC). Although CFC is registered with St. Catherine's as an official parish organization or ministry, it stands largely outside of its local authority and control. Bibingka, on the other hand, is not registered with any parish. Although one group is registered with the Church and is larger in its institutional reach, while the other is not registered with the Church and is smaller in its reach, the two share similar attributes on varying levels. CFC households, the formal sites for fellowship meetings, comprise roughly twenty-five people or fewer per group. However, CFC is a rather large international organization. In Houston CFC has twelve household units, compared to just one for Bibingka, which consists of only twenty-five people for the whole group/organization. Both CFC and Bibingka meet weekly in members' houses to conduct their business and worship. In both cases, household shrines form the center of their respective worship spaces by venerating various images of Jesus, Mary, and provincial saints and martyrs with candles, lights, and, in some cases, food offerings. Both groups worship through prayer, reading of scripture, and music—and in many cases in charismatic fashion. The age of both sets of group members ranges from thirty to seventy-eight. Given the familial focus of the groups, the members are equally constituted by men (48 percent) and women (52 percent). Socioeconomically, both groups are well educated, with college to post-bachelor degrees, and are largely middle to upper class, based on household income.

The group Bibingka—both its real name and that of this pseudonym—is named for a traditional Filipino sweet that is made by the group for special occasions. The group selected this name to represent something rare and special as well as something explicitly Filipino. They also wanted to highlight the importance of food to the group's fellowship. The couples in Bibingka have been together for over forty years. From their early years of adjusting to life in Houston in the late 1970s to the raising of their children and the birth of grandchildren, these couples have been a vital part of what each considers their family and community. Although the group's membership has changed somewhat over the years, in the last ten or so years since one of its members became terminally ill, the group has not changed much and remains focused on spiritual growth of the group and the physical healing of its ill member.

CFC, on the other hand, originated as a charismatic Catholic family renewal movement in the Philippines in the early 1980s and quickly spread with the Filipino diaspora. Today CFC is a large international organization that has households around the world. The Houston CFC chapters were founded in 1996 with four couples, at the urging of Mark Casa (pseudonym), a recent immigrant from the Philippines to Houston. From the original four couples the group grew to twenty in a matter of months to form three households. Today, CFC in Houston comprises roughly 400 adults or about 200 couples, and this does not include their children.

Interviews, Survey, and Analysis

The majority of the data presented in this book come from 167 interviews I conducted with a combined snowball sample of first-generation Filipino Americans in Houston. Roughly 65 percent of the interviews were conducted with first-generation Filipino Americans who were or are active or former members of St. Catherine's parish. Included in this group are first-generation Filipino American members of St. Catherine's clergy, staff, and lay leadership. Another 30 percent of the interviews were conducted with Filipino immigrants from neighboring Houston-area parishes or those who are not involved in a parish; in some cases this included members of CFC and Bibingka who attend multiple churches. The remaining interviews (5 percent) were conducted with various community leaders around the country based on a convenience sample. Not all of those I interviewed were citizens, but roughly 83 percent were, and the overwhelming majority (93 percent) immigrated to the United States after 1965. The majority of the interviews were conducted in peoples' homes, but in some cases I interviewed people in unoccupied meeting halls at St. Catherine's during special events and celebrations or other locations. Face-to-face interviews typically lasted anywhere from one to four hours and were often followed up with email or phone conversations. In addition to these interviews, several focus groups were conducted over this period. Of the 160-plus interviews I conducted, 96 percent were face to face. All interviews were conducted in English, but, in some cases, Filipinos responded to questions in Taglish—a mixture of Tagalog and English. All interviews were transcribed verbatim by myself or a paid research assistant. I transcribed roughly 87 percent of the interviews myself. They were then later translated by me, if necessary, and were likewise coded and analyzed by me.

Although my primary interest in the interviews was structured around asking questions that would situate the ways in which religion informs and shapes Filipino American Catholic immigrants' civic lives, I started each interview by asking people to describe their life in the Philippines, their upbringing, and the importance of religion to them. I then asked what the circumstances were surrounding their immigration to the United States, why they came, and by what means. From there I asked people what it was like immigrating to the United States, any hardships they faced, and the ways they went about trying to establish a sense of community in their new homes. These questions provided a rich context to better understand peoples' answers about their current religious and civic lives in Houston. While the approach I took to analyzing these interviews was informed and shaped by previous scholarship on immigrant religious and civic life, it was not until certain patterns began to emerge from the transcriptions in the ways in which Filipinos described their community in familial terms that I began to build a more grounded theory about what faith and family means for Filipino American immigrants' civic life. I retested these themes by returning to the interviews and recoding them along these theoretical lines. In some cases I also returned to my original respondents for follow-up interviews, which were then analyzed in the context of the larger body of data.

In addition to the interviews above, I also surveyed over 200 first-generation Filipino Americans at St. Catherine's about issues ranging from religious and community participation to views on abortion and the Church's role in the community. The questions on the survey were largely drawn from survey questions from the 2000 Social Capital Community Benchmark Survey (SCCB), which is one of the largest nationally representative surveys of American civic and religious life ever conducted. Questions from the SCCB were used in part to allow for systematic comparisons between first-generation Filipino Americans and what we know about religious and civic life in America more generally.[4]

The Houston Filipino American Survey was conducted at the 112th anniversary of Philippine Independence celebrated at St. Catherine's Catholic Church in 2010. The celebration is the largest single annual gathering of first-generation Filipino Americans for a secular holiday in the city of Houston. Six first-generation Filipino American religious groups were represented at the event. These include Bibingka, Couples for Christ, Holy Rosary Crusade, Our Lady of Lourdes, Santo Niño, and Totus Tuo. Out of 350 surveys, 264 valid and completed surveys were returned, with a response rate of roughly 75 percent. The overall sample is roughly 35 percent male and 65 percent female, which is comparable to that of the general Filipino American population. Socioeconomically, the sample is likewise comparable to that of Filipinos in the 2010 United States census in terms of educational attainment and income. However, the sample is considerably older on average than the general Filipino American community, at a mean age of fifty-six years versus roughly forty-one according to the 2010 United States census.[5] The difference in mean age may be attributed to the Houston population itself and the sample criteria of foreign-born adults only. The age range of the survey respondents was eighteen to eighty-four years of age. Roughly 99 percent of the sample was Catholic. The two non-Catholic cases, one "other" and one "non-affiliated," were dropped from analyses. The sample is considerably more Catholic than most national estimates (65 to 83 percent) and can largely be attributed to the location of the survey site.

A second survey was administered to forty-two first-generation Filipino Americans attending a fundraising dance at the San Lorenzo de Manila center. The sample from the San Lorenzo event is roughly 45 percent male and 55 percent female, which is considerably more balanced than the Philippine Independence Survey (35 percent male and 65 percent female). This may be attributed to the fact that the event was a fundraising dance and the majority of those who attended typically come as a couple. In terms of socioeconomics and other demographic characteristics, the sample is identical to the prior survey. However, only 98 percent of the sample is Catholic, which is slightly lower than the previous survey at St. Catherine's.

In addition to the interviews and surveys, I monitored and engaged Filipino American community listserves and online group posts. Building on Emily Ignacio's pioneering work on Filipino immigrant cultural community formation online, I found these spaces important venues for better situating the ways in which Filipino American immigrants in Houston build and engage community.[6] These data provided yet another means to observe patterns in community relations and engage a host of hot issues as they made news on these posts. To gain a better sense of geographic space and dispersion, I also routinely asked people at events to fill out a short questionnaire to list their home parish, if they had one or more, and give both the city and zip code of their personal home address. Triangulating this unique and original data collection, I also situated them in the context of an extensive review of secondary literature on immigrant religious and civic life, including comparative census data about the wider United States Filipino American population.

NOTES

CHAPTER 1 — FAITHFULLY FILIPINO AND AMERICAN

1. The names of all individuals interviewed as well the names of the central churches in the study have been changed to maintain a measure of anonymity and confidentiality. Note that I use the term Filipino American throughout the book despite the fact that a host of terms can be to describe Filipinos. According to both interviews and findings from the Pew Research Center study on Asian Americans, Filipinos overwhelmingly describe themselves as Filipino American (69 percent); see Yen Le Espiritu, *Filipino American Lives* (Philadelphia, PA: Temple University Press, 1995); Yen Le Espiritu, *Home Bound: Filipino American Lives across Cultures, Communities, and Countries* (Berkeley: University of California Press, 2003); Pew Research Center, *The Rise of Asian Americans* (Pew Research Center's Social and Demographic Trends Project, June 19, 2012), http://www.pewsocialtrends .org/files/2012/06/The-Rise-of-Asian-Americans-Full-Report.pdf; Barbara Posadas, *The Filipino Americans* (Westport, CT: Greenwood, 1999).

2. See Christian Smith, *Moral Believing Animals: Human Personhood and Culture* (New York: Oxford University Press, 2003) on the importance of moral commitments in theorizing about the powerful influence of culture on motivations for social action.

3. Pui-Yan Lam, "As the Flocks Gather: How Religion Effects Voluntary Association Participation," *Journal for the Scientific Study of Religion* 41 (2002): 405–422, doi:10.1111/1468-5906.00127; Marc A. Musick and John Wilson, *Volunteers: A Social Profile* (Bloomington: Indiana University Press, 2008); Mark Regnerus, Christian Smith, and David Sikkink, "Who Gives to the Poor? The Role of Religious Tradition and Political Location on the Personal Generosity of Americans toward the Poor," *Journal for the Scientific Study of Religion* 37.3 (1998): 481–493, doi:10.2307/1388055; Sydney Verba, Kay Schlozman, and Henry Brady, *Voice and Equality* (Cambridge, MA: Harvard University Press, 1995).

4. Paul Lichterman, *Elusive Togetherness: Church Groups Trying to Bridge America's Divisions* (Princeton, NJ: Princeton University Press, 2005); Paul Lichterman and Charles Brady Potts, *The Civic Life of American Religion* (Stanford, CA: Stanford University Press, 2009).

5. See, for example, the case of Nigerian Catholics in Michael W. Foley and Dean R. Hoge, *Religion and the New Immigration: How Faith Communities Form Our Newest Citizens* (New York: Oxford University Press, 2007).

6. Jasso, Guillermina, Douglas S. Massey, Mark R. Rosenzweig, and James P. Smith, "Exploring Religious Preferences of Recent Immigrant to the United States: Evidence from the New Immigrant Survey Pilot," in *Religion and Immigration: Christian, Jewish, and Muslim Experiences in the United States*, edited by Yvonne Yazbeck Haddad, Jane I. Smith, and John L. Esposito (Walnut Creek, CA: AltaMira Press, 2003), 217–253; Aaron Terrazas and Jeanne Batalova, *Filipino Immigrants in the United States* (Migration Policy Institute report, 2010), www.migrationinformation.org/USFocus/display.cfm?ID=777.

7. See, for example, Smith, *Moral Believing Animals* in general; Elaine Howard Ecklund, *Korean American Evangelicals: New Models for Civic Life* (New York: Oxford University Press, 2006) on the case of Korean immigrants.

8. I define and discuss my use of cultural frameworks further in Chapter 2.

9. It is estimated that during this time the number of foreign-born immigrants rose from under four million (3.5) in 1890 to well over nine million by 1910, with the overwhelming majority being Catholic; see James D. Davidson, "Civic Engagement among American Catholics, Especially the Post Vatican II Generation," *Meeting of American Catholics in the Public Square Project* (New York, January 26–28, 2001), http://www.esosys.net/pew/papers/winter2001commonweal/davidson/davidson1.htm; James D. Davidson, *Catholicism in Motion: The Church in American Society* (Ligouri, MO: Ligouri and Triumph, 2005); Roger Finke and Rodney Stark, *The Churching of America 1776–1990* (New Brunswick, NJ: Rutgers University Press, 1992); Andrew M. Greely, *American Catholic: A Social Portrait* (New York: Basic Books, 1977); Robert F. Leavitt SS, "Lay Participation in the Catholic Church in America, 1789–1989," in *Perspectives, Politics, and Civic Participation*, edited by Stephen J. Vicchio and Virginia Geiger SSND (Westminster, MD: Christian Classics, 1989), 275–293.

10. As of 2010, the two largest American immigrant communities are Mexicans and Filipinos. Both Mexico and the Philippines are predominately Catholic countries and represent the two largest sources of Catholic immigration to the United States; see Jasso, Massey, Rosenzweig, and Smith, "Exploring Religious Preferences"; Terrazas and Batalova, *Filipino Immigrants in the United States*.

11. See discussion in chapter 3 of Helen Rose Ebaugh and Janet Saltzman Chafetz, *Religion and the New Immigrants: Continuities and Adaptations in Immigrant Congregations* (Walnut Creek, CA: AltaMira Press, 2000).

12. Digby E. Baltzell, *The Protestant Establishment* (New York: Random House, 1964); Ray Allen Billington, *The Protestant Crusade 1800–1960: A Study of the Origins of American Nativism* (New York: Quadrangle Books, 1964); M. Jeffrey Burns, Ellen Skerrett, and Joseph M. White, eds., *Keeping Faith: European and Asian Catholic Immigrants* (New York: Orbis Books, [2000] 2006), 80–86; James D. Davidson and Mark McCormick, "Catholics and Civic Engagement: Empirical Findings at the Individual Level," in *Civil Society, Civic Engagement and Catholicism in the U.S.*, edited by Antonius Liedhegener and Werner Kremp (Trier, Germany: WVT Wissenschaftlicher Verlag Trier, 2007), 119–134; John Higham, *Strangers in the Land: Patterns in the American Nativism, 1840–1925* (New Brunswick, NJ: Rutgers University Press, 2002).

13. Within a year of its founding, the Know Nothing Party elected eight governors, over one hundred members of Congress, countless local officials, and mounted a spirited presidential bid before its eventual quick demise; see Tyler G. Anbinder, *Nativism and Slavery: The Northern Know Nothings and the Politics of the 1850s* (New York: Oxford University Press, 199).

14. In the years leading up to World War I, nativism sparked a massive America for Americans campaign. Prior immigrant waves who now saw themselves as both American and ethnically something else, such as Irish-Americans, were criticized for not being 100 percent American. They were also asked to pick flags to defend for fear of dual loyalties. These sentiments paved the way for the 1917 Immigration Act and the literacy tests it enacted; see Bill Ong Hing, *Defining America through Immigration Policy* (Philadelphia, PA: Temple Press University, 2004).

15. See the detailed history of American colonial occupation of the Philippines in Julian Go and Anne L. Foster, *The American Colonial State in the Philippines: Global Perspectives* (Durham, NC: Duke University Press, 2003); Julian Go, *American Empire and the Politics of Meaning: Elite Political Cultures in the Philippines and Puerto Rico during U.S. Colonialism* (Durham, NC: Duke University Press, 2008).

16. United States Census Bureau, *Census of the Philippine Islands*, Volume 1, directed by General J. P. Sanger (Washington, DC: Bureau of the Census, 1905), 411–431, http://www.archive.org/details/censusphilippino3ganngoog.

17. From 1929 through 1930, for example, anti-Filipino riots broke out in rural communities such as Watsonville, California, in response to Filipino men dancing with white women at local bars. On numerous occasions Filipinos were beaten by angry mobs; see Stephen Bogardus, *Anti-Filipino Race Riots* (San Diego, CA: Ingram Institute of Social Science, 1976); Fred Cordova, *Filipinos: Forgotten Asian Americans, A Pictorial Essay* (Dubuque, IA: Kendall/ Hunt, 1983); Ronald Takaki, *Strangers from a Different Shore: A History of Asian Americans* (New York: Penguin, 1987); Ronald Takaki, *India in the West: South Asians in America* (New York: Chelsea House, 1995); Ronald Takaki, *In the Heart of Filipino America: Immigrants from the Pacific Isles* (New York: Chelsea House, 1996).

18. See further on the racialization and discrimination of Filipinos in Stephen Bogardus, "American Attitudes toward Filipinos," *Sociology and Social Research* 14 (1929): 56–69; Rick Bonus, *Locating Filipino Americans: Ethnicity and the Cultural Politics of Space* (Boston, MA: Temple University Press, 2000); Hing, *Defining America through Immigration Policy*.

19. Burns, Skerrett, and White, *Keeping Faith*, 263–269.

20. See discussion on the ghettoization of American Catholics in John Cogley and Rodger Van Allen, *Catholic America* (Kansas City, MO: Sheed and Ward, 1986); Davidson, *Catholicism in Motion*; Jay P. Dolan, *The American Catholic Experience: A History from Colonial Times to the Present* (Garden City, NY: Doubleday, 1985).

21. Chapter 2 will discuss this at greater length, looking specifically at the case of Filipino immigrants.

22. Charles R. Morris, *American Catholic: The Saints and Sinners Who Built America's Most Powerful Church* (New York: Random House, 1997).

23. Davidson, *Catholicism in Motion*; Robin Gill, *Churchgoing and Christian Ethics* (New York: Cambridge University Press, 1999); Robin Gill, *The Empty Church Revisited: Explorations in Practical, Pastoral, and Empirical Theology* (Burlington, VT: Ashgate, 2003); Norval Glenn and Ruth Hyland, "Religious Preference and Worldly Success: Some Evidence from National Surveys," *American Sociological Review* 32 (1967): 73–85; Greely, *American Catholic*.

24. Mary J. Oats, "Faith and Good Works: Catholic Giving and Taking," in *Charity, Philanthropy, and Civility in American History*, edited by L. J. Friedman and M. D. McGarvie (New York: Cambridge University Press, 2003), 284.

25. Frank Adloff, "Civil Society, Civic Engagement, and Religion: Findings and Research Problems in Germany and the U.S.," in *Civil Society, Civic Engagement and Catholicism in*

the U.S., edited by Antonius Liedhegener and Werner Kremp (Trier, Germany: WVT Wissenschaftlicher Verlag Trier, 2007), 63–92.

26. See discussion in David R. Roediger, *Working toward Whiteness: How America's Immigrants Became White: The Strange Journey from Ellis Island to the Suburbs* (Cambridge MA: Basic Books, 2005), on the historical processes by which newly arriving immigrants in the nineteenth century confronted racism and struggled to become American by working toward whiteness.

27. Vatican II is the Second Vatican Council held between 1962 and 1965 at St. Peter's Basilica in order to address relations between the Roman Catholic Church and the so-called modern world. The proceedings from Vatican II brought about many changes both institutionally and culturally to Roman Catholicism; see further Michael Novak, *The Catholic Ethic and the Spirit of Capitalism* (New York: New York Free Press, 1993). The important role of Vatican II and Catholicism in the civic life of Filipinas, women from the Philippines, will be discussed at greater length in Chapter 2; see José Casanova, *Public Religions in the Modern World* (Chicago, IL: University of Chicago Press, 1994); Thomas Gannon, *World Catholicism in Transition* (New York: MacMillan, 1988). Also see the discussion of the role of women in specific Catholic churches in Houston in Ebaugh and Chafetz, *Religion and the New Immigrants*.

28. William V. D'Antonio, James D. Davidson, Dean R. Hoge, and Katherine Meyer, *American Catholics: Gender, Generation, and Commitment* (Walnut Creek, CA: AltaMira Press, 2001); Meghan Davis and Antonius Liedhegener, "Catholic Civic Engagement at the Local Level: The Parish and Beyond," in *Civil Society, Civic Engagement and Catholicism in the U.S.*, edited by Antonius Liedhegener and Werner Kremp (Trier, Germany: WVT Wissenschaftlicher Verlag Trier, 2007), 135–160; Kathleen Joyce, "The Long Loneliness: Liberal Catholics and the Conservative Church," in *"I Come away Stronger": How Small Groups are Shaping American Religion*, edited by Robert Wuthnow (Grand Rapids, MI: Wm. B. Eerdmans, 1994), 55–76; Novak, *The Catholic Ethic and the Spirit of Capitalism*.

29. Chapters 1 and 4 in John F. Kennedy, *A Nation of Immigrants* (New York: HarperCollins, 1964).

30. Ebaugh and Chafetz, *Religion and the New Immigrants*; Stephen R. Warner and Judith G. Wittner, *Gatherings in Diaspora: Religious Communities and the New Immigration* (Philadelphia, PA: Temple University Press, 1998).

31. George Borjas, *Friends or Strangers: The Impact of Immigrants on the U.S. Economy* (New York: Basic Books, 1990); Peter Brimelow, *Alien Nation: Common Sense about America's Immigration Disaster* (New York: Random House, 1995); Stephen Moore, *Immigration and the Rise and Decline of American Cities* (Stanford, California: Hoover Institute on War, Revolution, and Peace, Stanford University, 1997); Wayne Lutton and John Tanton, *The Immigration Invasion* (Petosky, MI: Social Contract Press, 1994).

32. Virginia Abernathy, *Population Politics: The Choices That Shape Our Future* (New York: Insight Books, 1993); Brent Nelson, *America Balkanized: Immigration's Challenge to Government* (Monterey, VA: American Immigration Control Foundation, 1994).

33. Samuel P. Huntington, "The Hispanic Challenge," *Foreign Policy* 141 (March/April 2004): 30-45, http://dx.doi.org/10.2307/4147547; Samuel P. Huntington, *Who Are We? The Challenges to America's National Identity* (New York: Simon and Schuster, 2004).

34. Huntington, "Hispanic Challenge" and *Who Are We?*

35. Catherine Choy, *Empire of Care: Nursing and Migration in Filipino American History* (Durham, NC: Duke University Press, 2003); John Cox, "Filipino Nurses File Suit to Join Federal Action against Delano Regional Hospital," *Bakersfield Californian*, December 8,

2010,   http://www.bakersfield.com/news/local/x998656883/Filipino-nurses-file-suit-to
-join-federal-action-against-Delano-Regional-hospital; Law Offices of Rheuban and
Greeson, "Filipino Nurses Accuse California Hospital of Discrimination," blog, December 10, 2010, http://www.losangelesemploymentlaws.com/2010/12/filipino-nurses-accuse
-california-hospital-of-discrimination.shtml.

36. For a broader discussion of Asian American racialization and their perceived sta-
tus as perpetual foreigners, see Keith Osajima, "Asian Americans as the Model Minority:
An Analysis of the Popular Images in the 1960s and 1980s," in *Reflections on Shattered
Windows: Promises and Prospects for Asian American Studies*, edited by Gary Y. Okihiro
(Pullman: Washington State University Press, 1988), 449–458; Mia Tuan, *Forever Foreign-
ers or Honorary Whites: The Asian Ethnic Experience Today* (New Brunswick, NJ: Rutgers
University Press, 1998); Deborah Woo, *Glass Ceilings and Asian Americans: The New Faces
of Workplace Barriers* (Walnut Creek, CA: AltaMira Press, 2000).

37. See discussions on assimilation, acculturation, and incorporation in Elizabeth Arias,
"Change in Nuptiality Patterns among Cuban Americans: Evidence of Cultural and
Structural Assimilation," *International Migration Review* 35 (2001): 525–556; Elizabeth
Wildsmith, "Race/Ethnic Differences in Female Headship: Exploring the Assumptions of
Assimilation Theory," *Social Science Quarterly* 85.1 (2004): 89–106. For the classical para-
digm, see Milton Gordon, *Assimilation in American Life* (New York: Oxford University
Press, 1964); Robert E. Park and Ernest W. Burgess, *Introduction to the Science of Sociology*
(Chicago, IL: University of Chicago Press, 1924).

38. See, for example, Richard D. Alba and Victor Nee, "Rethinking Assimilation Theory for a New Era of Immigration,"*International Migration Review* 31 (1997): 826–874,
doi:10.2307/2547416.

39. Rodger Brubaker, "The Return of Assimilation? Changing Perspectives and its
Sequels in France, Germany, and the United States," *Ethnic and Racial Studies* 24 (2001):
531–548, doi:10.1080/01419870120049770; Alejandro Portes and Min Zhou, "The New Sec-
ond Generation: Segmented Assimilation and Its Variants among Post-1965 Immigrant
Youth," *Annals of American Academy of Political and Social Sciences* 530 (1993): 140–174;
Stephen R. Warner, "The De-Europeanization of American Christianity," in *A Nation of
Religions: Pluralism in the American Public Square*, edited by Stephen Prothero (Chapel
Hill: University of North Carolina Press, 2005), 233–255; Warner and Wittner, *Gatherings
in Diaspora.*

40. See further Joyce, "The Long Loneliness"; Novak, *The Catholic Ethic and the Spirit
of Capitalism.*

41. William V. D'Antonio, James D. Davidson, Dean R. Hoge, and Mary L. Gautier,
American Catholics Today: New Realities of Their Faith and Their Church (Lanham, MD:
Rowman & Littlefield, 2007); Jay P. Dolan, *In Search of an American Catholicism* (New
York: Oxford University Press, 2002); Gill, *The Empty Church Revisited: Explorations in
Practical, Pastoral, and Empirical Theology*, 39–50. Also see more generally Philip Jenkins,
The Next Christendom: The Coming of Global Christianity (New York: Oxford University
Press, 2002), a discussion of the Western Hemisphere's reaction to the immigration of
southern Christianity from the global South.

42. Tuan, *Forever Foreigners or Honorary Whites* draws further attention to this with the
case of Michelle Kwan, who despite skating for the United States in the Olympics was subject to news of her loss as "American beats Kwan." Kwan lost to her fellow American team-
mate but was deemed non-American in the media. See further Osajima, "Asian Americans
as the Model Minority"; Woo, *Glass Ceilings and Asian Americans.*

43. Tuan, *Forever Foreigners or Honorary Whites*; also see Philip Perlmutter, *The Legacy of Hate: A Short History of Ethnic, Religious and Racial Prejudice in America* (Armonk, NY: M. E. Sharpe, 1999) on the intersection of religious and racial prejudice in America.

44. Foley and Hoge, *Religion and the New Immigration*; Alejandro Portes and Jozsef Borocz, "Contemporary Immigration: Theoretical Perspectives on Its Determinates and Modes of Incorporation," *International Migration Review* 23.3 (1989): 606–630, doi:10.2307/2546431.

45. Civic incorporation does not necessarily involve politics or formal civic engagement such as volunteerism, but also the ways in which a sense of community is built through active participation with others: Alejandro Portes and Robert Manning, "The Immigrant Enclave: Theory and Empirical Examples," in *Competitive Ethnic Relations*, edited by Susan Olzak and Joane Nagel (Orlando, FL: Academic Press, 1986), 47–63; John A. Arthur, *Invisible Sojourners: African Immigrant Diaspora in the United States* (Westport, CT: Praeger, 2000); David M. Cutler, Edward L. Glaeser, and Jacob L. Vigdor, "Is the Melting Pot Still Hot? Explaining the Resurgence of Immigrant Segregation," *Review of Economics and Statistics* 90.3 (2008): 478–497, doi:10.1162/rest.90.3.478; David M. Cutler, Edward L. Glaeser, and Jacob L. Vigdor, "When Are Ghettos Bad? Lessons from Immigrant Segregation in the United States," *Journal of Urban Economics* 63.3 (2008): 759–774, doi:10.1016/j.jue.2007.08.003; Guillermo Grenier and Lisandro Perez, *The Legacy of Exile: Cubans in the United States* (Boston, MA: Allyn and Bacon, 2003); Alejandro Portes and Ruben Rumbaut, *Immigrant America: A Portrait*, third edition (Berkeley: University of California Press, 2006).

46. Cutler, Glaeser, and Vigdor, "Is the Melting Pot Still Hot?"; Cutler, Glaeser, and Vigdor, "When Are Ghettos Bad?"; Portes and Rumbaut, *Immigrant America: A Portrait*.

47. Arthur, *Invisible Sojourners*; Grenier and Perez, *The Legacy of Exile*; Portes and Manning, "The Immigrant Enclave: Theory and Empirical Examples"; Portes and Rumbaut, *Immigrant America: A Portrait*; Kenneth Wilson and W. Allen Martin, "Ethnic Enclaves: A Comparison of the Cuban and Black Economies in Miami," *American Journal of Sociology* 88.1 (1982): 135–160.

48. Richard D. Alba, Albert J. Raboteau, and Josh DeWind, eds., *Immigration and Religion in America: Comparative and Historical Perspectives* (New York: New York University Press, 2009); Tony Carnes and Fenggang Yang, eds., *Asian American Religions: The Making and Remaking of Borders and Boundaries* (New York: New York University Press, 2004); Carolyn Chen, *Getting Saved in America: Taiwanese Immigration and Religious Experience* (Princeton, NJ: Princeton University Press, 2008); Ebaugh and Chafetz, *Religion and the New Immigrants*; Ecklund, *Korean American Evangelicals*; Foley and Hoge, *Religion and the New Immigration*; Joaquin Gonzalez III, *Filipino American Faith in Action: Immigration, Religion, and Civic Engagement* (New York: New York University Press, 2009); Fred Kniss and Paul D. Numrich, *Sacred Assemblies and Civic Engagement: How Religion Matters for America's Newest Immigrants* (New Brunswick, NJ: Rutgers University Press, 2007); Alex Stepick, Terry Rey, and Sarah J. Mahler, eds., *Churches and Charity in the Immigrant City* (New Brunswick, NJ: Rutgers University Press, 2009); Warner and Wittner, *Gatherings in Diaspora*; Fenggang Yang, *Chinese Christians in America: Conversion, Assimilation, and Adhesive Identities* (University Park: Pennsylvania State University Press, 1999); David Yoo, *New Spiritual Homes: Religion and Asian Americans* (Honolulu: University of Hawaii Press, 1999).

49. Mary Jo Bane, "The Catholic Puzzle: Parishes and Civic Life," in *Taking Faith Seriously*, edited by Mary Jo Bane, Brent Coffin, and Richard Higgins (Cambridge, MA: Harvard University Press, 2005), 63–93.

50. Several scholars have proposed that a distinctive Catholic Ethic exists that fosters a more communitarian spirit than Protestantism. For these scholars, the Catholic Ethic emphasizes communal relationships through what Ferdinand Tonnies, *Community and Society / Gemeinschaft and Gesellschaft*, translated and edited by C. P. Loomis (New Brunswick, NJ: Transaction Publishers, [1887] 1988) defined as more personal or Gemeinschaft orientations; see Bane, "The Catholic Puzzle"; Andrew M. Greely, *The Great Mysteries: An Essential Catechism* (New York: Seabury Press, 1976); Greely, *American Catholic: A Social Portrait*, 253–267; Andrew M. Greely, *The Catholic Imagination* (Berkeley: University of California Press, 2000); Novak, *The Catholic Ethic and the Spirit of Capitalism*; Daniel Rigney, Jerome Matz, and Armondo Abney, "Is There a Catholic Sharing Ethic?: A Research Note," *Sociology of Religion* 65.2 (2004): 155–165; J. M. Thompson, "The Catholic Ethic in American Society: An Exploration of Values (review)," *Choice* 33.6 (1996): 966; John Tropman, *The Catholic Ethic in American Society* (San Francisco, CA: Jossey-Bass, 1995).

51. Mary Jo Bane, Brent Coffin, and Richard Higgins, eds., *Taking Faith Seriously* (Cambridge, MA: Harvard University Press, 2005); Mark E. Brewer, *Relevant No More? The Protestant / Catholic Divide in American Electoral Politics* (Lanham, MD: Lexington Books, 2003); D'Antonio, Davidson, Hoge, and Gautier, *American Catholics Today*; James D. Davidson and Mark McCormick, "Catholics and Civic Engagement: Empirical Findings at the Individual Level," in *Civil Society, Civic Engagement and Catholicism in the U.S.*, edited by Antonius Liedhegener and Werner Kremp (Trier, Germany: WVT Wissenschaftlicher Verlag Trier, 2007), 119–134; Dean R. Hoge, William D. Dinges, Mary Johnson, and Juan L. Gonzales, *Young Adult Catholics: Religion in the Culture of Choice* (Notre Dame, IN: University of Notre Dame Press, 2001); Rigney, Matz, and Abney, "Is There a Catholic Sharing Ethic?" Note there is also some disagreement over the degree to which Catholic youth are receiving and acting on messages of community service; see Christian Smith and Melinda L. Denton, *Soul Searching: The Religious and Spiritual Lives of American Teenagers* (New York: Oxford University Press, 2005).

52. See literature summary and discussion in Davidson and McCormick, "Catholics and Civic Engagement." Of particular interest is their finding that Catholics are for the most part no more or less involved in voluntary associations than other religious denominations, and like these groups, tend to be most involved in groups that stress personal and family needs over the needs of other collective groups; this is important to Tocquevillian arguments about American civil society.

53. See, for example, the discussion in Foley and Hoge, *Religion and the New Immigration*, on the comparative differences between Vietnamese and Salvadoran Catholics churches and Chinese and Korean Protestant churches.

54. David Carlin, *The Decline and Fall of the Catholic Church in America* (Manchester, NH: Sophia Institute, 2003); Meghan Davis and Antonius Liedhegener, "Catholic Civic Engagement at the Local Level: The Parish and Beyond," in *Civil Society, Civic Engagement and Catholicism in the U.S.*, edited by Antonius Liedhegener and Werner Kremp (Trier, Germany: WVT Wissenschaftlicher Verlag Trier, 2007), 135–160; Joseph A. Varacalli, *The Catholic Experience in America* (Westport, CT: Greenwood, 2005).

55. Lam, "As the Flocks Gather"; Marc A. Musick and John Wilson, *Volunteers: A Social Profile* (Bloomington: Indiana University Press, 2008); Regnerus, Smith, and Sikkink, "Who Gives to the Poor?" Note that this is not necessarily the case in comparison with non-Christian traditions, at least in the Asian American context: see discussions on Asian American civic life in Stephen M. Cherry, "Engaging the Spirit of the East:

Asian American Christians and Civic Life," *Sociological Spectrum* 29.2 (2009): 249–272; Elaine Ecklund and Jerry Park, "Religious Diversity and Community Volunteerism among Asian Americans," *Journal for the Scientific Study of Religion* 46.2 (2007): 233–244, doi:10.1111/j.1468-5906.2007.00353.x.

56. Verba, Scholzman, and Brady, *Voice and Equality.*

57. Pui-Yan Lam, "Religion and Civic Culture: A Cross-National Study of Voluntary Association Membership," *Journal for the Scientific Study of Religion* 45.2 (2006): 177–293, doi:10.1111/j.1468-5906.2006.00300.x.

58. See further Kniss and Numrich, *Sacred Assemblies and Civic Engagement* on the locus of moral authority in the American Catholic Church.

59. Mark Chavez, *Congregations in America* (Cambridge, MA: Harvard University Press, 2004), 122.

60. Foley and Hoge, *Religion and the New Immigration*, 218–219.

61. Kniss and Numrich, *Sacred Assemblies and Civic Engagement*, 47–53.

62. In 2005, the most important issue ranked in the Diocesan Social Action Offices was immigration; see Jeffrey Odell Korgen, "State Catholic Conferences, Local Bishops, and Volunteer Leaders: A Pastoral Reflection on Catholic Legislative Advocacy on the Diocesan Level," in *Civil Society, Civic Engagement and Catholicism in the U.S.*, edited by Antonius Liedhegener and Werner Kremp (Trier, Germany: WVT Wissenschaftlicher Verlag Trier, 2007), 233–237.

63. Gerald P. Fogarty, "Volunteerism in the Land of Voluntarism: The American Catholic Church," in *Civil Society, Civic Engagement and Catholicism in the U.S.*, edited by Antonius Liedhegener and Werner Kremp (Trier, Germany: WVT Wissenschaftlicher Verlag Trier, 2007): 110.

64. Alexis de Tocqueville, *Democracy in America: Historical-Critical Edition of De la démocratie en Amérique*, edited by Eduardo Nolla, translated from the French by James T. Schleifer, bilingual French-English edition, 4 vols. (Indianapolis, IN: Liberty Fund, [1835] 2010), 468–469.

65. Richard D. Alba and Robert Orsi, "Passages in Piety: Generational Transitions and the Social and Religious Incorporation of Italian Americans," in *Immigration and Religion in America: Comparative and Historical Perspectives*, edited by Richard Alba, Albert J. Raboteau, and Josh DeWind (New York: New York University Press, 2009), 32–55; Huntington, "José Can You See?"; Huntington, *Who Are We?*

66. David Lopez, "Whither the Flock? The Catholic Church and the Success of Mexicans in America," in *Immigration and Religion in America: Comparative and Historical Perspectives*, edited by Richard Alba, Albert Raboteau, and Josh DeWind (New York: New York University Press, 2007), 71–98.

67. Ana Maria Diaz-Stevens and Anthony M. Stevens-Arroyo, *Recognizing the Latino Resurgence in U.S. Religion: The Emmaus Paradigm* (Boulder, CO: Westview, 1998); Michael Jones-Correa and David Leal, "Political Participation: Does Religion Matter?" *Political Research Quarterly* 54.4 (2001): 751–770; Peggy Levitt, *The Transnational Villagers* (Berkeley: University of California Press, 2001); Cecilia Menjivar, "Religion and Immigration in Comparative Perspective: Catholic and Evangelical Salvadorans in San Francisco, Washington, D.C., and Phoenix," *Sociology of Religion* 64.1 (2003): 21–46, doi:10.2307/3712267; Alejandro Portes and Ruben Rumbaut, *Legacies: The Story of the Immigrant Second Generation* (Berkeley: University of California Press, 2001); Min Zhou and Carl Bankston, *Growing Up American: How Vietnamese Children Adapt to Life in the United States* (New York: Russell Sage Foundation, 1998).

68. United States Conference of Catholic Bishops estimates that 83 percent of Filipino Americans (1.54 million), 29 percent of Vietnamese Americans (0.33 million), 17 percent of Indian Americans (0.29 million), roughly 12 percent of Chinese Americans (0.30 million), 7 percent of Korean Americans (0.07 million), and 4 percent of Japanese Americans (0.03 million) are Catholic: United States Council of Catholic Bishops (USCCB), *Asian and Pacific Presence: Harmony and Faith* (Washington DC: USCCB online, 2001), http://old.usccb.org/mrs/harmony.shtml. There is some debate over the exact percentages for each, but regardless of variability by data set, Filipino Americans are overwhelmingly Catholic across them; see Jasso, Massey, Rosenzweig, and Smith, "Exploring Religious Preferences of Recent Immigrant to the United States"; Pei-te Lien and Tony Carnes, "Religious Demography of Asian American Boundary Crossing," in *Asian American Religions*, edited by Tony Carnes and Fenggang Yang (New York: New York University Press, 2004), 38–54; Warner, "The De-Europeanization of American Christianity"; Jerry Z. Park, "Assessing the Sociological Study of Asian American Christians," *Society of Asian North American Christianity Studies Journal* 1 (2009): 57–94; Pew, *The Rise of Asian Americans*; Pew Research Center, *Asian Americans: A Mosaic of Faith* (Pew Research Center, July 19, 2012), http://www.pewforum.org/uploadedFiles/Topics/Demographics/Asian%20Americans%20religion%20full%20report.pdf.

69. Pew, *The Rise of Asian Americans.*

70. It is estimated that the number of Filipino Americans in the United States prior to 1946 was roughly 109,000; see the discussion of early Filipino settlements in California and Louisiana in Eloisa Gomez Borah, "Filipinos in Unamuno's California Expedition of 1587," *Amerasia Journal* 21.3 (1995): 175–183; Carl Nolte, "400th Anniversary of Spanish Shipwreck, Rough First Landing in the Bay Area," *San Francisco Chronicle*, November 14, 1995, http://articles.sfgate.com/1995-11-14/news/17820166_1_spanish-galleon-california-coast-ship; Antonio Pido, *The Pilipinos in America: Macro/ Micro Dimensions of Immigration and Integration* (New York: Center for Immigration Studies, 1986); Posadas, *The Filipino Americans.*

71. Signage at West Coast hotels in the 1930s that read "Positively No Filipinos Allowed" exemplifies the extent of anti-Filipino sentiments of the time; see chapter 3 in Yen Le Espiritu, *Home Bound: Filipino American Lives across Cultures.*

72. Bonus, *Locating Filipino Americans*; Hing, *Defining America through Immigration Policy.*

73. Alvar Carlson, "The Settling of Recent Filipino Immigrants in Midwestern Metropolitan Areas," *Crossroads* 1.1 (1983): 13–19; Cordova, *Filipinos: Forgotten Asian Americans*; Espiritu, *Home Bound: Filipino American Lives across Cultures*; Espiritu, *Filipino American Lives*; Pilpinos in American History Workgroup, ed., *Iriri Ti Pagsayaatan Ti Sapasap: A Reader of the History of Pilipinos in America* (San Francisco, CA: Pilpinos in America History Workgroup, 1975); Bruno Lasker, *Filipino Immigration to the United States and Hawaii* (New York: Arno, 1969); Posadas, *The Filipino Americans*; United States Census Bureau, *U.S. Census 2000*, www.census.gov.

74. See discussion in Ma Reinaruth D. Carlos, "On the Determinates of International Migration in the Philippines," *International Migration Review* 36.1 (2002): 81–102; chapter 2 of Espiritu, *Home Bound: Filipino American Lives across Cultures.*

75. Terrazas and Batalova, *Filipino Immigrants in the United States*

76. From 2001 to 2010, the Philippines were also recipients of more immigrant visas issued by the United States than any other Asian country (350,694); see Asian American Center for Advancing Justice, *A Community of Contrasts: Asian Americans in the United*

States: 2011, http://www.apalc.org/pdffiles/Community_of_Contrast.pdf. In terms of undocumented Asians, we might compare the Filipino figures to an estimated 130,000 undocumented immigrants from China; see ibid. For a general discussion of all Filipino demographic trends, also see Gonzalez III, *Filipino American Faith in Action*; Pew, *The Rise of Asian Americans*; Terrazas and Batalova, *Filipino Immigrants in the United States*.

77. Note that Chinese, according to these estimates, does not include Taiwanese; see Asian American Center for Advancing Justice, *A Community of Contrasts*. For comparison, see Pew, *The Rise of Asian Americans*, which estimates Filipino growth to be only 30 percent, compared to Chinese growth at 38 percent.

78. The Filipino American population constitutes roughly 20 percent of the overall Asian American population, surpassed only by Chinese Americans at 23 percent; see Bonus, *Locating Filipino Americans*; Pew, *The Rise of Asian Americans*.

79. Filipinas, women, are roughly 59 percent of the Filipino immigrant population; Terrazas and Batalova, *Filipino Immigrants in the United States*.

80. Ibid.; also see Choy, *Empire of Care* on the history of Filipino nurse migration to the United States.

81. Terrazas and Batalova, *Filipino Immigrants in the United States*.

82. Ibid.; also see Asian American Center for Advancing Justice, *A Community of Contrasts*.

83. Fenella Cannell, *Power and Intimacy in the Christian Philippines* (Cambridge, UK: Cambridge University Press, 1999); Joaquin L. Gonzalez III and Andrea Maison, "We Do Not Bowl Alone: Social and Cultural Capital from Filipinos and Their Church," in *Asian American Religions: The Making and Remaking of Borders and Boundaries*, edited by Tony Carnes and Fenggang Yang (New York: New York University Press, 2004), 21–38; Park, "Assessing the Sociological Study of Asian American Christians"; Pido, *The Pilipinos in America*; France Viana, "Philippine Culture 101," *Filipino Express*, March 6, 2005, http://www.filipinasmag.com/free_fvi_focusonfilams.html.

84. Jenkins, *The Next Christendom*; Social Weather Survey, *SWS Select Surveys on Filipino Religiosity*, Vol. 3 (March 2002), www.sws.org.ph.

85. Cannell, *Power and Intimacy in the Christian Philippines*; Jenkins, *The Next Christendom; The Official Catholic Directory* (Berkeley Heights, NJ: National Register Publishing, 1999).

86. Social Weather Survey, *SWS Select Surveys on Filipino Religiosity*, Vol. 3.

87. Gonzalez III, *Filipino American Faith in Action*.

88. Park, "Assessing the Sociological Study of Asian American Christians."

89. Gonzalez III, *Filipino American Faith in Action*; Gonzalez III and Maison, "We Do Not Bowl Alone"; Jonathan Okamura, *Imagining the Filipino American Diaspora* (New York: Garland, 1998); Steffi San Buenaventura, "Filipino Folk Spirituality and Immigration: From Mutual Aid to Religion," in *New Spiritual Homes*, edited by David K. Yoo (Honolulu: University of Hawaii Press, 1999), 52–86.

90. Dovelyn Agunias, *Linking Temporary Worker Schemes with Development* (Washington, DC: Migration Policy Institute, February 2007), http://www.migrationinformation.org/Feature/display.cfm?ID=576.

91. See discussion of diaspora people in Espiritu, *Home Bound: Filipino American Lives across Cultures*; Paul Gilroy, *The Black Atlantic: Modernity and Double Consciousness* (Cambridge, MA: Harvard University Press, 1993).

92. Within the Philippines, there is considerable concern over the future impact of migration on the country. Although economically remittances make up 10 percent of the nation's

GNP, the continual brain drain may not be worth it. Even if the nation survives losing its most educated and skilled workers, migration has seriously eroded traditional family structures and placed enormous anxieties on the people themselves: see further Dovelyn Agunias and Kathleen Newland, *Developing a Road Map for Engaging Diasporas in Development* (Washington, DC: Migration Policy Institute, April 2007), http://www.migrationpolicy. org/pubs/thediasporahandbook.pdf); Rhacel Parreñas, *Servants of Globalization: Women, Migration, and Domestic Work* (Stanford, CA: Stanford University Press, 2001).

93. Jenkins, *The Next Christendom*, 118.

94. USCCB, *Asian and Pacific Presence.*

95. See, for example, Park, "Assessing the Sociological Study of Asian American Christians," and Pew, *Asian Americans: A Mosaic of Faith.* Also note that according to Pew findings, Asian American Catholics, of which Filipinos constitute the largest majority, have the second highest religious affiliation retention rate from childhood to adulthood (second only to Hindus); Pew, *Asian Americans: A Mosaic of Faith.*

96. Gonzalez III, *Filipino American Faith in Action*; Okamura, *Imagining the Filipino American Diaspora*; San Buenaventura, "Filipino Folk Spirituality and Immigration."

97. Gonzalez III, *Filipino American Faith in Action.*

98. Ibid.

99. Pauline Agbayani-Siewert and Linda Revilla, "Filipino Americans," in *Asian Americans: Contemporary Trends and Issues*, edited by Pyong Gap Min (London: Sage, 1995), 134–168; Clay White, "Residential Segregation among Asians in Long Beach: Japanese, Chinese Filipino, Korean, Indian, Vietnamese, Hawaiian, Guamian, and Samoan," *Sociology and Social Research* 70 (1986): 266–267.

100. Cordova, *Filipinos: Forgotten Asian Americans*; Espiritu, *Filipino American Lives*; Espiritu, *Home Bound: Filipino American Lives across Cultures*; Oscar Peñaranda, Serafin Syquia, and Sam Tagatac, "An Introduction to Filipino American Literature," in *Aiiieeeee! An Anthology of Asian American Writers*, edited by Frank Chin et al. (Washington, DC: Howard University Press, 1974), 227–236; Epifanio San Juan Jr., *Writing and National Liberation: Essays in Critical Practice* (Quezon City, Philippines: University of the Philippines Press, 1991), 117.

101. Jessica Chao, "Asian-American Philanthropy: Expanding Circles of Participation," in *Cultures of Caring: Philanthropy in America's Diverse Communities* (Washington, DC: Council on Foundations, 1999), 189–253, for example, suggests that Filipino Americans tend to stress obligations to family, ethnic organizations, and their religious institutions in their giving and community engagements, but does not elaborate on the cultural frameworks that may facilitate these processes.

102. For further specifics about my entry into the community, the research sites, and the methods by which I collected data, see the Methodological Appendix.

103. Bibingka, both its real name and its pseudonym, is named for a traditional Filipino sweet that is made by the group for special occasions. Thus the name was selected to represent something special and explicitly Filipino. For further specifics about my selection of these two groups and the methods by which I collected data, see the Methodological Appendix.

104. The history and structure of these groups will be discussed at greater length in subsequent chapters.

105. See the study by Emily Noelle Ignacio, *Building Diaspora* (New Brunswick, NJ: Rutgers University Press, 2005) for details on the importance of studying the Filipino diaspora on-line.

106. Arturo B. Rodriquez, *U.S. Citizenship Guidebook* (Kearney, NE: Morris, 2000).

107. Ebaugh and Chafetz, *Religion and the New Immigrants*; Helen Rose Ebaugh and Janet Saltzman Chafetz, *Religion across Borders: Transnational Immigrant Networks* (Walnut Creek, CA: AltaMira Press, 2002).

108. Beyond the clear academic reasons for studying the first-generation Filipino American community in Houston, the selection of this particular locale was also somewhat personal and stems from my long-standing relationship with the community; see further comments in the Methodological Appendix.

109. According to the 2010 census, the Filipino American community in Texas grew by 77 percent since 2000 in the Filipino Alone category; see National Federation of Filipino American Associations (NaFFAA), "U.S. 2010 Census: Filipinos in the U.S. Increased by 38%; Nevada has fastest growing population" (NaFFAA press release June 29, 2011), http://www.scribd.com/doc/58979501/US-2010-Census-Filipinos-in-the-US-Increased-by-38-Percent-Nevada-Has-Fastest-Growing-Population. Note that Texas now has the third largest Asian American population, overtaking New Jersey and Hawaii, and Harris County in particular now has the twelfth largest Asian American population of all United States counties; see Asian American Center for Advancing Justice, *A Community of Contrasts*.

110. Roughly 7 percent of all Asian immigrants live in Texas. This is third only to California and New York, which have had a longer history as gateway states for immigration; Jeanne Batalova, *Asian American Immigrants in the United States* (Migration Policy Institute report 2011), http://www.migrationinformation.org/USfocus/display.cfm?id=841.

111. Estimates include Fort Bend and Harris Counties. Note that the surrounding counties of Montgomery, Galveston, and Brazoria have an additional combined 8,059 Filipino Americans beyond this estimate; see Stephen Klineberg, *Houston's Ethnic Communities, Third Edition: Updated and Expanded to Include the First-Ever Survey of the Asian Communities* (Houston Area Survey Report, Houston Ethnic Communities, Rice University, Kinder Institute for Urban Research online 1996, http://has.rice.edu/downloads/?ekmensel=c580fa7b_8_0_1748_5); Stephen Klineberg, "Religious Diversity and Social Integration among Asian Americans in Houston," in *Asian American Religions: The Making and Remaking of Borders and Boundaries*, edited by Tony Carnes and Yang Fenggang (New York, NY: New York University Press, 2004), 247–262; Pew, *The Rise of Asian Americans*.

112. United States Census Bureau, *Economic Census, Minority and Women Owned Businesses* (Washington DC: Bureau of the Census, 1997), http://www.census.gov/epcd/mwb97/tx/TX.html.

113. Wendy Lee, "Filipinotown Searching for Its Center; Leaders Are Trying to Lure Filipino Americans Back to a Historic Neighborhood by Building a Sense of Community," *Los Angeles Times*, September 13, 2005, B3; http://articles.latimes.com/2005/sep/13/local/me-filipinotown13.

114. Carolina G. Hernandez, "The Philippines in 1996: A House Finally in Order?" *Asian Survey* 37.2 (1997): 204–211, doi:10.1525/as.1997.37.2.01p0223l; Ebaugh and Chafetz, *Religion across Borders*; Fenggang Yang, "Chinese Christian Transnationalism: Diverse Networks of a Houston Church," in *Religion across Borders: Transnational Immigrant Networks*, edited by Helen Rose Ebaugh and Janet Saltzman Chafetz (Walnut Creek, CA: AltaMira Press, 2002), 129–148.

115. Bicol (also spelled Bikol) is one of the seventeen major regions of the Philippines, comprising four provinces on the Bicol Peninsula near the southeastern end of the island of Luzon.

CHAPTER 2 — CATHOLIC CULTURE AND FILIPINO FAMILIES

1. The Philippine Declaration of Independence from Spain was made on June 12, 1898.

2. France Viana, "Philippine Culture 101," *Filipino Express*, March 6, 2005, http://www.filipinasmag.com/free_fvi_focusonfilams.html.

3. The barrangay will be defined and discussed at greater length later in this chapter.

4. Viana, "Philippine Culture 101."

5. Royal Morales, "Pilipino American Studies: A Promise and an Unfinished Agenda," *Amerasia Journal* 13.1 (1987): 124.

6. Beyond Yen Le Espiritu's use of Catholic churches in San Diego to build her ethnographic sample (see *Home Bound: Filipino American Lives across Cultures, Communities, and Countries* [Berkeley: University of California Press, 2003]), scholars Joaquin Gonzalez III, *Filipino American Faith in Action: Immigration, Religion, and Civic Engagement* (New York: New York University Press, 2009), and Steffi San Buenaventura, "Filipino Religion at Home and Abroad: Historical Roots and Immigrant Transformations," in *Religions in Asian America: Building Faith Communities*, edited by Pyong G. Min and Jung H. Kim (Walnut Creek, CA: AltaMira Press, 2002), 143–184 have been two of a select few to draw attention to the importance of Catholicism in Filipino American studies.

7. For a more complete history of Spanish colonial rule in the Philippines, see Eufronio Alip, *Political and Cultural History of the Philippines*, Volumes 1 and 2 (Manila, Philippines: Alip and Brion, 1950); Gerald Anderson, ed., *Studies in Philippine Church History* (Ithaca, NY: Cornell University Press, 1969); Gayo Aragon, "The Controversy over Justification of Spanish Rule in the Philippines," in *Studies in Philippine Church History*, edited by Gerald Anderson (Ithaca, NY: Cornell University Press, 1969), 368–389; Vicente Rafael, *Contracting Colonialism* (Ithaca, NY: Cornell University Press, 1988); Robert Reed, *Hispanic Urbanism in the Philippines: A Study of the Impact of Church and State* (Manila, Philippines: University of Manila Press, 1967); Nilda Rimonte, "Colonialism's Legacy: The Inferiorization of the Filipino," in *Filipino Americans: Transformation and Identity*, edited by Maria P. P. Root (London: Sage, 1997), 39–61.

8. Peter Gowing, *Islands under the Cross: The Story of the Church in the Philippines* (Manila, Philippines: National Council of Churches in the Philippines, 1967).

9. Horacio De la Costa, "The Development of a Native Clergy in the Philippines," in *Studies in Philippine Church History*, edited by Gerald Anderson (Ithaca, NY: Cornell University Press, 1969), 65–104; Rafael, *Contracting Colonialism*.

10. John Leddy Phelan, "Prebaptismal Instruction and the Administration of Baptism in the Philippines during the Sixteenth Century," in *Studies in Philippine Church History*, edited by Gerald Anderson (Ithaca, NY: Cornell University Press, 1969), 3–23.

11. Reynaldo Clemena Ileto, *Pasyon and Revolution: Popular Movements in the Philippines, 1840–1910* (Manila, Philippines: Ateneo de Manila University Press, 1979), describes how Catholicism became an indigenous rallying point for opposition to the Spanish crown from 1840 to 1910. Had Catholicism not become a vital force among many Filipinos, this would not have been possible. Further evidence of this may be taken from the fact that Filipinos are still very active Catholics today; also see Gowing, *Islands under the Cross*; Rafael, *Contracting Colonialism*; Rimonte, "Colonialism's Legacy"; Social Weather Station Survey, *SWS Select Surveys on Filipino Religiosity*, Vol. 3 (March 2002), www.sws.org.ph.

12. De la Costa, "The Development of a Native Clergy in the Philippines"; Ileto, *Pasyon and Revolution*; Barbara Posadas, *The Filipino Americans* (Westport, CT: Greenwood, 1999).

13. Phelan, "Prebaptismal Instruction and the Administration of Baptism"; Gowing, *Islands under the Cross.*

14. Pre-Hispanic barangays were kinship networks of thirty to one hundred families and were the only political entities in existence prior to colonial conquest. Spain standardized the barangays into a set size of around forty-five to fifty people that could be counted as a uniform census block. By 1768, among the 6,000 known or registered barangays, the size had dropped to under thirty; see Robert Fox, "The Filipino Family and Kinship," *Philippine Quarterly* 2 (1961): 6–9; John Leddy Phelan, *The Hispanization of the Philippines: Spanish Aims and Filipino Responses 1565–1700* (Madison: University of Wisconsin Press, [1959] 1967).

15. Fox, "The Filipino Family and Kinship"; Posadas, *The Filipino Americans*; Viana, "Philippine Culture 101."

16. See Phelan, "Prebaptismal Instruction and the Administration of Baptism" further for historical estimates on Filipino baptisms; also Gowing, *Islands under the Cross* on the historical nature of Filipino conversions.

17. Phelan, *The Hispanization of the Philippines*; Antonio Pido, *The Pilipinos in America: Macro/ Micro Dimensions of Immigration and Integration* (New York: Center for Immigration Studies, 1986); Viana, "Philippine Culture 101."

18. Pido, *The Pilipinos in America*; Reed, *Hispanic Urbanism in the Philippines.*

19. Before Spanish conquest and the spread of Catholicism, datus (chiefs) often served barangays as shaman or quasi-religious leaders: Fox, "The Filipino Family and Kinship"; Pido, *The Pilipinos in America.*

20. Pido, *The Pilipinos in America.*

21. De la Costa, "The Development of a Native Clergy in the Philippines"; Gowing, *Islands under the Cross*; Ileto, *Pasyon and Revolution*; Rimonte, "Colonialism's Legacy."

22. Alip, *Political and Cultural History of the Philippines*; Renato. L. Constantino, *The Philippines: A Past Revisited*, Vol. 1 (Manila: Rentato Constantino, 1998); Richard Deats, *Nationalism and Christianity in the Philippines* (Dallas, TX: Southern Methodist University Press, 1968); Pido, *The Pilipinos in America.*

23. Gonzalez III, *Filipino American Faith in Action*; Stanley Karnow, *In Our Image: America's Empire in the Philippines* (New York: Random House, 1989).

24. The Benedictine Sisters were sent in response to the Church's desire to bring Filipinas back into the fold: Gowing, *Islands under the Cross.*

25. Laubach cited in San Buenaventura, "Filipino Religion at Home and Abroad."

26. Peter Ackerman and Jack Duvall, *A Force More Powerful: A Century of Nonviolent Conflict* (New York: Palgrave, 2000).

27. Florentino Rodao and Felice Noelle Rodriguez, eds., *The Philippine Revolution of 1896: Ordinary Lives in Extraordinary Times* (Quezon City, Philippines: Ateneo de Manila University Press, 2001).

28. The name EDSA 1 originates from the main highway in Metro Manila, *Epifanio de los Santos Avenue*, where the bulk of the demonstrations over Marcos's election stolen from Aquino took place (1 being the first of subsequent revolutions).

29. Rodao and Rodriguez, *The Philippine Revolution of 1896.*

30. John L. Allen Jr, *The Future Church: How Ten Trends Are Revolutionizing the Catholic Church* (New York: Doubleday, 2009). Also note that according to a Pew study 88 percent of Filipinos in the Philippines state that they consider religion very important to their lives, the fourth highest percentage globally, compared to only 59 percent of Americans who state the same, ranking sixth as a nation globally; Pew Research Center, *U.S. Stands Alone in Its Embrace of Religion among Wealthy Nations* (Pew Global Attitudes Project, 2002), http://www.pewglobal.org/2002/12/19/among-wealthy-nations/.

31. Steffi San Buenaventura, "Filipino Folk Spirituality and Immigration: From Mutual Aid to Religion," in *New Spiritual Homes*, edited by David K. Yoo (Honolulu: University of Hawaii Press, 1999), 52–86; Jonathan Okamura, *Imagining the Filipino American Diaspora* (New York: Garland, 1998).

32. See Fred Cordova, *Filipinos: Forgotten Asian Americans, A Pictorial Essay* (Dubuque, IA: Kendall/ Hunt, 1983); Jonathan Okamura, "Filipino Hometown Associations in Hawaii," *Ethnology* 22.4 (1983): 341–353, doi:10.2307/3773681. Note that in addition to the Catholic clubs, early Filipino immigrants, primarily men, also turned to quasi-Masonic lodges and associations such as the Knights of Rizal as an outlet for civic life; M. Jeffrey Burns, Ellen Skerrett, and Joseph M. White, eds., *Keeping Faith: European and Asian Catholic Immigrants* (New York: Orbis, [2000] 2006); Joaquin L. Gonzalez III and Andrea Maison, "We Do Not Bowl Alone: Social and Cultural Capital from Filipinos and their Church," in *Asian American Religions: The Making and Remaking of Borders and Boundaries*, edited by Tony Carnes and Fenggang Yang (New York: New York University Press, 2004), 21–38. Similar patterns of religious and ethnic organization can be seen in other Asian American immigrant communities; see Sharmila Rudrappa, *Ethnic Routes to Becoming American: Indian Immigrants and the Cultures of Citizenship* (New Brunswick, NJ: Rutgers University Press, 2004).

33. The Church's attitude toward Filipino Americans during this time was "one of indifference if not benign condescension"; Cordova, *Filipinos: Forgotten Asian Americans*, 172.

34. Cordova, *Filipinos: Forgotten Asian Americans*; San Buenaventura, "Filipino Religion at Home and Abroad."

35. Burns, Skerrett, and White, *Keeping Faith*.

36. Naomi Castillo, *Introduction to Filipino Ministry* (Washington, DC: Archdiocese of San Francisco in cooperation with the Pastoral Care of Migrants and Refugees-United States Catholic Council, 1986); Gonzalez III and Maison, "We Do Not Bowl Alone."

37. Castillo, *Introduction to Filipino Ministry*.

38. See United States Council of Catholic Bishops (USCCB), *Asian and Pacific Presence: Harmony and Faith* (Washington, DC: USCCB, 2001), http://old.usccb.org/mrs/harmony.shtml).

39. Suzanne E. Hall, *A Catholic Response to the Asian Presence,* (Washington D.C., 1990), http://www.eric.ed.gov/contentdelivery/servlet/ERICServlet?accno=ED337543 (document no longer available).The hearings were sponsored by the National Catholic Educational Association, the Office of Pastoral Research and Planning from the Archdiocese of New York, and the Office of Migration and Refugee Services.

40. See reports for further comments: Castillo, *Introduction to Filipino Ministry*; USCCB, *Asian and Pacific Presence*; United States Conference of Catholic Bishops (USCCB), *Welcoming the Stranger among Us: Unity in Diversity* (Washington, DC: USCCB, 2000), http://www.usccb.org/issues-and-action/cultural-diversity/pastoral-care-of-migrants-refugees-and-travelers/resources/welcoming-the-stranger-among-us-unity-in-diversity.cfm.

41. USCCB, *Asian and Pacific Presence*; USCCB, *Welcoming the Stranger among Us*.

42. Castillo, *Introduction to Filipino Ministry*; USCCB, *Asian and Pacific Presence*; USCCB, *Welcoming the Stranger among Us*; Naomi Castillo, *Pastoral Plan for Filipino Ministry* (San Francisco, CA: Archdiocese of San Francisco, 1988).

43. Networker, "History in the Making for Filipino American Catholics," *United States Conference of Catholic Bishops* 9.4 (2001), http://www.nccbuscc.org/pcmrt/newsletter/vol9no4.shtml#19.

44. Filipino-Express, "San Lorenzo Ruiz Chapel Blessing Set," *Filipino Express* online (November 21–27, 2005), http://www.filipinoexpress.net/19/47_eweek.html. The chapel is

the second church dedicated to Filipinos outside the Philippines; the first one, the Basilica of Santa Pudenciana, was established in Rome during the fall of 1991.

45. Gonzalez III, *Filipino American Faith in Action*; Gonzalez III and Maison, "We Do Not Bowl Alone."

46. Paul DiMaggio, "Culture and Cognition," *Annual Review of Sociology* 23 (1997): 263, doi:10.1146/annurev.soc.23.1.263.

47. Clifford Geertz, *The Interpretation of Cultures* (New York: Basic Books, 1973); Ann Swidler, *Talk of Love: How Americans Use Their Culture* (Chicago, IL: University of Chicago Press, 1997); Dennis H. Wrong, "The Oversocialized Conception of Man in Modern Sociology," *American Sociological Review* 26 (1961): 184–193, http://dx.doi.org/10.2307/2089854.

48. Pierre Bourdieu, "Structures, Habitus, Practices," in *The Logic of Practice*, translated by Richard Nice (Stanford, CA: Stanford University Press, [1980] 1990), 52–65; Ann Swidler, "Culture in Action: Symbols and Strategies," *American Sociological Review* 51 (1986): 273–286, doi:10.2307/2095521; Charles Tilly, "How to Detect, Describe, and Explain Repertoires of Contention," Working Paper No. 150, in Center for Studies of Social Change, New School for Social Research, *Annual Review* (New York, 1992); Robert Wuthnow, *Meaning and Moral Order* (Berkeley: University of California Press, 1987); Robert Wuthnow, *Poor Richard's Principle: Recovering the American Dream through Moral Dimensions of Work, Business, and Money* (Princeton, NJ: Princeton University Press, 1996).

49. DiMaggio, "Culture and Cognition"; Ronald L. Jepperson and Ann Swidler, "What Properties of Culture Should We Measure?" *Poetics* 22 (1994): 359–371, doi:10.1016/0304-422X(94)90014-0; Christian Smith, *Moral Believing Animals: Human Personhood and Culture* (New York: Oxford University Press, 2003); Swidler, "Culture in Action"; Wuthnow, *Meaning and Moral Order*; Michael P. Young, *Bearing Witness against Sin: The Evangelical Birth of the American Social Movement* (Chicago, IL: University of Chicago Press, 2006).

50. William H. Sewell Jr., "A Theory of Structure: Duality, Agency, and Transformation," *American Journal Sociology* 98.1 (1992): 1–29, doi:10.1086/229967; Smith, *Moral Believing Animals*; Swidler, "Culture in Action."

51. Kathleen Mary Carley, "A Theory of Group Stability," *American Sociology Review* 56 (1991): 331–354, doi:10.2307/2096108; DiMaggio, "Culture and Cognition"; Elaine Howard Ecklund, *Korean American Evangelicals: New Models for Civic Life* (New York: Oxford University Press, 2006); Barry Schwartz, *Vertical Classification: A Study in Structuralism and the Sociology of Knowledge* (Chicago, IL: University of Chicago Press, 1981); Smith, *Moral Believing Animals*, 23; Harrison C. White, *Identity and Control: A Structural Theory of Social Action* (Princeton, NJ: Princeton University Press, 1992); Wuthnow, *Meaning and Moral Order*; Young, *Bearing Witness against Sin*.

52. See DiMaggio, "Culture and Cognition," 267; Young, *Bearing Witness against Sin*, 30.

53. See further the discussion in Bourdieu, "Structures, Habitus, Practices" on the relationship between habitus and doxa. Bourdieu suggests that habitus is an important part of social reproduction. While much of this process is explicitly conscious, unconscious beliefs and values play an equally important role in mobilizing peoples' social actions.

54. Erving Goffman, in *Frame Analysis* (New York: Harper & Row, [1947] 1997), originally defined frames as "interpretive schemata" that form the basic frameworks of understanding available to members of society for making sense out of events and social interaction; also see Kathleen Mary Carley, "The Value of Cognitive Foundations for Dynamic Social Theory," *Journal Mathematical Sociology* 14 (1989): 171–208; Carley, "A Theory of Group Stability."

55. Smith, *Moral Believing Animals.*

56. Pierre Bourdieu, *Distinction: A Social Critique of the Judgment of Taste*, translated by Richard Nice (Cambridge, MA: Harvard University Press, 1984); Geert Hofstede, *Culture's Consequences: International Differences in Work-Related Values* (Beverly Hills, CA: Sage, 1980).

57. David Reisman, Nathan Glazer, and Reuel Denny, *The Lonely Crowd*, abridged edition (New Haven, CT: Yale University Press, 1961), discuss this in terms of traditional-directed guidance from memory and past experience, inner-directed guidance from more self-orientations, and other-directed guidance that is weighed in the context of family and community.

58. John Tropman, *The Catholic Ethic in American Society* (San Francisco, CA: Jossey-Bass, 1995).

59. Catholic Church, *Catechism of the Catholic Church* (New York: Doubleday Religious, 2003), http://www.scborromeo.org/ccc/p3s2c2a4.htm.

60. Ibid., 599.

61. Tropman, *The Catholic Ethic in American Society.*

62. Jonah Dycus, "St. Joseph Is the Quintessential Model for Fathers," *Texas Catholic Herald* 47.3 (June 15, 2010): 1 & 7.

63. See, for example, Milgros Peña and Lisa M. Frehill, "Latina Religious Practice." *Journal for the Scientific Study of Religion* 37.4 (1998): 620–635, doi:10.2307/1388145.

64. Smith, *Moral Believing Animals*, 16.

65. Alexis de Tocqueville, *Democracy in America: Historical-Critical Edition of De la démocratie en Amérique*, edited by Eduardo Nolla, translated from the French by James T. Schleifer, bilingual French-English edition, 4 vols. (Indianapolis, IN: Liberty Fund, [1835] 2010): 469.

66. Sewell, "A Theory of Structure."

67. Ibid., 11; Young's *Bearing Witness against Sin* discussion, 31–32.

68. Michele Dillon, *Catholic Identity: Balancing Reason, Faith, and Power* (Cambridge, UK: Cambridge University Press, 1999); Anthony Giddens, *The Constitution of Society* (Berkeley: University of California Press, 1984); Laura A. Leming, "Sociological Explorations: What Is Religious Agency?" *Sociological Quarterly* 48 (2007): 73–92.

69. Richard D. Alba, Albert J. Raboteau, and Josh DeWind, eds., *Immigration and Religion in America: Comparative and Historical Perspectives* (New York: New York University Press, 2009): 10; José Casanova, "Globalizing Catholicism and the Return of the 'Universal' Church," in *Transnational Religion and Fading States*, edited by Susanne Hoeber Rudolph and James Piscatori (Boulder, CO: Westview, 1997), 121–143.

70. Pido, *The Pilipinos in America.*

71. Teodoro A. Agoncillo and Oscar M. Alphonso, *History of the Filipino People* (Quezon City, Philippines: Malaya Books, 1967), 42; Emma H. Blair and James A. Robertson, eds., *The Philippine Islands, 1493–1898* (Cleveland, OH: A. H. Clark, 1903); John Nance, *The Gentle Tasadays: A Stone Age People in the Philippine Rain Forest* (New York: Harcourt, Brace, Javanovich, 1972).

72. Agoncillo and Alphonso, *History of the Filipino People*; Pido, *The Pilipinos in America.*

73. Rafael, *Contracting Colonialism.*

74. Naomi Castillo, *Filipino Devotionals and Religiocultural Celebrations* (San Francisco, CA: Archdiocese of San Francisco, 1997).

75. Both of these celebrations will be discussed in greater length in the coming chapters.

76. Pido, *The Pilipinos in America.*

77. Tropman, *The Catholic Ethic in American Society*; John Tropman, *The Catholic Ethic and the Spirit of Community* (Washington, DC: Georgetown University Press, 2002).

78. See further Michael W. Foley and Dean R. Hoge, *Religion and the New Immigration: How Faith Communities Form Our Newest Citizens* (New York: Oxford University Press, 2007), 46 on organizational culture and the relationship between houses of worship, family, and community.

79. Belen T. G. Medina, *The Filipino Family*, second edition (Quezon City, Philippines: University of the Philippines Press, 2001); Isabel Panopio and Realidad Rolda, *Society and Culture* (Quezon City, Philippines: JMC Press, 2000).

80. Of Filipino Americans 69 percent state that being a good parent is "one of the most important things" in their lives; see Pew Research Center, *The Rise of Asian Americans* (Pew Research Center's Social and Demographic Trends Project, June 19, 2012), http://www.pewsocialtrends.org/files/2012/06/The-Rise-of-Asian-Americans-Full-Report.pdf.

81. Stella P. Go, *The Filipino Family in the Eighties* (Manila, Philippines: De La Salle University, Social Development Research Center, 1993).

82. Pido, *The Pilipinos in America*; Posadas, *The Filipino Americans*.

83. Grace T. Cruz, Elma P. Laguna, and Corazon M. Raymundo, "Family Influences on the Lifestyle of Filipino Youth," Working Paper, Population Series No. 108–8, East-West Center Working Papers (Honolulu, HI, 2001); Yen Le Espiritu, *Filipino American Lives* (Philadelphia, PA: Temple University Press, 1995); Yen Le Espiritu, *Home Bound*; Rhacel Parreñas, *The Force of Domesticity: Filipina Migrants and Globalization* (New York: New York University Press, 2008); Rhacel Parreñas, *Servants of Globalization: Women, Migration, and Domestic Work* (Stanford, CA: Stanford University Press, 2001); Posadas, *The Filipino Americans*.

84. Rhacel Parreñas, "Transnational Mothering: A Source of Gender Conflict in the Family," *North Carolina Law Review* 88 (2010): 1825–1855; Parreñas, *The Force of Domesticity*; Rhacel Parreñas, *Children of Global Migration: Transnational Families and Gender Woes* (Stanford, CA: Stanford University Press, 2005); Parreñas, *Servants of Globalization*; Posadas, *The Filipino Americans*.

85. Cruz, Laguna, Raymundo, "Family Influences on the Lifestyle of Filipino Youth"; Parreñas, *Children of Global Migration*; Rachel H. Racelis and Emily Cabegin, *A Household Model for Economic and Social Studies: Updated Household and Macro/Sectoral Projections* (Pasig City, Philippines: National Economic Authority, 1998), 1990–2030.

86. Parreñas, "Transnational Mothering"; Parreñas, *The Force of Domesticity*; Parreñas, *Children of Global Migration*; Parreñas, *Servants of Globalization*.

87. It is not surprising that "family reasons" are the main reason Filipinos give when asked why they came to the United States in 2012. Forty-three percent of Filipinos gave this reason, more than any other Asian group; see Pew, *The Rise of Asian Americans*.

88. See for example Cruz, Laguna, Raymundo, "Family Influences on the Lifestyle of Filipino Youth."

89. Pew, *The Rise of Asian Americans*.

90. Rick Bonus, *Locating Filipino Americans: Ethnicity and the Cultural Politics of Space* (Philadelphia, PA: Temple University Press, 2000).

91. Dovelyn Agunias and Kathleen Newland, *Circular Migration and Development: Trends, Policy Routes, and Ways Forward* (Washington, DC: Migration Policy Institute online, April 2007), http://www.migrationpolicy.org/pubs/MigDevPB_041807.pdf.

92. Parreñas, *Servants of Globalization*.

93. See Floyd Whaley, "Philippines Moves Forward with Bill to Improve Contraceptive Access," *New York Times* online August 6, 2012, http://www.nytimes.com/2012/08/07/world/asia/philippines-set-to-vote-on-reproductive-health-bill.html?_r=1.

94. The mention of "thick descriptions" here is in reference to Clifford Geertz, *The Interpretation of Cultures.* I agree with Geertz that before an interpretation of culture can be fully undertaken, the contours of the subject and context must be richly detailed. I attempt to do this in mapping the Filipino American community in Houston in the next chapter.

CHAPTER 3 — COMMUNITY OF COMMUNITIES

1. Both the Mapua Institute of Technology in the Philippines and the University of Santo Tomas are Philippine institutions.

2. See further chapter 4 of Joaquin Gonzalez III, *Filipino American Faith in Action: Immigration, Religion, and Civic Engagement* (New York: New York University Press, 2009).

3. Gawad Kalinga was originally a social ministry of Couples for Christ (CFC). Its relationship to CFC and the particulars of the project will be discussed in greater depth in the coming chapters.

4. The first year a Filipino doctor practiced in Harris County (Houston) was actually 1959, but it was not until 1965 that a sizeable group of Filipino doctors and nurses joined him in the city; Jimmy Viray, "Filipino-American Community in Houston," in *Philippine Centennial Review: One Hundred Years in the Life of a Nation* (Houston, TX: Filipino-American Council of Southern Texas, June 12, 1898).

5. See, for example, chapter 2 of Yen Le Espiritu, *Home Bound: Filipino American Lives across Cultures, Communities, and Countries* (Berkeley: University of California Press, 2003), and her description of the Filipino American community in San Diego. See also Celan Alo and Josélito Uy, eds., *CIPAS Silver Anniversary, 1970–1995* (Springfield, IL: Privately printed, 1995), 43.

6. See further Carlos Buloson, *America Is in the Heart: A Personal History* (New York: Harcourt, Brace, 1946) and his semi-autobiographical novel that describes some of the early infighting and politicking between first-generation Filipino American associations and groups on the West Coast; also see Rick Bonus, *Locating Filipino Americans: Ethnicity and the Cultural Politics of Space* (Philadelphia, PA: Temple University Press, 2000), and Espiritu, *Home Bound.*

7. It is important to note that these organizations are important transnational spaces that link Filipinos to the specific regions and providences from which they migrated. They allow them to engage in the politics and concerns of their homelands and provide a means to resist being forcibly homogenized into a singular catchall Filipino American category in the United States. Although the proliferation of these organizations may be taken as evidence of divisiveness and disunity, their numbers serve as better evidence of the diversity and complexity that is the Filipino diaspora. However, these organizations do struggle to forge unity across groups, as is the case with many other immigrant communities; see further Bonus, *Locating Filipino Americans*; Buloson, *America Is in the Heart*; Espiritu, *Home Bound*; Antonio Pido, *The Pilipinos in America: Macro/Micro Dimensions of Immigration and Integration* (New York: Center for Immigration Studies, 1986).

8. See Viray, "Filipino-American Community in Houston" on the growth and associational foundations of the Filipino American community in Houston. See Espiritu, *Home Bound,* on similar trends in San Diego.

9. See chapter 4 of Bonus, *Locating Filipino Americans* on the history of Filipino American associations in San Diego and their relationship to American civil society and normative politics.

10. See further Espiritu's comments in *Home Bound* on the processes by which Filipinos in San Diego "make home" and build community.

11. Perry Diaz, "The Filipino-American Barangay," *Global Balita* online, October 22, 2004, http://globalbalita.com/2004/the-filipino-american-barangay/.

12. Pierrette Hondagneu-Sotelo, *Gendered Transitions: Mexican Experiences of Immigration* (Berkeley: University of California Press, 1994); Cecilia Menjivar, *Fragmented Ties: Salvadorian Immigrant Networks in America* (Berkeley: University of California Press, 2000).

13. The history of the San Lorenzo Ruiz de Manila and its relationship to St. Catherine's will be discussed in more depth in Chapter 5.

14. Robert Wuthnow, "Small Groups and Spirituality: Exploring the Connections," in *"I Come away Stronger": How Small Groups are Shaping American Religion*, edited by Robert Wuthnow (Grand Rapids, MI: Wm. B. Eerdmans, 1994), 1–6.

15. Kathleen Joyce, "The Long Loneliness: Liberal Catholics and the Conservative Church," in *"I Come away Stronger": How Small Groups are Shaping American Religion*, edited by Robert Wuthnow (Grand Rapids, MI: Wm. B. Eerdmans, 1994).

16. See, for example, Andrew M. Greely, *American Catholic: A Social Portrait* (New York: Basic Books, 1977); Robert A. Orsi, *The Madonna of 115th Street: Faith and Community in Italian Harlem* (New Haven, CT: Yale University Press, 2002); United States Council of Catholic Bishops (USCCB), *Asian and Pacific Presence: Harmony and Faith* (Washington, DC: USCCB online 2001) http://old.usccb.org/mrs/harmony.shtml.

17. Joyce, "The Long Loneliness."

18. Wuthnow, "Small Groups and Spirituality"; Robert Wuthnow, *Sharing the Journey: Support Groups and America's New Quest for Community* (New York: Free Press, 1994).

19. According to Robert D. Putnam, *Bowling Alone: The Collapse and Revival of American Community* (New York: Simon and Schuster, 2000), 74, and his prognostications about the ills befalling American civil society, privatized religion is morally compelling and psychologically fulfilling but also embodies less social capital and hence mobilizes fewer resources to civic life. Putnam suggests that people who exemplify this trend, surfing from one congregation to another, may still be religious, but they are also less committed to a particular religious community. For many first-generation Filipino Americans, however, it is important to note that this more privatized religiosity can often hold the community together as individuals cross parishes and frequently attend more than one church and home devotional or prayer group. This will be discussed in greater depth in Chapter 5.

20. See, for example, Paul Lichterman, *Elusive Togetherness: Church Groups Trying to Bridge America's Divisions* (Princeton, NJ: Princeton University Press, 2005); Wuthnow, "Small Groups and Spirituality"; Wuthnow, *Sharing the Journey.*

21. Wuthnow, "Small Groups and Spirituality"; Wuthnow, *Sharing the Journey.*

22. See further Bonus, *Locating Filipino Americans*; Gonzalez III, *Filipino American Faith in Action*; Antonio J. Pido, "Macro/Micro Dimensions of Pilipino Immigration to the United States," in *Filipino Americans: Transformation and Identity*, edited by Maria P. Root (Thousand Oaks, CA: Sage, 1997), 21–38.

23. PAMAT is the oldest Filipino Masonic lodge in the Southwest and one the oldest Filipino lodges in the United States.

24. Chapters 4 and 5 of Espiritu, *Home Bound*.

25. Richard L. Wood and Mark R. Warren, "A Different Face of Faith-Based Politics: Social Capital and Community Organizing in the Public Arena," *International Journal of Sociology and Social Policy* 22, no. 11/12 (2002): 6–54, doi:10.1108/01443330210790148.

26. See Methodological Appendix for survey specifics.

27. An index was created to measure relative importance of each of the items to the respondents' sense of community. First, each item was given a point allotment for each time it was mentioned as important to a respondent's sense of community. For example, if an item was mentioned as the most important factor in a respondent's sense of community, it received three points. Mentions of second and third most important factors received two and one points, respectively. If the respondent did not indicate the item was an important factor in his or her sense of community, that item did not receive any points. Next, the respondent level scores were summed to determine an overall importance score for each item across all respondents. The overall scores were then scaled, such that the highest value was one hundred.

28. This percentage is comparable to findings from the Social Capital Community Benchmark survey, a nationally representative survey of Americans, in which 82 percent of Filipino Americans indicated that their church or place of worship gives them a sense of community; independent ancillary analysis. See Roper Center, *Social Capital Community Benchmark Survey*, Roper Center online, 2006, http://www.cfsv.org/community survey/docs/exec_summ.pdf.

29. Joaquin L. Gonzalez III and Andrea Maison, "We Do Not Bowl Alone: Social and Cultural Capital from Filipinos and Their Church," in *Asian American Religions: The Making and Remaking of Borders and Boundaries*, edited by Tony Carnes and Fenggang Yang (New York: New York University Press, 2004), 21–38; Gonzalez III, *Filipino American Faith in Action*.

30. This mission statement is found in all church correspondence such as newsletters, on boards through the parish halls, and on the church homepage online.

31. Ferdinand Tonnies, *Community and Society/Gemeinschaft und Gesellschaft* (New Brunswick, NJ: Transaction Publishers, [1887] 1988).

32. I emphasize that these are often forced categorizations because more often than not nationally representative samples of the United States lack sufficient numbers of Filipinos or any other Asian population for independent analyses. Clearly the scholars working with these secondary data sources are not to blame but are limited nonetheless. I join others here in highlighting the need for better national data collections.

33. Pei-te Lien, "Asian Americans and Voting Participation: Comparing Racial and Ethnic Differences in Recent U.S. Elections," *International Migration Review* 38.2 (2004): 493–517, doi:10.1111/j.1747-7379.2004.tb00207.x; Pei-te Lien and Tony Carnes, "Religious Demography of Asian American Boundary Crossing," in *Asian American Religions*, edited by Tony Carnes and Fenggang Yang (New York: New York University Press, 2004), 38–54; Jerry Z. Park, "Assessing the Sociological Study of Asian American Christians," *Society of Asian North American Christianity Studies Journal* 1 (2009): 57–94, http://www.baylorisr .org/wp-content/uploads/park_assessing.pdf.

34. See further the importance of majority to minority religious immigrant transitions discussed in Helen Rose Ebaugh and Janet Saltzman Chafetz, *Religion and the New Immigrants: Continuities and Adaptations in Immigrant Congregations* (Walnut Creek, CA: AltaMira Press, 2000).

35. Gonzalez III, *Filipino American Faith in Action*; Park, "Assessing the Sociological Study of Asian American Christians."

36. Gonzalez III, *Filipino American Faith in Action*; Park, "Assessing the Sociological Study of Asian American Christians."

37. Social Weather Survey, *SWS Select Surveys on Filipino Religiosity*, Vol. 3 (March 2002), www.sws.org.ph.

CHAPTER 4 — COMMUNITIES IN CONFLICT

1. Pancit is the national noodle dish of the Philippines.

2. This will be explained in greater depth throughout the present chapter.

3. Ben Ongoco, "2010 New Paradigm," *Manila-Headline*, December 18–January 13, 2010, 5.

4. Rick Bonus, *Locating Filipino Americans: Ethnicity and the Cultural Politics of Space* (Philadelphia, PA: Temple University Press, 2000), 92. Also see the case of other Asian communities: Angie Chung, *Legacies of Struggle: Conflict and Cooperation in Korean American Politics* (Stanford, CA: Stanford University Press, 2007).

5. Perry Diaz, "Are Filipino-Americans Electable?," *Global Balita* online, October 15, 2004, http://globalbalita.com/2004/are-filipino-americans-electable/.

6. Ray Colorado, "The Steps to Political Power—Part 1, 'Pioneer Syndrome,'" *Pinoy Texas* online, November 27, 1999, http://www.pinoytexas.com/editorapr2000.htm.

7. Colorado, "The Steps to Political Power." Pinoy (men) or pinay (women) are terms many Filipinos use to describe themselves.

8. Ibid.

9. Robert D. Putnam, *Bowling Alone: The Collapse and Revival of American Community* (New York: Simon and Schuster, 2000).

10. For example, see Margarita A. Mooney, *Faith Makes Us Live: Surviving and Thriving in the Haitian Diaspora* (Berkeley: University of California Press, 2009) on the role of the Catholic Church in the lives of those in the Haitian diaspora. More generally, see the contributions in Alex Stepick, Terry Rey, and Sarah J. Mahler, eds., *Churches and Charity in the Immigrant City* (New Brunswick, NJ: Rutgers University Press, 2009) on the role of the Church in multiple immigrant communities in Miami and the impact it has not only on social relations but the effect of these relations on civic life.

11. See the documents presented in M. Jeffrey Burns, Ellen Skerrett, and Joseph M. White, eds., *Keeping Faith: European and Asian Catholic Immigrants* (New York: Orbis Books, [2000] 2006), 277–281, that chart the Santo Niño de Cebu controversy in St. Patrick's parish in San Francisco during the late 1970s through the mid-1980s. Like the Bicol case that I present later in this chapter, these documents highlight the volatile nature of first-generation Filipino community politics and the relationship of regional associations, in this case Cebuanos, to the Catholic Church. These documents illustrate the precarious position that local Filipino priests can be placed in and highlight both the centrality of the parish to Filipino community life and the role it can play in mediating conflicts.

12. Our Lady of Peñafrancia is the patroness of Bicol and an apparition of Mary, beloved by all in the region. Although the origins of the devotion are somewhat enigmatic, it is believed that the devotion in the Philippines began around 1712; Our Lady of Peñafrancia Basilica website, http://penafrancia.org.ph/.

13. See Couples for Christ website, http://www.couplesforchristglobal.org/; Antonio Meloto, *Builder of Dreams* (Mandaluyong City, Philippines: Gawad Kalinga Community Development Foundation, 2009).

14. Meloto, *Builder of Dreams*.

15. See Methodological Appendix for more about the history and structure of CFC in Houston.

16. Vatican, "Pontifical Council for the Laity" (Vatican document Couples for Christ, 2000), http://www.vatican.va/roman_curia/pontifical_councils/laity/documents/rc_pc _laity_doc_20051114_associazioni_en.html#COUPLES%20FOR%20CHRIST.

17. Meloto, *Builder of Dreams*.

18. Ibid.

19. Ibid.; also see Gawad Kalinga website, http://www.gk1world.com/.

20. Meloto, *Builder of Dreams*.

21. See, for example, *Philippine Daily Inquirer*, "Meloto Not the Founder of Gawad Kalinga," January 28, 2007, http://services.inquirer.net/print/print.php?article_id=20070206-47677.

22. I was given a photocopy of this correspondence, but it has also been posted on the Couples for Christ Foundations for Family and Life (CFC-FFL), Documents Archive website, updated July 9, 2010, http://www.cfcffl.org/documents/documents.htm.

23. Ibid.

24. See letter from the CBC of the Philippines, June 7, 2007 to the Elders' Assembly of CFC. I was given a photo copy of this correspondence but it has also been posted on CFC-FFL, Documents Archive website.

25. Ibid.

26. See the Decree of Recognition from the Roman Catholic Bishop of Antipolo August 1, 2007. I was given a photo copy of this correspondence but it has also been posted on CFC-FFL, Documents Archive website; also see Perry Diaz, "Quo Vadis Couples for Christ?" *Philippine Daily Inquirer* online, August 28, 2007, http://www.inquirer.net/specialreports/couplesforchristrift/view.php?db=1&article=20070828-85120.

27. See editorials throughout the month of August on the *Philippine Daily Inquirer* website, http://www.inquirer.net/; for specifics, see Rina Jimenez-David, "Crabs in God's Design" August 31, 2007, http://business.inquirer.net/money/topstories/view/20070831 -85730/Crabs_and_God%92s_design; or Ma. José Montelibano, "The Good, the Crab, and the Ugly," August 31, 2007, http://opinion.inquirer.net/viewpoints/columns/view/ 20070831-85684/The_good,_the_crab,_and_the_ugly.

28. Cited in Perry Diaz, "Time for GK to Break Away from CFC," April 30, 2008, http:// globalnation.inquirer.net/mindfeeds/mindfeeds/view/20080430-133598/Time-for-GK-to -Break-Away-from-CFC.

29. I was given a photo copy of this correspondence but it has also been posted on CFC-FFL, Documents Archive website.

30. For more on GK today, both its continued spread and successes, see my chapter contribution to Stephen M. Cherry and Helen Rose Ebaugh, eds., *Global Religious Movements across Borders: Sacred Service* (Burlington, VT: Ashgate Publishing, 2014).

31. See a similar discussion in Laura A. Leming, "Sociological Explorations: What Is Religious Agency?" *Sociological Quarterly* 48 (2007): 73–92 on strategies for gaining agency in the Church among Catholic women.

CHAPTER 5 — BUILDING CENTERS OF COMMUNITY

1. Although the focus of this book is on the religious and civic lives of first-generation Filipino Americans, it is important to note that fears for the second generation or what scholars refer to as 1.5ers—those born in the Philippines but raised in the United States— often arise when talking to the first generation about the current state of community affairs. Keeping in mind that there is a fairly large percentage of Filipinos immigrating to

Houston today in their mid-twenties and early thirties with young children, it is not so much an issue of youth per se as an issue of subsequent American-born generations; see Yen Le Espiritu, *Home Bound: Filipino American Lives Across Cultures, Communities and Countries* (Berkeley: University of California Press, 2003) for a discussion of generational issues in the Filipino American community of San Diego.

2. See Ben Ongoco, "2010 New Paradigm," *Manila-Headline*, December 18–January 13, 2010, 5.

3. Ibid.

4. Ibid.

5. The canonization and importance of San Lorenzo Ruiz de Manila will be discussed at greater length in subsequent sections.

6. See Methodological Appendix for survey details.

7. John Leddy Phelan, *The Hispanization of the Philippines: Spanish Aims and Filipino Responses 1565–1700* (Madison: University of Wisconsin Press, [1959] 1967); Antonio Pido, *The Pilipinos in America: Macro/ Micro Dimensions of Immigration and Integration* (New York: Center for Immigration Studies, 1986); Naomi Castillo, *Introduction to Filipino Ministry* (Washington D.C.: Archdiocese of San Francisco in cooperation with the Pastoral Care of Migrants and Refugees-United States Catholic Council, 1986).

8. Castillo, *Introduction to Filipino Ministry.*

9. Ibid.; Barbara Posadas, *The Filipino Americans* (Westport, CT: Greenwood, 1999).

10. During this particular night I passed around a sheet and asked people to write down their home parish as well as where they live by city and zip code.

11. See original message by Monsignor Seth Hermosa, "Simbang Gabi," *Tambuli ng Panginoon*, October–December 1, 2006, 1.

12. Naomi Castillo, *Filipino Devotionals and Religiocultural Celebrations* (San Francisco, CA: Archdiocese of San Francisco, 1997), 2.

13. See, for example, Sydney Verba, Kay Schlozman, and Henry Brady, *Voice and Equality* (Cambridge, MA: Harvard University Press, 1995).

14. Cecilia Menjivar, "Religion and Immigration in Comparative Perspective: Catholic and Evangelical Salvadorans in San Francisco, Washington D.C., and Phoenix," *Sociology of Religion* 64.1 (2003): 21–46, doi:10.2307/3712267, notes similar differences between Salvadoran Protestant and Catholic churches. Although in both cases Menjivar found that the churches equally supported new immigrants and connected them to their community, they did so on a different scale. Protestants were more homogeneous, smaller in congregational size, focused on a specific ethnic or regional group, and were more inclined to split. Catholics, on the other hand, were more diverse ethnically and concerned with uniting all people in the parish through an extended communitarian ethic.

15. Lorenzo Ruiz was beatified in Manila on February 18, 1981, by Pope John Paul II during his papal visit to Manila—the first beatification ceremony held outside the Vatican; United States Council of Catholic Bishops (USCCB), *Asian and Pacific Presence: Harmony and Faith* (Washington D.C.: USCCB online 2001), http://old.usccb.org/mrs/harmony .shtml.

16. Castillo, *Introduction to Filipino Ministry*; Castillo, *Filipino Devotionals and Religiocultural Celebrations.*

17. Santacruzan is a pageant held in honor of Reyna Elena (Helena) and Constantine finding the true cross in Jerusalem. It is held on the last day of Flores de Mayo, which is a month-long festival in the Philippines honoring the Virgin Mary during the month of May; see Castillo, *Introduction to Filipino Ministry*; Posadas, *The Filipino Americans.*

18. The survey instrument used for this event was identical to that used at the Philippine Independence celebration held at St. Catherine's. For particulars, see Methodological Appendix.

19. Juliette Gran Ringer, "Houston's Best Kept Secret: The San Lorenzo Ruiz de Manila Center," *Manila-Headline*, October 7, 2008, 5.

CHAPTER 6 — CARING FOR COMMUNITY

1. Alief is a suburb in southwestern Houston.

2. See additional coverage on various aspects of the health fair and its partners in Betty L. Martin, "Alief-area Medical Clinic Expands Care for Uninsured," *Houston Chronicle* online July 14, 2005, http://www.chron.com/news/article/Alief-area-medical-clinic -expands-care-for-1657446.php.

3. See, for example, comments made by Mazur Javed Khan during Houston City Council Briefing, October 28, 2004.

4. Ibid.

5. PSA (prostate specific antigen) testing is a screening for prostate cancer. CHIP stands for Children's Health Insurance Program.

6. Khan, Houston City Council Briefing.

7. Charles Demangin, "Alief Health Fair Is Deemed Success," *Houston Chronicle*, August 16, 2005, http://www.chron.com/news/article/Alief-health-fair-is-deemed-a -success-1944009.php.

8. Ibid.

9. "Alief Super Neighborhood Meeting," notes taken by Henry Williams, secretary, March 22, 2005, at Alief Super Neighborhood #25.

10. Note that according to the fact pamphlet distributed by the Philippines Nurses Association of Metropolitan Houston, *Fact Pamphlet* (2006), there were a total of 158 volunteers.

11. See estimates in Demangin, "Alief Health Fair Is Deemed Success"; Khan, Houston City Council Briefing; "Alief Super Neighborhood Meeting."

12. See, for example, Karen Hastings, "Catholic Agencies, Community Active during Freeze," *Texas Catholic Herald*, February 9, 2010, 8.

13. See further discussion in Chapter 5; also Stephen M. Cherry and Kody Allred, "Models of Disaster Response: Lessons Learned from Filipino Immigrant Mobilizations for Hurricane Katrina Evacuees," *Criminal Justice Studies* 25.4 (2012): 391–408.

14. According to members of the Philippine American Chamber of Congress, Texas won first place among all United States communities for the number of people it served in the outreach; see Ethel Mercado, *PACC Texas Report to the Community*, Philippine American Chamber of Commerce of Texas, 2011, http://www.pacctexas.org/documents/PACC -Texas-Report-to-the-Community-August2011.pdf.

15. Richard D. Sundeen, Cristina Garcia, and Lili Wang, "Volunteer Behavior among Asian American Groups in the United States," *Journal of Asian American Studies* 10 (2007): 3243–3281.

16. Rick Bonus, *Locating Filipino Americans: Ethnicity and the Cultural Politics of Space* (Philadelphia, PA: Temple University Press, 2000); Jessica Chao, "Asian-American Philanthropy: Expanding Circles of Participation," in *Cultures of Caring: Philanthropy in America's Diverse Communities* (Washington, DC: Council on Foundations, 1999), 189–253; Stephen M. Cherry and Helen Rose Ebaugh, eds., *Global Religious Movements across*

Borders: Sacred Service (Burlington, VT: Ashgate, 2013); Pei-te Lien, *The Making of Asian America through Political Participation* (Philadelphia, PA: Temple University Press, 2001).

17. Drawing on survey analysis of the Social Capital Community Benchmark survey (SCCB), a study has found significant differences not only in the influence of religion on Filipino American volunteering versus community participation but in the rates Filipino Americans actually volunteer versus participate in their communities. Filipino Americans report to participate more than they volunteer, and Catholicism appears to contribute more to Filipino American community participation than community volunteerism. Although it is not clear what volunteering versus participating actually meant to those Filipino Americans surveyed in the SCCB, it is a clear indication that studying immigrant volunteerism through survey analysis only can be hampered by a host of linguistic and methodological issues; see, for example, Stephen M. Cherry, "Catholicism and Filipino American Community Volunteerism and Participation," *Sociological Spectrum* 33.1 (2013): 36–56.

18. See, for example, Christopher Troppe, "Measuring Volunteering: A Behavioral Approach," *Circle Working Paper 42* (2005), www.civicyouth.org, on how volunteers may define "volunteerism" more narrowly or differently from what is presented in surveys.

19. Archdiocese of Galveston-Houston, *Annual Report 2008–2009* (Houston: Archdiocese of Galveston-Houston, 2009).

20. Marc A. Musick and John Wilson, *Volunteers: A Social Profile* (Bloomington: Indiana University Press, 2008).

21. Project CURE boxes medical supplies and sends them to international destinations such as the Philippines.

22. See discussion in Chapter 5.

23. See Methodological Appendix for survey specifics.

24. Elaine Ecklund and Jerry Park, "Asian American Community Participation and Religion," *Journal of Asian American Studies* 8 (2005): 1–21, doi:10.1353/jaas.2005 .0027; Ecklund and Park, "Religious Diversity and Community Volunteerism among Asian Americans," *Journal for the Scientific Study of Religion* 46.2 (2007): 233–244, doi:10.1111/j.1468-5906.2007.00353.x.

25. David E. Campbell and Stephen J. Yonish, "Religion and Volunteering in America," in *Religion and Social Capital*, edited by Corwin E. Schmidt (Waco, TX: Baylor University Press, 2003), 87–106; Musick and Wilson, *Volunteers: A Social Profile*; Robert D. Putnam, *Bowling Alone: The Collapse and Revival of American Community* (New York: Simon and Schuster, 2000); John Wilson and Marc Musick, "Who Cares? Toward an Integrated Theory of Volunteer Work," *American Sociological Review* 62 (1997): 694–713, doi:10.2307/2657355; Robert Wuthnow and C. Hackett, "The Social Integration of Practitioners of Non-Western Religions in the United States," *Journal for the Scientific Study of Religion* 42.4 (2003): 651–657, doi:10.1046/j.1468-5906.2003.00209.x.

26. Virginia A. Hodgkinson, "The Connection between Philanthropic Behavior Directed to Religious Institutions and Small Religious Nonprofit Organizations," presentation at the Conference on Small Religious Nonprofits: From Vulnerability to Viability, DePaul University, Chicago, IL, October 1995; Musick and Wilson, *Volunteers: A Social Profile*; Wilson and Musick, "Who Cares?" Note that only education rivals frequent church attendance as a predictor of volunteerism: Campbell and Yonish, "Religion and Volunteering in America"; Putnam, *Bowling Alone*, 65–79. However, Musick and Wilson, *Volunteers: A Social Profile*, also point out that Catholics are less likely to volunteer than liberal Protestants, regardless of church attendance.

27. Virginia A. Hodgkinson, "The Connection"; Christopher G. Ellison, "Are Religious People Nice People?: Evidence from the National Survey of Black Americans," *Social Forces* 71 (1992): 411–430; Musick and Wilson, *Volunteers: A Social Profile*; Wilson and Musick, "Who Cares?"; Robert Wuthnow, "Religion and the Voluntary Spirit in the United States," in *Faith and Philanthropy in America*, edited by R. Wuthnow, V. Hodgkinson, et al. (San Francisco, CA: Jossey-Bass, 1990), 3–21; Robert Wuthnow, *Acts of Compassion* (Princeton, NJ: University of Princeton Press, 1991).

28. Jonah Dycus, "Acts of Charity, Social Justice Help the Faithful Fulfill Baptismal Call," *Texas Catholic Herald* 47.1 (May 11, 2010): 1 & 7.

29. See similar patterns among other fellowship groups discussed in Paul Lichterman, *Elusive Togetherness: Church Groups Trying to Bridge America's Divisions* (Princeton, NJ: Princeton University Press, 2005).

30. Dennis Marzan and Andrea Maison, "Sarap Ng Samba! Food and Community at Two Bay Area Filipino Churches," *Call of Nature*, August/September 2001.

31. As of September 2008, prior to the CFC split, GK had built over 30,000 homes and 2,000 communities in sixty-four of the Philippines' eighty provinces. It had housed over 500,000 people in a nation in which 70 percent of the population is landless: Antonio Meloto, "Is There Hope for This Country? The Case for Optimism," Lecture presented at the 2006 Magsaysay Awardees' Lecture Series, Magsaysay Center, Manila, August 29, 2006, http://www.rmaf.org.ph/Awardees/Lecture/LectureMelotoAnt.htm; *Gawad Kalinga Annual Report*, 2010, http://gk1world.com/Media/PDFs/GK_Annual _Report_2010_Final_Resized.pdf. Today, the project has begun to expand beyond the Philippines to Indonesia, Cambodia, Papua New Guinea, Jakarta Indonesia, India, and East Timor: see John Alayon, "Migration, Remittance, and Development: The Filipino New Zealand Experience," Master's thesis, Institute of Public Policy, Auckland University of Tchnology, Auckland, NZ, 2009; Cherry and Ebaugh, *Global Religious Movements across Borders*.

32. See Chapter 5 discussion of the controversy surrounding the GK project.

33. See discussions on this debate in Chapter 3.

34. Bernard Lazerwitz, "Membership in Voluntary Associations and Frequency of Church Attendance," *Journal for the Scientific Study of Religion* 2 (1962): 74–84, doi:10.2307/1384095; Putnam, *Bowling Alone*; Robert Wuthnow, "Small Groups and Spirituality: Exploring the Connections," in *"I Come away Stronger": How Small Groups are Shaping American Religion*, edited by Robert Wuthnow (Grand Rapids, MI: Wm. B. Eerdmans, 1994), 1–6; Robert Wuthnow, *Sharing the Journey: Support Groups and America's New Quest for Community* (New York: Free Press, 1994); Robert Wuthnow, Conrad Hackett, and Becky Yang Hsu, "The Effectiveness and Trustworthiness of Faith-based and other Service Organizations: A Study of Recipients' Perceptions," *Journal for the Scientific Study of Religion* 43 (2004): 1–17, doi:10.1111/j.1468-5906.2004.00214.x.

35. Six first-generation Filipino American religious groups and fellowships were surveyed as part of the Philippine Independence Day survey. These include Bibingka, Couples for Christ, Holy Rosary Crusade, Our Lady of Lourdes, Santo Niño, and Totus Tuo; see Methodological Appendix.

36. Compare to Cecilia Menjivar, "Religion and Immigration in Comparative Perspective: Catholic and Evangelical Salvadorans in San Francisco, Washington D.C., and Phoenix," *Sociology of Religion* 64.1 (2003): 21–46, doi:10.2307/3712267.

37. In general, see Musick and Wilson, *Volunteers: A Social Profile*; Troppe, "Measuring Volunteering: A Behavioral Approach."

38. Ecklund and Park, "Religious Diversity and Community Volunteerism."

39. Peter Brimelow, *Alien Nation: Common Sense about America's Immigration Disaster* (New York: Random House, 1995); George Borjas, *Friends or Strangers: The Impact of Immigrants on the U.S. Economy* (New York: Basic Books, 1990); Wayne Lutton and John Tanton, *The Immigration Invasion* (Petosky, MI: Social Contract Press, 1994); Stephen Moore, *Immigration and the Rise and Decline of American Cities* (Stanford, CA: Hoover Institute on War, Revolution, and Peace, Stanford University, 1997).

40. Virginia Abernathy, *Population Politics: The Choices That Shape Our Future* (New York: Insight Books, 1993); Brent Nelson, *America Balkanized: Immigration's Challenge to Government* (Monterey, VA: American Immigration Control Foundation, 1994).

41. Among Asian Americans, Filipino Americans are the most likely to say that they have worked with other people from their neighborhood to fix or improve a condition in their community in the past year—48 percent. Although there were only modest differences between Asian groups, the fact that Filipinos are the most active is not surprising; see Pew Research Center, *The Rise of Asian Americans* (Pew Research Center's Social and Demographic Trends Project, June 19, 2012), http://www.pewsocialtrends.org/files/2012/06/The-Rise-of-Asian-Americans-Full-Report.pdf.

CHAPTER 7 — PROTECTING FAMILY AND LIFE

1. Michael A. Fletcher, "Bush Immigration Plan Meets GOP Opposition: Lawmakers Resist Temporary-Worker Proposal," *Washington Post*, January 2, 2005, http://www.washingtonpost.com/wp-dyn/articles/A41340-2005Jan1.html.

2. HR 4437 directs the Secretary of Homeland Security to take all appropriate actions to maintain operational control over the United States international land and maritime borders, including prosecuting those harboring illegal immigrants. The Church feared that by serving its parish, among whom are illegal immigrants, it would be subject to prosecution; HR4437 (2005–2006), http://thomas.loc.gov/cgi-bin/bdquery/z?d109:H.R.4437; "Nonpunitive Immigration Reform Urged at Catholic Gathering," *Texas Catholic Herald* 42.19 (February 24, 2006): 1 & 17; "Open Letter to Our Senators," *Texas Catholic Herald* 42.19 (February 24, 2006), inserted flyer.

3. See Justice for Immigrants website, www.justiceforimmigrants.org.

4. The center is part of the vast network of programs within Catholic Charities.

5. These same four questions were outlined in the "Justice for Immigrants" article (card) in the *Texas Catholic Herald* 40.20 (March 26, 2004), inserted card; see also "Conscience Formation on Immigration Reform," *Texas Catholic Herald* 43.22 (April 28, 2006), 1 & 24.

6. Also see Richard Vara and Barbara Karkabi, "Catholics Are Urged to Join Debate as 'The People of God': House Immigration Bill Also Opposed by Other Denominations," *Houston Chronicle*, April 1, 2006, http://www.chron.com/life/houston-belief/article/Catholics-are-urged-to-join-immigration-debate-as-1848008.php.

7. Also see "Conscience Formation on Immigration Reform."

8. Critical Filipina and Filipino Studies Collective, *Resisting Homeland Security: Organizing against Unjust Removals of U.S. Filipinos* (San José, CA: CFFSC, 2004), http://www.bayanusa.org/downloads/resisting_home_sec.pdf.; "Immigrants as Terrorists?," *Filipino Express*, April 17–23, 2006, http://www.filipinoexpress.net/20/16_op-ed.html#editorial.

9. Statement released via email by the Gabriela Network, August 2, 2004; for general information on GabNet (now AF3IRM), see Gabriela Network website/ Association of Filipinas, Feminists Fighting Imperialism, Re-feudalization, and Marginalization (AF3IRM), http://af3irm.org/home.

10. In general, it should be noted that 70 percent of Filipinos believe that immigration today strengthens the United States because of immigrants' hard work and talents—the highest among Asian Americans surveyed; Pew Research Center, *The Rise of Asian Americans* (Pew Research Center's Social and Demographic Trends Project, June 19, 2012), http://www.pewsocialtrends.org/files/2012/06/The-Rise-of-Asian-Americans-Full-Report.pdf.

11. Sixty-one percent of Filipino Americans, for example, are dissatisfied with the direction or way things are going in the United States today; ibid.

12. Julius's concerns also mirror those of the wider Church. According to the Catholic Church, the issue of immigration is connected to a global state of poverty that forces people to move from country to country; see "Nonpunitive Immigration Reform Urged at Catholic Gathering," "Open Letter to Our Senators."

13. "Conscience Formation on Immigration Reform."

14. "Filipinos Join Protest for Immigrants," *Filipino Express* online, April 17–23, 2008, http://www.filipinoexpress.net/20/16_news.html#1.

15. See discussion of the EDSA 1 People Power Movement in Chapter 2.

16. Filipino Americans might be best described as "liberal conservatives" when it comes to national American politics. They are rather conservative on social issues such as abortion but are more liberal on issues such as taxes, education, health care, and immigration, as we might expect; see discussion in chapter 3 of Janelle S. Wong, Karthick Ramakrishnan, and Taeku Lee, *Asian American Political Participation: Emerging Constituents and Their Political Identities* (New York: Russell Sage Foundation, 2011); Barbara Posadas, *The Filipino Americans* (Westport, CT: Greenwood, 1999); Gus Mercado, "Obama Wins Filipino Vote at Last Hour," *Global Nation* online, November 10, 2008, http://globalnation.inquirer.net/mindfeeds/mindfeeds/view/20081110-171290/Obama-wins-Filipino-vote-at-last-hour; David D. Kirkpatrick, "A Fight among Catholics over Which Party Best Reflects Church Teachings," *New York Times* online, October 4, 2008, http://www.nytimes.com/2008/10/05/us/politics/05catholic.html.

17. For example, President Clinton nominated Maria Luisa Mabilangan Haley to the Board of Directors for the Export-Import Bank of the United States, a position that required Senate approval. He also appointed Paula Bagasao as the senior policy advisor in the Agency for International Development, Ferdinand Aranza as the deputy director of insular affairs in the Interior Department, Irene Bueno as deputy to the assistant secretary for legislation in Department of Health and Human Services, Eugene Bae as senior program analyst of the environment at the Defense Department, Christian Balida as senior policy analyst of domestic financing at the Treasury Department, Tyrone Cabulu as confidential assistant in the Bureau of Export Affairs at the Department of Commerce, and Bob Santos as the head of the Northwest and Alaskan office of the Department of Housing and Urban Development: Jim Dwyer, "Catholic Vote Is Harbinger of Success for Clinton," *New York Times* online, February 9, 2008, http://www.nytimes.com/2008/02/09/nyregion/09about.html; Rodel E. Rodis, "The Filipino-American Catholic Vote," *Inquirer.net* online, February 13, 2008, http://globalnation.inquirer.net/mindfeeds/mindfeeds/view/20080213-118569/The-Filipino-American-Catholic-Vote.

18. Sixty-four percent of Filipino Americans voted for Gore, according to analysis of the NAAP survey; results from this study also suggest that in 2000 a little over 22 percent of Filipino-Americans considered themselves to be "strong" Democrats, compared to just 7 percent who considered themselves "strong" Republicans: Pei-te Lien, M. Margaret Conway, and Janelle Wong, *The Politics of Asian Americans: Diversity and Community* (New York: Routledge, 2004).

19. See, for example, Perry Diaz, "The Fil-Am Vote and the Electoral College," *Global Balita* online, August 13, 2004, http://globalbalita.com/2004/perryscope-the-fil-am-vote-and-the-electoral-college/.

20. This split or uncertainty was somewhat different from that among other Asian Americans. A national poll of Asian Americans and Pacific Islanders found that most APIs supported Kerry; only Vietnamese and Filipinos strongly supported Bush: New America Media, "National Poll of Asian Pacific Islanders on the 2004 Election," *New America Media* online, September 14, 2004, http://news.newamericamedia.org/news/view_article.html?article_id=318ff90e5420209eaa2f8aa20e65d592.

21. See, for example, coverage in the *Filipino-Express* throughout 2004; Diaz, "The Fil-Am Vote and the Electoral College."

22. See Diaz, "The Fil-Am Vote and the Electoral College."

23. Ratzinger cited in Phil Brennan, "Cardinal Ratzinger Orders Kerry Communion Ban," *Virtue Online*, July 2, 2004, http://www.virtueonline.org/portal/modules/news/print.php?storyid=1021.

24. Ray's reference to comedian Bill Maher's interpretation of the Republicans definition of moral values was meant to be a joke highlighting the comedian's belief that republicans use moral values for political gain but are in fact less moral in their actions.

25. Findings from the National Asian American Survey suggest that 41 percent of registered Filipino Americans voted for Hillary Clinton in the primaries, compared to 32 percent for Obama: S. Karthick Ramakrishnan, Janelle Wong, Taeku Lee, and Jane Junn, "Race Based Considerations and the Obama Vote: Evidence from the 2008 National Asian American Survey," *Du Bois Review* 6.1 (2009): 219–238.

26. Findings from the National Asian American Survey suggest that 31 percent of Filipino Americans voted for Obama versus 26 percent for McCain—42 percent were undecided; see National Asian American Survey, "Different or Similar? Asian American Public Opinion and Intergroup Relations," 2008, http://www.naasurvey.com/publications_assets/naas-ajconf-2009-final.pdf. Also note that as of 2012 Filipino Americans are still split between the Republican Party, 40 percent, and the Democratic Party, 43 percent; Pew Research Center, *The Rise of Asian Americans*.

27. Grassfire Alliance, now called Grassfire Nation, is not a Filipino American group, nor is it affiliated with any particular religious group. It is an independent conservative group. Grassfire Alliance was started in 2000 by Steve Elliot as a grassroots on-line conservative advocacy group.

28. Roughly 51 percent of Filipino Americans think abortion should be illegal in all or most cases; Pew, *The Rise of Asian Americans*.

29. Quoting the *New Oxford Annotated Bible* (New York: Oxford University Press, 1977), John 6:68.

30. I counted thirteen other Filipino Americans that I recognized or talked to in the crowd that day, but did not have much opportunity to talk with them while walking with members of CFC.

31. Patrick George, "Decry Abortion, War," *Austin American Statesman*, January 28, 2007, B01.

32. Ibid.

33. See Methodological Appendix.

34. Karin Aguilar-San Juan, ed., *The State of Asian America: Activism and Resistance in the 1990s* (Boston, MA: South End Press, 1994); Joaquin L. Gonzalez III and Andrea Maison, "We Do Not Bowl Alone: Social and Cultural Capital from Filipinos and Their Church," in *Asian American Religions: The Making and Remaking of Borders and Boundaries*, edited by Tony Carnes and Fenggang Yang (New York: New York University Press, 2004), 21–38.

35. Perry Diaz, "The Core of Our Values," *Global Balita* online, October 29, 2004, http://globalbalita.com/2004/the-core-of-our-values/.

36. Robert Wuthnow, "Small Groups and Spirituality: Exploring the Connections," in *"I Come away Stronger": How Small Groups Are Shaping American Religion*, edited by Robert Wuthnow (Grand Rapids, MI: Wm. B. Eerdmans, 1994): 2–3.

CHAPTER 8 — GROWING PRESENCE AND POTENTIAL IMPACTS

1. Naomi Castillo and Rev. Michael G. Kyte, *Journeying with Mary* (San Francisco; Journeying with Mary Foundation, 1996).

2. Ibid.

3. United States Census Bureau, *Overview of Race and Hispanic Origin: 2010* (Washington, DC: Bureau of the Census, 2010), http://www.census.gov/prod/cen2010/briefs/c2010br-02.pdf.

4. Pew Research Center, *The Rise of Asian Americans* (Pew Research Center's Social and Demographic Trends Project, June 19, 2012), http://www.pewsocialtrends.org/files/2012/06/The-Rise-of-Asian-Americans-Full-Report.pdf.

5. Asian American Center for Advancing Justice, *A Community of Contrast: Asian Americans in the United States*, Asian Pacific American Legal Center and Asian Justice Center online, 2011, http://www.apalc.org/pdffiles/Community_of_Contrast.pdf; National Federation of Filipino American Associations (NaFFAA), "U.S. 2010 Census: Filipinos in the U.S. Increased by 38%; Nevada has fastest growing population," NaFFAA online, June 29, 2011, http://www.scribd.com/doc/58979501/US-2010-Census-Filipinos-in-the-US-Increased-by-38-Percent-Nevada-Has-Fastest-Growing-Population.

6. NaFFAA, "U.S. 2010 Census."

7. Ibid.

8. Jean Batalova, *Asian American Immigrants in the United States* (Washington, DC: Migration Policy Institute, 2011), http://www.migrationinformation.org/USfocus/display.cfm?id=841.

9. Roughly 20,900 physicians or 9 percent of all practicing international medical graduates; see American Medical Association, "IMGs by Country of Origin: Top 20 Countries Where IMGs Received Medical Training," 2007, http://www.ama-assn.org/ama/pub/about-ama/our-people/member-groups-sections/international-medical-graduates/imgs-in-united-states/imgs-country-origin.page.

10. American Society of Registered Nurses, "Record Number of Philippine Nurses Seek Careers in the U.S.," September 1, 2007, http://www.asrn.org/journal-nursing-shortage-update/112-record-number-of-philippino-nurses-seek-careers-in-us.html; Barbara L. Brush, Julie Sochalski, and Anne M. Berger, "Imported Care: Recruiting Foreign Nurses to

U.S. Health Care Facilities," *Health Affairs* 23.3 (2004): 78–87, http://content.healthaffairs.org/content/23/3/78.full; doi:10.1377/hlthaff.23.3.78. Also see Catherine Choy, *Empire of Care: Nursing and Migration in Filipino American History* (Durham: Duke University Press, 2003) on the history of Filipino nurses in the United States.

11. Luciana E. Sweis and Albert H. Guay. "Foreign-Trained Dentists Licensed in the United States: Exploring Their Origins." *Journal of the American Dental Association* 138.2 (2007): 219–224, http://jada.ada.org/content/138/2/219.full?maxtoshow=&HITS=10 &RESULTFORMAT=1&andorexacttitle=and&andorexacttitleabs=and&fulltext=for eign+dentists&andorexactfulltext=and&searchid=1&FIRSTINDEX=0&SORTSPEC =relevance&resourcetype=HWCIT.

12. Filipino teachers, for example, are being recruited en masse to states such as Alabama, Georgia, and Virginia; see Mark J. Ubalde, "Filipino Teachers Leaving in Droves to the US," GMANews, 2007, http://www.gmanews.tv/story/56492/Filipino-teachers -leaving-in-droves-to-the-US.

13. Epifanio San Juan Jr., *Writing and National Liberation: Essays in Critical Practice* (Quezon City, Philippines: University of the Philippines Press, 1991), 117. Also see discussion in Oscar Penaranda, Serafin Syquia, and Sam Tagatac, "An Introduction to Filipino American Literature," in *Aiiieeeee! An Anthology of Asian American Writers*, edited by Frank Chin et al. (Washington, DC: Howard University Press, 1974), 227–236; Fred Cordova, *Filipinos: Forgotten Asian Americans: A Pictorial Essay* (Dubuque, IA: Kendall/Hunt, 1983); Yen Li Espiritu, *Filipino American Lives* (Philadelphia: Temple University Press, 1995); Yen Li Espiritu, *Home Bound: Filipino American Lives across Cultures, Communities, and Countries* (Berkeley: University of California Press, 2003).

14. Jacob Vigdor, "Measuring Immigrant Assimilation in the United States," Civic Report No. 53 (New York: Manhattan Institute, 2008), http://www.manhattan-institute.org/html/ cr_53.htm.

15. Nurith C. Aizenman, "Study Says Foreigners in U.S. Adapt Quickly," *Washington Post*, May 13, 2008, http://www.washingtonpost.com/wp-dyn/content/article/2008/05/12/ AR2008051202575.html.

16. Ed Langlois, "Filipino Catholics Bring Tradition to American Scene," *Catholic Sentinel*, October 1, 1999, http://www.catholicsentinel.org/main.asp?SectionID=2&SubSection ID=35&ArticleID=4055.

17. Ibid.

18. John L. Allen Jr., *The Future Church: How Ten Trends Are Revolutionizing the Catholic Church* (New York: Doubleday, 2009). Also note that according to a Pew study 88 percent of Filipinos in the Philippines state that they consider religion very important to their lives, fourth highest globally, compared to only 59 percent of Americans who state the same, ranking sixth as a nation globally; Pew Research Center, *U.S. Stands Alone In Its Embrace of Religion among Wealthy Nations*, Pew Global Attitudes Project, 2002, http:// www.pewglobal.org/2002/12/19/among-wealthy-nations/.

19. Dean Hoge and Aniedi Okure, *International Priests in America: Challenges and Opportunities* (Collegeville, MN: Liturgical Press, 2006), http://www.litpress.org/excerpts/ 0814618308.pdf.

20. "Mass Exodus: Filipino Priests Leave RP to Work Overseas," *Filipino Express*, January 9–15, 2006, http://www.filipinoexpress.net/20/02_news.html.

21. Allen, *The Future Church*.

22. Ibid.

23. Ibid. Also see David Gibson, *The Coming Catholic Church: How the Faithful Are Shaping a New American Catholicism* (San Francisco: Harper Collins, 2003), chapter 10; Hoge and Okure, *International Priests in America*; Stephen G. Vegh, "Foreign Priests Fill Persistent Vacancies in U. S. Dioceses," *Virginian-Pilot, Worldwide Religious News*, January 4, 2004, http://wwrn.org/articles/2621/?&place=united-states.

24. See Filipino Book Team, *Filipinos in America: A Journey of Faith* (San Francisco, CA: Filipinas Publishing, 2003).

25. San Lorenzo Ruiz de Manila Web Archive, 2011, http://web.archive.org/web/20080803000608/http://www.chapelofsanlorenzoruiz.org/Home.html.

26. First National Assembly of Filipino Priests website, 2011, http//www.filipino priestsusa.org.

27. See the Pew Forum on Religion and Public Life, *A Portrait of American Catholics on the Eve of Pope Benedict's Visit to the U.S.*, Pew Research Center, Migration Policy Institute, 2007, http://pewforum.org/Christian/Catholic/A-Portrait-of-American-Catholics-on-the-Eve-of-Pope-Benedicts-Visit-to-the-US-%282%29.aspx, for comparison.

28. Ibid. Also note that while part of this high percentage may be a result of the Houston data being collected at a community event at St. Catherine's, Filipinos have been found in other studies to have the second highest rate of weekly church attendance among Asian Americans surveyed in more secular settings; see, for example, Janelle S. Wong, Karthick Ramakrishnan, and Taeku Lee, *Asian American Political Participation: Emerging Constituents and their Political Identities* (New York: Russell Sage Foundation, 2011).

29. Pew Forum, *A Portrait of American Catholics.*

30. See Social Weather Survey, *SWS Select Surveys on Filipino Religiosity*, Vol. 3 (March 2002), www.sws.org.ph, compared to the findings of the Pew Forum, *A Portrait of American Catholics.*

31. Pew Forum, *A Portrait of American Catholics.*

32. See Trinidad Linares, "Review of Home Bound: Filipino American Lives across Cultures, Communities, and Countries," *Meridians: Feminism, Race, Transnationalism* 5.1 (2004): 261, for a review of Espiritu's *Home Bound.*

33. Laura Leming, "Sociological Explorations: What Is Religious Agency?," *Sociological Quarterly* 48 (2007): 73–92.

34. See discussion in Allen, *The Future Church*, chapter 5.

35. Philip Jenkins, *The Next Christendom: The Coming of Global Christianity* (New York: Oxford University Press, 2002); also see Pew Forum on Religion and Public Life, *Spirit and Power: A 10-Country Survey of Pentecostals*, Pew Research Center, Migration Policy Institute, 2006, http://pewforum.org/Christian/Evangelical-Protestant-Churches/Spirit-and-Power.aspx.

36. Allen, *The Future Church*; Joaquin Gonzalez III, *Filipino American Faith in Action: Immigration, Religion, and Civic Engagement* (New York: New York University Press, 2009); Jenkins, *The Next Christendom*; Katherine Wiegele, *Investing in Miracles: El Shaddai and the Transformation of Popular Catholicism in the Philippines* (Honolulu: University of Hawaii Press, 2005).

37. See full discussion and citations in Chapter 1.

38. See 2009 summary report in National Asian American Survey, *Different or Similar? Asian American Public Opinion and Intergroup Relations*, 2008, http://www.naasurvey.com/publications_assets/naas-ajconf-2009-final.pdf. Also see Wong, Ramakrishnan, and Lee, *Asian American Political Participation*; Karin Aguilar-San Juan, ed., *The State of Asian America: Activism and Resistance in the 1990s* (Boston, MA: South End Press, 1994).

39. This is the case both with various Asian and Latino immigrant Protestant churches; see, for example, Elaine Howard Ecklund, *Korean American Evangelicals: New Models for Civic Life* (New York: Oxford University Press, 2006), or Cecilia Menjivar, *Fragmented Ties: Salvadorian Immigrant Networks in America* (Berkeley: University of California Press, 2003).

40. Fred Kniss and Paul D. Numrich, *Sacred Assemblies and Civic Engagement: How Religion Matters for America's Newest Immigrants* (New Brunswick, NJ: Rutgers University Press, 2007), 47–53.

41. Menjivar, *Fragmented Ties*.

42. See, for example, Stephen M. Cherry, "Catholicism and Filipino American Community Volunteerism and Participation," *Sociological Spectrum* 33.1 (2013): 36–56; Elaine Howard Ecklund and Jerry Z. Park, "Religious Diversity and Community Volunteerism among Asian Americans," *Journal for the Scientific Study of Religion* 6.2 (2007): 233–244, doi:10.1111/j.1468-5906.2007.00353.x.

METHODOLOGICAL APPENDIX

1. This has since changed with the more recent work of Joaquin Gonzalez III, *Countries of the World: The Philippines* (New York; Gareth Stevens, 2002); Joaquin Gonzalez III, *Filipino American Faith in Action: Immigration, Religion, and Civic Engagement* (New York: New York University Press, 2009).

2. See Sandra Acker, "In/Out/Side: Positioning the Research in Feminist Qualitative Research," *Resources for Feminist Research* 28.1–2 (2000): 189. Also see Sonya Corbin Dwyer and Jennifer L. Buckle, "The Space Between: Being an Insider-Outsider in Qualitative Research," *International Journal of Qualitative Methods* 8.1 (2009): 45–63.

3. This was discussed and fully disclosed with all respondents in both of these groups. In the case of Couples for Christ, however, additional measures were taken to keep specific household meeting places and area groups anonymous even though the larger international organization would be identified. All research and procedures for this study, including the aforementioned, was approved by the Human Subjects Review Board at the University of Texas at Austin and subsequently, after 2009, by the University of Houston Clear Lake.

4. The SCCB did not ask respondents' nativity; see Roper Center, "Social Capital Community Benchmark Survey," 2006, http://www.cfsv.org/communitysurvey/docs/exec_summ.pdf.

5. Note the median age of Filipino American respondents in the 2012 American community is forty-one years of age; see Pew Research Center, *The Rise of Asian Americans* (Pew Research Center's Social and Demographic Trends Project, June 19, 2012), http://www.pewsocialtrends.org/files/2012/06/The-Rise-of-Asian-Americans-Full-Report.pdf.

6. See study by Emily Ignacio, *Building Diaspora: Filipino Cultural Community Formation on the Internet* (New Brunswick, NJ: Rutgers University Press, 2005) for details on the importance of studying the Filipino diaspora online.

SELECTED BIBLIOGRAPHY

Acker, Sandra. "In/Out/Side: Positioning the Research in Feminist Qualitative Research." *Resources for Feminist Research* 28.1–2 (2000): 189.

Agbayani-Siewert, Pauline, and Linda Revilla. "Filipino Americans." In *Asian Americans: Contemporary Trends and Issues,* edited by Pyong Gap Min, 134–168. London: Sage, 1995.

Agoncillo, Teodoro A., and Oscar M. Alphonso. *History of the Filipino People.* Quezon City, Philippines: Malaya Books, 1967.

Aguilar-San Juan, Karin, ed. *The State of Asian America: Activism and Resistance in the 1990s.* Boston, MA: South End Press, 1994.

Alba, Richard D. and Victor Nee. "Rethinking Assimilation Theory for a New Era of Immigration." *International Migration Review* 31 (1997): 826–874, doi:10.2307/2547416.

Alba, Richard D., and Robert Orsi. "Passages in Piety: Generational Transitions and the Social and Religious Incorporation of Italian Americans." In *Immigration and Religion in America: Comparative and Historical Perspectives,* edited by Richard Alba, Albert J. Raboteau, and Josh DeWind, 32–55. New York: New York University Press, 2009.

Alba, Richard D., Albert J. Raboteau, and Josh DeWind, eds. *Immigration and Religion in America: Comparative and Historical Perspectives.* New York: New York University Press, 2009.

Alip, Eufronio. 1950. *Political and Cultural History of the Philippines.* Volumes 1 and 2. Manila, Philippines: Alip and Brion, 1950.

Allen, John L. Jr. *The Future Church: How Ten Trends Are Revolutionizing the Catholic Church.* New York: Doubleday, 2009.

Anbinder, Tyler G. *Nativism and Slavery: The Northern Know Nothings and the Politics of the 1850s.* New York: Oxford University Press, 199.

Anderson, Gerald, ed. *Studies in Philippine Church History.* Ithaca, NY: Cornell University Press, 1969.

Arias, Elizabeth. "Change in Nuptiality Patterns among Cuban Americans: Evidence of Cultural and Structural Assimilation." *International Migration Review* 35 (2001): 525–556, doi:10.1111/j.1747-7379.2001.tb00028.x.

Baltzell, Digby E. *The Protestant Establishment.* New York: Random House, 1964.

Bane, Mary Jo. "The Catholic Puzzle: Parishes and Civic Life." In *Taking Faith Seriously*, edited by Mary Jo Bane, Brent Coffin, and Richard Higgins, 63–93. Cambridge, MA: Harvard University Press, 2005.

Bane, Mary Jo, Brent Coffin, and Richard Higgins, eds. *Taking Faith Seriously*. Cambridge, MA: Harvard University Press, 2005.

Billington, Ray Allen. *The Protestant Crusade 1800–1960: A Study of the Origins of American Nativism*. New York: Quadrangle Books, 1964.

Bogardus, Stephen. "American Attitudes toward Filipinos." *Sociology and Social Research* 14 (1929): 56–69.

Bonus, Rick. *Locating Filipino Americans: Ethnicity and the Cultural Politics of Space*. Philadelphia, PA: Temple University Press, 2000.

Bourdieu, Pierre. *Distinction: A Social Critique of the Judgment of Taste*. Translated by Richard Nice. Cambridge, MA: Harvard University Press, 1984.

———. "Structures, Habitus, Practices." In *The Logic of Practice*. Translated by Richard Nice, 52–65. Stanford, CA: Stanford University Press, [1980] 1990.

Brewer, Mark E. *Relevant No More? The Protestant/Catholic Divide in American Electoral Politics*. Lanham, MD: Lexington Books, 2003.

Brubaker, Rodger. "The Return of Assimilation? Changing Perspectives and Its Sequels in France, Germany, and the United States." *Ethnic and Racial Studies* 24 (2001): 531–548, doi:10.1080/01419870120049770.

Buloson, Carlos. *America Is in the Heart: A Personal History*. New York: Harcourt, Brace, 1946.

Burns, M. Jeffrey, Ellen Skerrett, and Joseph M. White, eds. *Keeping Faith: European and Asian Catholic Immigrants*. New York: Orbis Books, [2000] 2006.

Campbell, David E., and Stephen J. Yonish. "Religion and Volunteering in America." In *Religion and Social Capital*, edited by Corwin E. Schmidt, 87–106. Waco, TX: Baylor University Press, 2003.

Cannell, Fenella. *Power and Intimacy in the Christian Philippines*. Cambridge, UK: Cambridge University Press, 1999.

Carley, Kathleen Mary. "A Theory of Group Stability." *American Sociology Review* 56 (1991): 331–354, doi:10.2307/2096108.

Carlin, David. *The Decline and Fall of the Catholic Church in America*. Manchester, NH: Sophia Institute, 2003.

Carlos, Ma. Reinaruth D. "On the Determinates of International Migration in the Philippines." *International Migration Review* 36.1 (2002): 81–102.

Carnes, Tony, and Fenggang Yang, eds. *Asian American Religions: The Making and Remaking of Borders and Boundaries*. New York: New York University Press, 2004.

Casanova, José. "Globalizing Catholicism and the Return of the 'Universal' Church." In *Transnational Religion and Fading States*, edited by Susanne Hoeber Rudolph and James Piscatori, 121–143. Boulder, CO: Westview, 1997.

———. *Public Religions in the Modern World*. Chicago, IL: University of Chicago Press, 1994.

Castillo, Naomi. *Filipino Devotionals and Religiocultural Celebrations*. San Francisco, CA: Archdiocese of San Francisco, 1997.

———. *Pastoral Plan for Filipino Ministry*. San Francisco, CA: Archdiocese of San Francisco, 1988.

———. *Introduction to Filipino Ministry*. Washington, D.C.: Archdiocese of San Francisco in cooperation with the Pastoral Care of Migrants and Refugees–United States Catholic Council, 1986.

Chao, Jessica. "Asian-American Philanthropy: Expanding Circles of Participation." In *Cultures of Caring: Philanthropy in America's Diverse Communities*, 189–253. Washington, D.C.: Council on Foundations, 1999.

Chavez, Mark. *Congregations in America.* Cambridge, MA: Harvard University Press, 2004.

Chen, Carolyn. *Getting Saved in America: Taiwanese Immigration and Religious Experience.* Princeton, NJ: Princeton University Press, 2008.

Cherry, Stephen M. "Catholicism and Filipino American Community Volunteerism and Participation." *Sociological Spectrum* 33.1 (2013): 36–56.

———. "Engaging the Spirit of the East: Asian American Christians and Civic Life." *Sociological Spectrum* 29.2 (2009): 249–272.

Cherry, Stephen M., and Kody Allred. "Models of Disaster Response: Lessons Learned from Filipino Immigrant Mobilizations for Hurricane Katrina Evacuees," *Criminal Justice Studies* 25.4 (2012): 391–408.

Cherry, Stephen M., and Helen Rose Ebaugh, eds. 2013. *Global Religious Movements across Borders: Sacred Service.* Burlington, VT: Ashgate, 2014.

Choy, Catherine. *Empire of Care: Nursing and Migration in Filipino American History.* Durham, NC: Duke University Press, 2003.

Chung, Angie. *Legacies of Struggle: Conflict and Cooperation in Korean American Politics.* Stanford, CA: Stanford University Press, 2007.

Cogley, John, and Rodger Van Allen. *Catholic America.* Kansas City, MO: Sheed and Ward, 1986.

Constantino, Renato L. *The Philippines: A Past Revisited.* Volume 1. Manila: Rentato Constantino, 1998.

Cordova, Fred. *Filipinos: Forgotten Asian Americans, A Pictorial Essay.* Dubuque, IA: Kendall/Hunt, 1983.

Cutler, David M., Edward L. Glaeser, and Jacob L. Vigdor. "When Are Ghettos Bad? Lessons from Immigrant Segregation in the United States." *Journal of Urban Economics* 63.3 (2008): 759–774.

D'Antonio, William V., James D. Davidson, Dean R. Hoge, and Mary L. Gautier. *American Catholics Today: New Realities of Their Faith and Their Church.* Lanham, MD: Rowman & Littlefield, 2007.

D'Antonio, William V., James D. Davidson, Dean R. Hoge, and Katherine Meyer. *American Catholics: Gender, Generation, and Commitment.* Walnut Creek, CA: AltaMira Press, 2001.

Davidson, James D. *Catholicism in Motion: The Church in American Society.* Ligouri, MO: Ligouri and Triumph, 2005.

Davidson, James D., and Mark McCormick. "Catholics and Civic Engagement: Empirical Findings at the Individual Level." In *Civil Society, Civic Engagement and Catholicism in the U.S.,* edited by Antonius Liedhegener and Werner Kremp, 119–134. Trier, Germany: WVT Wissenschaftlicher Verlag Trier, 2007.

Davis, Meghan, and Antonius Liedhegener. "Catholic Civic Engagement at the Local Level: The Parish and Beyond." In *Civil Society, Civic Engagement and Catholicism in the U.S.,* edited by Antonius Liedhegener and Werner Kremp, 135–160. Trier, Germany: WVT Wissenschaftlicher Verlag Trier, 2007.

De Tocqueville, Alexis. *Democracy in America: Historical-Critical Edition of De la démocratie en Amérique,* edited by Eduardo Nolla. Translated from the French by James T. Schleifer. Bilingual French-English edition, 4 vols. Indianapolis, IN: Liberty Fund, [1835] 2010.

Diaz-Stevens, Ana Maria, and Anthony M. Stevens-Arroyo. *Recognizing the Latino Resurgence in U.S. Religion: The Emmaus Paradigm.* Boulder, CO: Westview, 1998.

Dillon, Michele. *Catholic Identity: Balancing Reason, Faith, and Power.* Cambridge, UK: Cambridge University Press, 1999.

DiMaggio, Paul. "Culture and Cognition." *Annual Review of Sociology* 23 (1997): 263–287, doi:10.1146/annurev.soc.23.1.263.

Dolan, Jay P. *In Search of an American Catholicism.* New York: Oxford University Press, 2002.

Dwyer, Sonya Corbin, and Jennifer L. Buckle. "The Space Between: Being an Insider-Outsider in Qualitative Research." *International Journal of Qualitative Methods* 8.1 (2009): 45–63.

Ebaugh, Helen Rose, and Janet Saltzman Chafetz. *Religion and the New Immigrants: Continuities and Adaptations in Immigrant Congregations.* Walnut Creek, CA: AltaMira Press, 2000.

———. *Religion across Borders: Transnational Immigrant Networks.* Walnut Creek, CA: AltaMira Press, 2002.

Ecklund, Elaine Howard. *Korean American Evangelicals: New Models for Civic Life.* New York: Oxford University Press, 2006.

Ecklund, Elaine, and Jerry Park. "Asian American Community Participation and Religion." *Journal of Asian American Studies* 8 (2005): 1–21, doi:10.1353/jaas.2005.0027.

———. "Religious Diversity and Community Volunteerism among Asian Americans." *Journal for the Scientific Study of Religion* 46.2 (2007): 233–244, doi:10.1111/j.1468-5906.2007.00353.x.

Ellison, Christopher G. "Are Religious People Nice People?: Evidence from the National Survey of Black Americans." *Social Forces* 71 (1992): 411–430.

Espiritu, Yen Le. *Filipino American Lives.* Philadelphia, PA: Temple University Press, 1995.

———. *Home Bound: Filipino American Lives across Cultures, Communities, and Countries.* Berkeley: University of California Press, 2003.

Finke, Roger, and Rodney Stark. *The Churching of America 1776–1990.* New Brunswick, NJ: Rutgers University Press, 1992.

Fogarty, Gerald P. "Volunteerism in the Land of Voluntarism: The American Catholic Church." In *Civil Society, Civic Engagement and Catholicism in the U.S.,* edited by Antonius Liedhegener and Werner Kremp, 109–118. Trier, Germany: WVT Wissenschaftlicher Verlag Trier, 2007.

Foley, Michael W., and Dean R. Hoge. *Religion and the New Immigration: How Faith Communities Form Our Newest Citizens.* New York: Oxford University Press, 2007.

Fox, Robert. "The Filipino Family and Kinship." *Philippine Quarterly* 2 (1961): 6–9.

Gannon, Thomas. *World Catholicism in Transition.* New York: MacMillan, 1988.

Geertz, Clifford. *The Interpretation of Cultures.* New York: Basic Books, 1973.

Gibson, David. *The Coming Catholic Church: How the Faithful Are Shaping a New American Catholicism.* San Francisco, CA: Harper Collins, 2003.

Giddens, Anthony. *The Constitution of Society.* Berkeley: University of California Press, 1984.

Gilroy, Paul. *The Black Atlantic: Modernity and Double Consciousness.* Cambridge, MA: Harvard University Press, 1993.

Go, Julian. *American Empire and the Politics of Meaning: Elite Political Cultures in the Philippines and Puerto Rico during U.S. Colonialism.* Durham, NC: Duke University Press, 2008.

Go, Julian, and Anne L. Foster. *The American Colonial State in the Philippines: Global Perspectives.* Durham, NC: Duke University Press, 2003.

Goffman, Erving. *Frame Analysis*. New York: Harper & Row, [1947] 1997.

Gonzalez, Joaquin III. *Filipino American Faith in Action: Immigration, Religion, and Civic Engagement*. New York: New York University Press, 2009.

Gonzalez, Joaquin L. III, and Andrea Maison. "We Do Not Bowl Alone: Social and Cultural Capital from Filipinos and Their Church." In *Asian American Religions: The Making and Remaking of Borders and Boundaries*, edited by Tony Carnes and Fenggang Yang, 21–38. New York: New York University Press, 2004.

Gordon, Milton. *Assimilation in American Life*. New York: Oxford University Press, 1964.

Gowing, Peter. *Islands under the Cross: The Story of the Church in the Philippines*. Manila, Philippines: National Council of Churches in the Philippines, 1967.

Greely, Andrew M. *American Catholic: A Social Portrait*. New York: Basic Books, 1977.

———. *The Catholic Imagination*. Berkeley: University of California Press, 2000.

Hing, Bill Ong. *Making and Remaking Asian America through Immigration Policy*. Stanford, CA: Stanford University Press, 1993.

Hoge, Dean R., William D. Dinges, Mary Johnson, and Juan L. Gonzales. *Young Adult Catholics: Religion in the Culture of Choice*. Notre Dame, IN: University of Notre Dame Press, 2001.

Hoge, Dean R., and Aniedi Okure. *International Priests in America: Challenges and Opportunities*. Collegeville, MN: Liturgical Press, 2006, http://www.litpress.org/excerpts/0814618308.pdf.

Hondagneu-Sotelo, Pierrette. *Gendered Transitions: Mexican Experiences of Immigration*. Berkeley: University of California Press, 1994.

Huntington, Samuel P. "The Hispanic Challenge." *Foreign Policy* 141 (March/April 2004): 30–45. http://dx.doi.org/10.2307/4147547.

———. *Who Are We? The Challenges to America's National Identity*. New York: Simon and Schuster, 2004.

Ignacio, Emily Noelle. *Building Diaspora*. New Brunswick, NJ: Rutgers University Press, 2005.

Ileto, Reynaldo Clemena. *Pasyon and Revolution: Popular Movements in the Philippines, 1840–1910*. Manila, Philippines: Ateneo de Manila University Press, 1979.

Jasso, Guillermina, Douglas S. Massey, Mark R. Rosenzweig. and James P. Smith. "Exploring Religious Preferences of Recent Immigrants to the United States: Evidence from the New Immigrant Survey Pilot." In *Religion and Immigration: Christian, Jewish, and Muslim Experiences in the United States,* edited by Yvonne Yazbeck Haddad, Jane I. Smith, and John L. Esposito, 217–253. Walnut Creek, CA: AltaMira Press, 2003.

Jenkins, Philip. *The Next Christendom: The Coming of Global Christianity*. New York: Oxford University Press, 2002.

Jepperson, Ronald L., and Ann Swidler. "What Properties of Culture Should We Measure?" *Poetics* 22 (1994): 359–371, doi:10.1016/0304-422X(94)90014-0.

Jones-Correa, Michael, and David Leal. "Political Participation: Does Religion Matter?" *Political Research Quarterly* 54.4 (2001): 751–770, doi:10.1177/106591290105400404.

Joyce, Kathleen. "The Long Loneliness: Liberal Catholics and the Conservative Church." In *"I Come away Stronger": How Small Groups Are Shaping American Religion*, edited by Robert Wuthnow, 55–76. Grand Rapids, MI: Wm. B. Eerdmans, 1994.

Karnow, Stanley. *In Our Image: America's Empire in the Philippines*. New York: Random House, 1989.

Kennedy, John F. *A Nation of Immigrants*. New York: HarperCollins, 1994.

Klineberg, Stephen. *Houston's Ethnic Communities, Third Edition: Updated and Expanded to Include the First-Ever Survey of the Asian Communities.* Houston Area Survey Report, Houston Ethnic Communities. Houston, TX: Rice University, Kinder Institute for Urban Research, 1996, http://has.rice.edu/downloads/?ekmensel=c58ofa7b_8_0_1748_5.

———. "Religious Diversity and Social Integration among Asian Americans in Houston." In *Asian American Religions: The Making and Remaking of Borders and Boundaries,* edited by Tony Carnes and Yang Fenggang, 247–262. New York: New York University Press, 2004.

Kniss, Fred, and Paul D. Numrich. *Sacred Assemblies and Civic Engagement: How Religion Matters for America's Newest Immigrants.* New Brunswick, NJ: Rutgers University Press, 2007.

Lam, Pui-Yan. "As the Flocks Gather: How Religion Effects Voluntary Association Participation." *Journal for the Scientific Study of Religion* 41 (2002): 405–422, doi:10.1111/1468-5906.00127.

———. "Religion and Civic Culture: A Cross-National Study of Voluntary Association Membership." *Journal for the Scientific Study of Religion* 45.2 (2006): 177–293, doi:10.1111/j.1468-5906.2006.00300.x.

Lasker, Bruno. *Filipino Immigration to the United States and Hawaii.* New York: Arno, 1996.

Leavitt, Robert F., SS. "Lay Participation in the Catholic Church in America, 1789–1989." In *Perspectives, Politics, and Civic Participation,* edited by Stephen J. Vicchio and Virginia Geiger SSND, 275–293. Westminster, MD: Christian Classics, 1998. Notre Dame Study of Catholic Parish Life 11.

Leming, Laura A. "Sociological Explorations: What Is Religious Agency?" *Sociological Quarterly* 48 (2007): 73–92.

Levitt, Peggy. *The Transnational Villagers.* Berkeley: University of California Press, 2001.

Lichterman, Paul. *Elusive Togetherness: Church Groups Trying to Bridge America's Divisions.* Princeton, NJ: Princeton University Press, 2005.

Lichterman, Paul, and Charles Brady Potts. *The Civic Life of American Religion.* Stanford, CA: Stanford University Press, 2009.

Lien, Pei-te. "Asian Americans and Voting Participation: Comparing Racial and Ethnic Differences in Recent U.S. Elections." *International Migration Review* 38, 2 (2004): 493–517, doi:10.1111/j.1747-7379.2004.tb00207.x.

———. *The Making of Asian America through Political Participation.* Philadelphia, PA: Temple University Press, 2001.

Lien, Pei-te, and Tony Carnes. "Religious Demography of Asian American Boundary Crossing." In *Asian American Religions,* edited by Tony Carnes and Fenggang Yang, 38–54. New York: New York University Press, 2004.

Lien, Pei-te, M. Margaret Conway, and Janelle Wong. *The Politics of Asian Americans: Diversity and Community.* New York: Routledge, 2004.

Lopez, David. "Whither the Flock? The Catholic Church and the Success of Mexicans in America." In *Immigration and Religion in America: Comparative and Historical Perspectives,* edited by Richard Alba, Albert Raboteau, and Josh DeWind, 71–98. New York: New York University Press, 2007.

Medina, Belen T. G. *The Filipino Family.* Quezon City, Philippines: University of the Philippines Press, 2001.

Meloto, Antonio. *Builder of Dreams.* Mandaluyong City, Philippines: Gawad Kalinga Community Development Foundation, 2009.

Menjivar, Cecilia. *Fragmented Ties: Salvadorian Immigrant Networks in America.* Berkeley: University of California Press, 2000.

———. "Religion and Immigration in Comparative Perspective: Catholic and Evangelical Salvadorans in San Francisco, Washington, D.C., and Phoenix." *Sociology of Religion* 64.1 (2003): 21–46, doi:10.2307/3712267.

Mooney, Margarita A. *Faith Makes Us Live: Surviving and Thriving in the Haitian Diaspora.* Berkeley: University of California Press, 2009.

Moore, Stephen. *Immigration and the Rise and Decline of American Cities.* Stanford, CA: Hoover Institute on War, Revolution, and Peace, Stanford University, 1997.

Morales, Royal. "Pilipino American Studies: A Promise and an Unfinished Agenda." *Amerasia Journal* 13.1 (1987): 119–124.

Morris, Charles R. *American Catholic: The Saints and Sinners Who Built America's Most Powerful Church.* New York: Random House, 1997.

Musick, Marc A., and John Wilson. *Volunteers: A Social Profile.* Bloomington: Indiana University Press, 2008.

Nelson, Brent. *America Balkanized: Immigration's Challenge to Government.* Monterey, VA: American Immigration Control Foundation, 1994.

Novak, Michael. *The Catholic Ethic and the Spirit of Capitalism.* New York: New York Free Press, 1993.

Oats, Mary J. "Faith and Good Works: Catholic Giving and Taking." In *Charity, Philanthropy, and Civility in American History,* edited by L. J. Friedman and M. D. McGarvie, 281–299. New York: Cambridge University Press, 2003.

Okamura, Jonathan. "Filipino Hometown Associations in Hawaii." *Ethnology* 22.4 (1983): 341–353, doi:10.2307/3773681.

———. *Imagining the Filipino American Diaspora.* New York: Garland, 1998.

Orsi, Robert A. *The Madonna of 115th Street: Faith and Community in Italian Harlem.* New Haven, CT: Yale University Press, 2002.

Osajima, Keith. "Asian Americans as the Model Minority: An Analysis of the Popular Images in the 1960s and 1980s." In *Reflections on Shattered Windows: Promises and Prospects for Asian American Studies,* edited by Gary Y. Okihiro, 449–458. Pullman: Washington State University Press, 1988.

Panopio, Isabel, and Realidad Rolda. *Society and Culture.* Quezon City, Philippines: JMC Press, 2000.

Park, Jerry Z. "Assessing the Sociological Study of Asian American Christians." *Society of Asian North American Christianity Studies Journal* 1 (2009): 57–94, http://www.baylorisr .org/wp-content/uploads/park_assessing.pdf.

Park, Robert E., and Ernest W. Burgess. *Introduction to the Science of Sociology.* Chicago, IL: University of Chicago Press, 1924.

Parreñas, Rhacel. *Children of Global Migration: Transnational Families and Gender Woes.* Stanford, CA: Stanford University Press, 2005.

———. *The Force of Domesticity: Filipina Migrants and Globalization.* New York: NewYork University Press, 2008.

———. *Servants of Globalization: Women, Migration, and Domestic Work.* Stanford, CA: Stanford University Press, 2001.

———. "Transnational Mothering: A Source of Gender Conflict in the Family." *North Carolina Law Review* 88 (2010): 1825–1855.

Peña, Milgros, and Lisa M. Frehill. "Latina Religious Practice." *Journal for the Scientific Study of Religion* 37.4 (1998): 620–635, doi:10.2307/1388145.

Perlmutter, Philip. *The Legacy of Hate: A Short History of Ethnic, Religious, and Racial Prejudice in America*. Armonk, NY: M. E. Sharpe, 1999.

Phelan, John Leddy. *The Hispanization of the Philippines: Spanish Aims and Filipino Responses 1565–1700*. Madison: University of Wisconsin Press, [1959] 1967.

Pido, Antonio. *The Pilipinos in America: Macro/Micro Dimensions of Immigration and Integration*. New York: Center for Immigration Studies, 1986.

Portes, Alejandro, and Jozsef Borocz. "Contemporary Immigration: Theoretical Perspectives on Its Determinates and Modes of Incorporation." *International Migration Review* 23.3 (1989): 606–630, doi:10.2307/2546431.

Portes, Alejandro, and Robert Manning. "The Immigrant Enclave: Theory and Empirical Examples." In *Competitive Ethnic Relations*, edited by Susan Olzak and Joane Nagel, 47–63. Orlando, FL: Academic Press, 1986.

Portes, Alejandro, and Ruben Rumbaut. *Immigrant America: A Portrait*. Third edition. Berkeley: University of California Press, 2006.

———. *Legacies: The Story of the Immigrant Second Generation*. Berkeley: University of California Press, 2001.

Portes, Alejandro, and Min Zhou. "The New Second Generation: Segmented Assimilation and Its Variants among Post-1965 Immigrant Youth." *Annals of American Academy of Political and Social Sciences* 530 (1993): 74–96.

Posadas, Barbara. *The Filipino Americans*. Westport, CT: Greenwood, 1994.

Putnam, Robert D. *Bowling Alone: The Collapse and Revival of American Community*. New York: Simon and Schuster, 2000.

Racelis, Rachel H., and Emily Cabegin. *A Household Model for Economic and Social Studies: Updated Household and Macro/Sectoral Projections, Philippines, 1990–2030*. Pasig City, Philippines: National Economic Authority, 1998.

Rafael, Vicente. *Contracting Colonialism*. Ithaca, NY: Cornell University Press, 1988.

Ramakrishnan, S. Karthick, Janelle Wong, Taeku Lee, and Jane Junn. "Race Based Considerations and the Obama Vote: Evidence from the 2008 National Asian American Survey." *Du Bois Review* 6.1 (2009): 219–238.

Reed, Robert. *Hispanic Urbanism in the Philippines: A Study of the Impact of Church and State*. Manila, Philippines: University of Manila Press, 1967.

Regnerus, Mark, Christian Smith, and David Sikkink. "Who Gives to the Poor? The Role of Religious Tradition and Political Location on the Personal Generosity of Americans toward the Poor." *Journal for the Scientific Study of Religion* 37.3 (1998): 481–493, doi:10.2307/1388055.

Reisman, David, Nathan Glazer, and Reuel Denny. *The Lonely Crowd*. Abridged edition. New Haven, CT: Yale University Press, 1961.

Rigney, Daniel, Jerome Matz, and Armando Abney. "Is There a Catholic Sharing Ethic?: A Research Note." *Sociology of Religion* 65.2 (2004): 155–165.

Rimonte, Nilda. "Colonialism's Legacy: The Inferiorization of the Filipino." In *Filipino Americans: Transformation and Identity*, edited by Maria P. P. Root, 39–61. London: Sage, 1997.

Rodao, Florentino, and Felice Noelle Rodriguez, eds. *The Philippine Revolution of 1896: Ordinary Lives in Extraordinary Times*. Quezon City, Philippines: Ateneo de Manila University Press, 2001.

Roediger, David R. *Working toward Whiteness: How America's Immigrants Became White: The Strange Journey from Ellis Island to the Suburbs*. Cambridge, MA: Basic Books, 2005.

Rudrappa, Sharmila. *Ethnic Routes to Becoming American: Indian Immigrants and the Cultures of Citizenship.* New Brunswick, NJ: Rutgers University Press, 2004.

San Buenaventura, Steffi. "Filipino Folk Spirituality and Immigration: From Mutual Aid to Religion." In *New Spiritual Homes,* edited by David K. Yoo, 52–86. Honolulu: University of Hawaii Press, 1999.

———. "Filipino Religion at Home and Abroad: Historical Roots and Immigrant Transformations." In *Religions in Asian America: Building Faith Communities,* edited by Pyong G. Min and Jung H. Kim, 143–184. Walnut Creek, CA: AltaMira Press, 2002.

San Juan, Epifanio Jr. *Writing and National Liberation: Essays in Critical Practice.* Quezon City, Philippines: University of the Philippines Press, 1991.

Schwartz, Barry. *Vertical Classification: A Study in Structuralism and the Sociology of Knowledge.* Chicago, IL: University of Chicago Press, 1981.

Sewell, William H. Jr. "A Theory of Structure: Duality, Agency, and Transformation." *American Journal of Sociology* 98.1 (1992): 1–29, doi:10.1086/229967.

Smith, Christian. *Moral Believing Animals: Human Personhood and Culture.* New York: Oxford University Press, 2003.

Stepick, Alex, Terry Rey, and Sarah J. Mahler, eds. *Churches and Charity in the Immigrant City.* New Brunswick, NJ: Rutgers University Press, 2009.

Sundeen, Richard D., Cristina Garcia, and Lili Wang. "Volunteer Behavior among Asian American Groups in the United States." *Journal of Asian American Studies* 10 (2007): 3243–3281.

Swidler, Ann. "Culture in Action: Symbols and Strategies." *American Sociological Review* 51 (1986): 273–286, doi:10.2307/2095521.

———. *Talk of Love: How Americans Use Their Culture.* Chicago, IL: University of Chicago Press, 1997.

Takaki, Ronald. *In the Heart of Filipino America: Immigrants from the Pacific Isles.* New York: Chelsea House, 1996.

———. *Strangers from a Different Shore: A History of Asian Americans.* New York: Penguin, 1987.

Terrazas, Aaron, and Jeanne Batalova. *Filipino Immigrants in the United States.* Migration Policy Institute, 2010, www.migrationinformation.org/USFocus/display.cfm?ID=777.

Tilly, Charles. "How to Detect, Describe, and Explain Repertoires of Contention." Working Paper 150. In *Annual Review,* Center for Studies of Social Change, New School for Social Research. New York, 1992.

Tonnies, Ferdinand. *Community and Society (Gemeinschaft and Gesellschaft).* Translated and edited by C. P. Loomis. New Brunswick, NJ: Transaction Publishers, [1887] 1988.

Tropman, John. *The Catholic Ethic and the Spirit of Community.* Washington, D.C.: Georgetown University Press, 2002.

———. *The Catholic Ethic in American Society.* San Francisco, CA: Jossey-Bass, 1995.

Tuan, Mia. *Forever Foreigners or Honorary Whites: The Asian Ethnic Experience Today.* New Brunswick, NJ: Rutgers University Press, 1998.

Varacalli, Joseph A. *The Catholic Experience in America.* Westport, CT: Greenwood, 2005.

Verba, Sydney, Kay Schlozman, and Henry Brady. *Voice and Equality.* Cambridge, MA: Harvard University Press, 1995.

Warner, R. Stephen. "The De-Europeanization of American Christianity." In *A Nation of Religions: Pluralism in the American Public Square,* edited by Stephen Prothero, 233–255. Chapel Hill: University of North Carolina Press, 2005.

Warner, R. Stephen, and Judith G. Wittner. *Gatherings in Diaspora: Religious Communities and the New Immigration.* Philadelphia, PA: Temple University Press, 1998.

Wiegele, Katherine. *Investing in Miracles: El Shaddai and the Transformation of Popular Catholicism in the Philippines.* Honolulu: University of Hawaii Press, 2005.

Wildsmith, Elizabeth. "Race/Ethnic Differences in Female Headship: Exploring the Assumptions of Assimilation Theory." *Social Science Quarterly* 85.1 (2004): 89–106, doi:10.1111/j.0038-4941.2004.08501007.x.

Wilson, John, and Marc Musick. "Who Cares? Toward an Integrated Theory of Volunteer Work." *American Sociological Review* 62 (1997): 694–713, doi:10.2307/2657355.

Wilson, Kenneth, and W. Allen Martin. "Ethnic Enclaves: A Comparison of the Cuban and Black Economies in Miami." *American Journal of Sociology* 88.1 (1982): 135–160, doi:10.086/227637.

Wong, Janelle S., Karthick Ramakrishnan, and Taeku Lee. *Asian American Political Participation: Emerging Constituents and Their Political Identities.* New York: Russell Sage Foundation, 2011.

Woo, Deborah. *Glass Ceilings and Asian Americans: The New Faces of Workplace Barriers.* Walnut Creek, CA: AltaMira Press, 2000.

Wrong, Dennis H. "The Oversocialized Conception of Man in Modern Sociology." *American Sociological Review* 26 (1961): 184–93. http://dx.doi.org/10.2307/2089854.

Wuthnow, Robert. *Meaning and Moral Order.* Berkeley: University of California Press, 1987.

———. *Sharing the Journey: Support Groups and America's New Quest for Community.* New York: Free Press, 1994.

———. "Small Groups and Spirituality: Exploring the Connections." In *"I Come away Stronger": How Small Groups are Shaping American Religion,* edited by Robert Wuthnow, 1–6. Grand Rapids, MI: Wm. B. Eerdmans, 1994.

Wuthnow, Robert, and C. Hackett. "The Social Integration of Practitioners of Non-Western Religions in the United States." *Journal for the Scientific Study of Religion* 42.4 (2003): 651–667, doi:10.1046/j.1468-5906.2003.00209.x.

Yang, Fenggang. "Chinese Christian Transnationalism: Diverse Networks of a Houston Church." In *Religion across Borders: Transnational Immigrant Networks,* edited by Helen Rose Ebaugh and Janet Saltzman Chafetz, 129–148. Walnut Creek, CA: AltaMira Press, 2002.

———. *Chinese Christians in America: Conversion, Assimilation, and Adhesive Identities.* University Park: Pennsylvania State University Press, 1999.

Yoo, David. *New Spiritual Homes: Religion and Asian Americans.* Honolulu: University of Hawaii Press, 1999.

Young, Michael P. *Bearing Witness against Sin: The Evangelical Birth of the American Social Movement.* Chicago, IL: University of Chicago Press, 2006.

Zhou, Min, and Carl Bankston. *Growing Up American: How Vietnamese Children Adapt to Life in the United States.* New York: Russell Sage Foundation, 1998.

INDEX

Note to index: an *f* following a page number indicates a figure on that page.

volunteerism, 1–2, 4, 108–17, 122–23, 125–26, 162–63
voting laws, 7

Warner, Stephen, 166
Welch, Louie, 46
Wells Fargo Bank, 24

Wilk, Dylan, 78
women: impact of immigration of, 28–29; importance of, 15; in labor force, 152; politics and, 147; power of, 83; role of, 35, 157–58; San Lorenzo Center and, 98

Youth for Christ, 78

ABOUT THE AUTHOR

Stephen M. Cherry is an assistant professor of sociology at the University of Houston Clear Lake. He is coeditor of *Global Religious Movements across Borders: Sacred Service* (Ashgate, expected 2014).

CPSIA information can be obtained at www.ICGtesting.com
Printed in the USA
LVOW08s2157041214

417296LV00002B/251/P